CW00819226

By the same author

Last Voyages

(Published by Fernhurst Books in 2017)
with a foreword by Sir Chay Blyth

The book describes the lives and tragic loss of eleven remarkable sailors who were lost at sea and never returned from their final voyage. Included are world-renowned sailors like Eric Tabarly, Rob James and Francis Walwyn and highly experienced adventurers like Bill Tilman and Peter Tangvald. All the sailors were known to the author.

'An excellent tribute to truly great sailors' - Sir Chay Blyth

'This is an unusual and absorbing book which describes the exploits and adventures of eleven great sailors, some very well known and others less so, all of whom lost their lives at sea. The subject matter is not as depressing as it sounds. Nicholas Gray has succeeded in making it more of a celebration of the lives and achievements of these remarkable people' - Royal Cruising Club

ASTRONAUTS OF CAPE HORN

by the time twelve men went to the moon,
only eleven extraordinary sailors had
rounded Cape Horn alone

Nicholas Gray

Astronauts of Cape Horn

Published by The Conrad Press in the United Kingdom 2018

Tel: +44(0)1227 472 874
www.theconradpress.com
info@theconradpress.com

ISBN 978-1-911546-38-2

Typesetting and Cover Design by:
Charlotte Mouncey, www.bookstyle.co.uk

The Conrad Press logo was designed by Maria Priestley.

Printed and bound in Great Britain
by Clays Ltd, St Ives plc

In memory of the late, great Edward Allcard,
who was an inspiration to so many
and who lived his life to the full.

(born on 31 October 1914 and died on 28 July 2017, aged 102)

'It is only the starting that is hard.'
Harry Pidgeon
(the second man to sail alone around the world)

Familiarity with danger makes a brave man braver,
but less daring. Thus with seamen:
he who goes the oftenest round Cape Horn
goes the most circumspectly.
Herman Melville

Cape Horn Fever:

An imaginary disease from which malingerers at sea were supposed to suffer.
  Its origin lay in the reluctance of many seamen to sign articles in a ship making a passage of Cape Horn from east to west under sail, the contrary winds and heavy seas frequently entailing almost non-stop work on the yards in numbing conditions.

The Oxford Companion to Ships and the Sea (1976)

Contents

Preface

I have seen Cape Horn from the deck of my own small yacht, and I can tell you it is a truly bleak sight. And a surprising one in that it is not as mighty as you expect. In terms of physical presence, this lump of black granite is easily eclipsed by many of our own headlands such as the Lizard, St Albans, or Cape Wrath; all of these are every bit as imposing as the Horn.

But the Horn is much more than the sum of its rocks and reefs. It is one of the major maritime turning-points of the world, standing as a gatekeeper between the Atlantic and Pacific Oceans, its nose pointing southwards towards Antarctica, daring you to venture there. It is also a monument; a massive gravestone marking the watery graves of countless thousands who were lost from the decks of sailing ships of old whose trade required them to make a passage round this headland at the ends of the earth. Cape Horn is their only memorial.

Several quirks of geography combine to make this one of nastiest places on the face of any ocean. The deep depressions which spin across the southern ocean at this latitude meet no land until they collide with the Horn. The result is that they vent their fury and produce winds almost beyond bearable. The rolling swells these storms produce gallop round the globe unhindered, until they meet the Horn where the sea shallows and funnels into the constriction created by icy finger of the Antarctic peninsula pointing towards the Horn itself. The result is that the sea boils with anger, whipped even higher by the wind, until you have all the conditions needed for the creation of a true hell hole.

Like Nicholas Gray, the author of this book, I too was surprised that so few had ever sailed singlehanded around Cape Horn, and I was intrigued to read their stories and marvel at their achievements. My passage round the Horn was a far more modest affair, I'm afraid. I had the luxury of being able to lurk in the Beagle Channel in the charming Chilean naval port of Puerto Williams, sitting in perfect shelter till the weather was just right. From here it was a mere sixty miles, so not much more than a day trip. Even so, the weather hereabouts is volatile and forecasts come with no guarantees. I left from the Beagle Channel in a calm, and had light winds with twenty miles to go. Even then, with the Horn nearly in my grasp, the breeze rose to force seven in a matter of ten minutes and even though I was so close to fulfilling a life-long ambition, I sensed I might have to retrace my steps with my tail between my legs. Far better sailors than me have been defeated by the Horn.

But we hung on, just able to make enough westing to safely bear away and pay our respects to the Horn and its wind-torn lightkeepers' houses clinging to the barren rock. Within an hour of our passing the wind had risen to a full gale and a couple of hours later, when we were thankfully in shelter, it was reported to be blowing a destructive sixty-five knots. How grateful we were to be round, and how typical of Cape Horn weather.

The achievement of the 'astronauts' in this book is on a far greater scale. They were sailing without any of the electronic aids even a modest sailing yacht is fitted with these days. They would have crossed the entire Southern Ocean, navigating by sextant, and relying on shaky observations of the sun from the heaving decks of their modest craft. On the basis of such shaky evidence, they will have nervously plotted a course to get them safely round this fearsome headland. It would not take much error for them to end up on the unforgiving shores of Chile and how their fingers must have been crossed as they peered into the distance to try and spot the Horn's craggy profile and confirm the safety or otherwise of their position.

And when the Horn was passed, I wonder how they felt? Clearly, relief must have been a considerable portion of the overwhelming emotions this headland inspires. But for me it was a sense of remembrance. So many have lost their lives here that I felt unable to conjure up any feelings of celebration, but sailed away believing I had been privileged to visit the site of one of the world's legendary battlefields.

The stories you will read in this book represent the achievements of some of greatest adventurers who have ever sailed the seas in small craft. And they have proved themselves worthy of that description by facing the terrors of Cape Horn and overcoming them. One famous astronaut spoke of 'a small step for man, one great leap for mankind. For those who go to sea, rather than into space, there's no greater step than rounding the Horn.

Paul Heiney
Suffolk 2018

TIMELINE

Year		'Lunar' Astronauts		'Cape Horn' Astronauts
1936			01/06/36	Al Hansen - 1st man round alone
1943			12/06/43	Vito Dumas - 2nd man round alone
1952			12/05/52	Marcel Bardiaux - 3rd man round alone
1965	16/02/65	Saturn I - successful first test flight - prototype of rocket used on all Apollo flights	07/01/65	Bill Nance - 4th man round alone
1966	26/02/66	Saturn 1B launched with first flight of Apollo Command/Service Module (CSM)	12/04/66	Edward Allcard - 5th man round alone
1967	21/02/67	Apollo 1 explodes on take off. Grissom, White and Chaffee killed	21/01/67	Francis Chichester - 6th man round alone
	09/11/67	Saturn V launched - CSM heat shield tested at lunar re-entry speed	07/11/67	Alec Rose nearly dismasted in Indian Ocean
1968	22/01/68	1st test flight of Lunar Module (LM)	01/04/68	Alec Rose - 7th man round alone
	04/04/68	2nd flight of Saturn V rocket - used in all Apollo landings	31/10/68	Bill King capsizes 200 miles from Cape Town and retires from Golden Globe Challenge
1969	03/03/69	Apollo 9 - first manned flight of CSM. Borman, Lovell and Anders	17/01/69	Robin Knox-Johnston - 8th man round alone
	18/05/69	Apollo 10 - 'dress rehearsal' for moon landing - descended to within 8 miles of moon's surface	05/02/69	Bernard Moitessier - 9th man round alone
	16/07/69	Apollo 11 - 1st moon landing in Sea of Tranquility. Armstrong, Collins (and Aldrin)	19/03/69	Nigel Tetley - 10th man round alone (the last three were all competitors in the Sunday Times Golden Globe Challenge)

Year		'Lunar' Astronauts		'Cape Horn' Astronauts
1969	14/11/69	Apollo 12 - 2nd moon landing. Conrad, Gordon (and Bean)	11/04/69	Donald Crowhurst breaks radio silence with claim to have rounded Cape Horn - would have been 11th man - later it was proved to be a fake claim
			23/04/69	Robin Knox-Johnston lands home in Falmouth after 313 days alone at sea
			20/05/69	Nigel Tetley sinks off Azores
			21/06/69	Moitessier lands in Pacific Ocean ('the Tranquil Sea') after sailing 1½ times round the world
1970	11/04/70	Apollo 13 - landing aborted after CSM oxygen tank exploded. LM used as 'lifeboat' and crew returned safely to earth. Lovell, Swingen and Halse	23/12/70	Chay Blyth - 11th man round alone
1971	31/01/71	Apollo 14 - 3rd moon landing. Shepard, Roosa (and Mitchell)	12/08/71	Chay Blyth lands after his non-stop circumnavigation
	26/07/71	Apollo 15 - 4th Moon landing. Scott, Worden (and Irwin).		
	07/08/71	Apollo 15 lands back on the Earth.		
1972	16/04/72	Apollo 16 - 5th moon landing. Young, Mattingly (and Duke)		
	07/12/72	Apollo 17 - 6th and last moon landing. Cernan, Evans (and Schmitt)		
1973			05/02/73	Bill King finally rounds alone after two failed attempts -would have been 12th man had his second attempt been successful -was two months too late!

INTRODUCTION

It was Sir Robin Knox-Johnston, featured later in this book, who first brought to my attention the astounding fact that more men had landed on the moon than had at that time sailed alone round Cape Horn - twelve against eleven (Sir Robin being one of the eleven). This is the tale of those eleven men, and the pioneers who explored those treacherous and often deadly waters before them.

Is it really relevant to compare and contrast the two endeavours? I think it is. Landing men on the moon cost the government of the United States of America over US$ 25 billion (just over US$ 2 billion per person landed) and stretched the available technology of the time to the maximum. Whilst the moon walkers had the full resources of the National Aeronautics and Space Administration (NASA) and its many thousands of employees and sub-contractors behind them, in the end it all came down to the astronauts' own bravery and tenacity, quite alone in deep space, thrown back entirely on their own resources. There was no question of any rescue attempt if something went wrong and they knew it. Despite all the money thrown at the project, these twelve men in space had to rely on exactly the same courage and emotional and physical strength as was demonstrated by the eleven Cape Horn sailors in the successful outcome of their earth-bound voyages. These cost their nations nothing.

The task of 'doubling' Cape Horn alone under sail in a small boat was for years known by sailors as the equivalent of conquering 'the Everest of the Sea'; in other words something nearly impossible and one of the hardest things to do on this planet. Remember that Mount Everest was not even climbed until after the first three men had been round Cape Horn alone. At that time 'going to the moon' was also thought of as being well-nigh impossible.

The first man to sail round the Horn alone was a Norwegian, Alfon Hansen, in 1934. He was followed by Vito Dumas in 1943 (in the middle of World War II) and then by Marcel Bardiaux in 1952. The young Australian Bill Nance, the fourth, rounded in a tiny boat in 1965.

Between 1952 and 1965, the interval between these last two voyages, the USA's mission to land a man on the moon got under way. In 1961

President John F Kennedy, looking for a project to capture the public's attention hit on the idea of a manned landing on the moon before the end of the decade. This would capture world imagination and function as a great propaganda coup for the USA, who were falling badly behind in the space race - earlier in 1961 the USSR had beaten them by putting Yuri Gagarin into space, the first man to orbit the earth.

Kennedy promised NASA all the funding it required and they went to work. In early 1965, whilst Bill Nance was at sea on his epoch-making voyage, NASA launched several flights to test the vehicles and systems that would take men to the moon.

In 1966, whilst the fifth man, Edward Allcard, was rounding the Horn and foraging for food in Patagonian waters on his long drawn out solo circumnavigation, NASA made several unmanned test launches of the Apollo-Saturn rockets. In August 1966 the Command Module (designed to bring the astronauts safely home to earth) made its first re-entry from a sub-orbital flight, landing safely in the Atlantic Ocean. In January 1967, exactly six days after Sir Francis Chichester, the sixth man, had rounded Cape Horn on his one-stop circumnavigation in *Gipsy Moth IV,* disaster struck the moon project. On 27 January, a fire erupted in the Apollo 1 Command Module during a test on the launch pad, destroying the module and killing the three astronauts, Virgil Grissom, Ed White and Roger Chaffee. These three had been scheduled to be on the first manned mission to the moon.

On 9 November 1967, two days after the yacht of Alec Rose (the seventh), *Lively Lady*, had been nearly dismasted in the Indian Ocean, NASA made an unmanned test flight of Apollo 4, successfully testing the Command Module heat shield at lunar re-entry speeds. A test like this was essential before any manned missions could take place.

Between December 1968 and May 1969, NASA made four successful manned test flights (Apollos 7, 8, 9 and 10), the last one being a full dress rehearsal for a landing. During this flight the Lunar Module descended to within sixteen kilometres of the moon's surface. These flights took place whilst four Cape Horn men were at sea trying to win the *Sunday Times* Golden Globe award for the first man to sail around the world alone and non-stop.

At last, on 20 July 1969, Apollo 11 landed on the moon in the Sea of Tranquillity and, for the first time ever, two men stepped out of the Lunar Module on to the moon's surface. On the earth things were happening too. Robin Knox-Johnston (the eighth) finished his solo non-stop circum-navigation on 22 April, just three months before the moon landing. Nigel

Tetley (the tenth) landed in the sea after his trimaran *Victress* sank under him in the Atlantic on 20 May, exactly two months before the moon landing and on 21 June 1969, one month before the landing in the lunar Sea of Tranquillity, Bernard Moitessier (the ninth) landed at Tahiti in the earth's 'tranquil' or peaceful sea, known as the Pacific Ocean, after sailing non-stop one and a half times round the world. If Moitessier was aware of what was happening far above him he would have thought there was some mystical significance to it all.

The eleventh and last Cape Horn 'astronaut', Sir Chay Blyth, was at sea from October 1970 to August 1971. During that time the third and fourth moon landings took place, the last one landed back on earth on 7 August 1971, only five days before Chay landed ashore in the Hamble River at the conclusion of his non-stop circumnavigation. The final two moon landings took place during 1972.

Getting the twelve men to the moon exhausted the resources of the government of the USA, it turned out to be far more expensive than budgeted for (the original budget given to President Kennedy in 1962 was $7 billion) and drained NASA financially and emotionally. Originally a further three moon landings had been planned. These Apollo missions, 18, 19 and 20, were cancelled because budget cuts had led to NASA running out of money. This makes the achievement of the Cape Horn 'astronauts' even more remarkable, as these missions would possibly have brought the total number of the actual astronauts up to eighteen as against only the eleven Cape Horn men.

Compared with US$ 25 billion, the costs of the Cape Horn ventures were minimal and the use of technology virtually zero. Most of the early sailors spent only hundreds of pounds or dollars on their voyages. Edward Allcard, for example, bought his boat for US$ 250 in New York in 1950. Only Sir Francis Chichester and Sir Chay Blyth spent (or rather their sponsors spent) serious money in building their boats. Pretty well all the others used whatever boat they happened to have and, unlike today's multi-million dollar (or euro) sponsorship deals, there was virtually no commercial involvement. These were personal private endeavours undertaken by brave and determined men, quite alone and self-reliant.

Like the astronauts, for whom there was no question of any rescue or assistance from the earth if things went wrong, the same applied to most of the Cape Horn sailors. Few of them had any form of life-saving equipment or life-rafts, not that they would have done them much good deep in the Southern Ocean, before the days of any effective ship-to-shore radios, satellite phones or emergency location beacons. Modern rescue and life-saving facilities and equipment all came much later.

Luckily, there was little need for rescue efforts in either the space flights or the solo Cape Horn voyages. It was only in the first 'flight' of each that lives were lost. The first man to attempt to solo Cape Horn was lost at sea after having successfully doubled the Horn. Likewise, it was only on the first Apollo mission (Apollo I), that lives were lost. As mentioned earlier the command module of Apollo I caught fire and exploded on the launch pad during a test firing killing the three astronauts. Otherwise, NASA never lost a man in flight until many years later, when in 1986, the Challenger Space Shuttle exploded soon after being launched. Given the dangers involved in both endeavours, this was an amazing achievement.

Today's sailors who race past Cape Horn in hugely expensive highly-stressed foil-assisted carbon-fibre sailing machines are more akin to the astronauts than to the first Cape Horners. With their satellite phones and fast broadband systems, they too rely on shore-based 'Mission Control' centres staffed by weather, technological, medical (and nutritional) and routing experts telling the sailor where to go and what to do (and what to eat) at every stage of the voyage. The technology and computing power available to these sailors far surpasses anything that was available to the astronauts in the 1970s. This all makes what the original eleven sailors did, with absolutely no shore based back up or contact, quite outstanding. They were as alone at sea as the astronauts were when on the far side of the moon, out of sight of and out of any contact with the earth. Once they had sailed over the horizon these sailors were to all intents and purposes 'lost' until they approached land again at the conclusion of their voyages. For a long time during Robin Knox-Johnston's voyage no one at home or on shore had any idea whether he was still alive or not.

Even today, the number of astronauts who have been shot into space far outnumbers those who have sailed alone round Cape Horn. Some 700 astronauts as against only 200 or so lone sailors.

So, apart from the money and technology behind the astronauts and the fact that they flew deep into space whilst the others sailed deep into the Southern Ocean, there is little to differentiate between their achievements. We should salute them all equally.

Another thought. When NASA was first established during the Presidency of Dwight Eisenhower and long before the White House had dumped on it the goal to land a man on the moon, NASA undertook an internal debate as to the type of man, and the attributes required, to become an 'astronaut' (then a newly minted term) prepared to be shot into space atop a highly inflammable rocket. NASA did not, at first, look toward the air-force or the military at all but considered that 'daredevil' types such as skydivers, deep-sea divers, circus performers or other extreme endurance adventurers would make the most suitable astronauts. Amongst these, long distance solo sailors would most certainly have been considered.

In the event this was not to be. President Eisenhower, being a military man, directed NASA to only use fliers and test pilots drawn from the United States Army and Air-Force. This was partly because they were already on the USA government payroll and also because they came cheap and were working for peanuts.

Thus it could easily have happened for the ranks of the real live lunar astronauts to have included one or more of the Cape Horn astronauts. When you have read this book consider whether you could see the likes of Chay Blyth, Robin Knox-Johnston, or even Bernard Moitessier, space-suited and strapped into the Command and Service Module on an Apollo mission on its way to the moon. I can certainly envisage any one of those doing just that and revelling in it. The title of this book is therefore not that fanciful.

Note: I personally know the three remaining survivors of the eleven Cape Horn astronauts, namely Bill Nance, Robin Knox-Johnston and Chay Blyth and I also knew two who are no longer with us, Edward Allcard and Francis Chichester. When writing about these five, I have used their Christian names as well as their surnames in the text.

PART I
CAPE HORN

5° 59' South and 67° 12' West. The uttermost end of the earth. To those in the northern hemisphere, it is the bottom of the world. To those in the southern hemisphere they say the same, but it is a lot nearer. Cape Horn lies 1,300 sea miles south of the Cape of Good Hope in Africa and 600 sea miles south of anywhere in Australia or New Zealand. Cape Horn is the farthest south of any piece of land, apart from ice-shrouded Antarctica.

To the east there is nothing. To the west nothing. To the south only the ice 400 miles away. To the north, the whole of the rest of the world.

We think little of Cape Horn these days. No longer is the 'Cape Stiff' of old the prime trade route for goods coming to the Old World from the Orient. No longer do European navies sail fighting ships past it to take their wars to the Pacific. No longer do American ships full of gold diggers and prospectors, seeking their fortunes in California, struggle their way against the incessant westerly winds to reach their goal.

In the year 1520, the early Portuguese voyager Magellan was the first European to discover a way through the myriad inlets and islands that litter south America to get from the Atlantic Ocean into the Pacific. This route is known today as the Magellan Strait. It was for many years the only known route to get from the Atlantic to the Pacific, except the long way eastabout via the Cape of Good Hope and the Indian Ocean.

In 1525, a ship from a Spanish expedition under the command of Francisco de Hoces was blown south by a gale whilst at the eastern entrance to the Magellan Strait. Its crew thought they saw 'land's end' at 56° South.

In 1578 Sir Francis Drake passed from east to west through the Magellan Strait during his circumnavigation. Upon leaving the western end of the Strait and whilst trying to head north into the Pacific Ocean, a storm blew his ships far to the south, whereupon they came across an expanse of open water. Sir Francis worked out that the land to the south of the Magellan Strait known as Tierra del Fuego was not part of a large southern continent, as was previously thought, but was merely an island with open sea to its south. This stretch of water later became known as the Drake Passage but went unused for some time.

In 1615 an expedition left Holland to try to find an alternative route to the Far East and to see if the unknown 'Terra Australis' really existed. It was led by a merchant, Isaac Le Maire, and a ship's captain, Willem Schouten, both from the town of Hoorn in Holland. They went south and then south-west past Tierra del Fuego. They saw land to the north of them as they passed into the Pacific. They called this headland Cape Horne (named after the town in Holland from whence they came). It was not until 1624 that the Cape was discovered to be on a small island of its own. Not until 1820 was land found to the south of the Drake Passage. That land was Antarctica some 400 miles away.

After the opening of the Panama Canal in 1914 little commercial traffic passed the Cape any more. Today only a few very large crude oil carriers, too wide to pass through the Canal, and the occasional passenger or cruise ship pass that way. The only regular traffic consists of myriad pleasure yachts and adventurers bent on attempting the fastest sailing route around the world, each seeking their own 'Mount Everest' moment.

The passage around Cape Horn is one of the most hazardous sea routes in the world. Depressions rush unceasingly eastwards uninterrupted by any land. These bring with them north-westerly gales which back to the south-west as weather fronts pass (the reverse of what happens in the northern hemisphere). Below 40° South these winds are known as the 'Roaring Forties', then the 'Furious Fifties' and finally the 'Screaming Sixties'. Cape Horn lies at a latitude of 56° South (the southern tip of south Africa lies at only 35° South). The strength of the winds is affected by the narrowing effect of the gap between the mountains of south America and the Antarctica land mass to the south. The winds funnel through the narrow Drake Passage increasing in speed as they pass.

These winds build up gigantic waves which march round the world uninterrupted by any land and they create an almost continual strong east going current. When this current meets the occasional opposing strong easterly winds even larger waves can build up which can be dangerous to all shipping.

Another factor affecting wave size is the shoaling of the sea to the west of the Horn and across the Drake Passage. This makes the already large waves shorter and steeper as they approach. Rogue waves one-hundred feet high can build up.

Ice is another hazard affecting sailors venturing into these waters. In the summer months, ice is generally confined to below 50° South but during the rest of the year it can be found as far north as 40° South. 'Growlers' and icebergs more than a mile long can be encountered in the vicinity of the Horn.

Newfoundland whalers frequenting these waters in the old days had a saying: 'Below 40° South - no law, below 50° South - no God'.

In the days of the old square-rigged sailing ships, which found it hard to make to windward even in good conditions, these winds, currents and icebergs made the passage extremely hazardous; especially when passing from east to west. Often little progress could be made against the winds and the oncoming seas. In 1905 a clipper ship called the *British Isles,* one of the largest three masted vessels ever built, tried for seventy-two days to round the Horn to reach Chile. Earlier still, in 1788, Captain William Bligh on HMS *Bounty* made only eighty-five miles headway in thirty-one days trying to sail from east to west. Facing a near mutiny, he gave up and turned east to reach the Pacific via South Africa and the Indian Ocean. Many ships were wrecked and many men lost when trying to double the Horn.

The last commercial sailing ship to round the Horn was the German four-masted barque *Pamir* carrying grain from Australia to England in 1949.

Today's fore and aft rigged yachts find it less difficult in making the east-west passage and are able to make to windward in almost any conditions. They are able to take advantage of today's reliable weather forecasts to wait until conditions improve and then make a dash for it. However, despite all of this, a voyage round the Horn is still an extremely hazardous undertaking and the winds and high seas have lost none of their ferocity, especially in a small boat with a small crew. To do the passage single-handed is even more of an achievement. It is these early voyages which are described in this book.

The book starts with a brief account of the life and voyages of the first and greatest single-hander of all time. Indeed, perhaps the greatest sailor of all time. He wrote one of the best sailing books ever published but did not actually sail round Cape Horn. As the first man to sail alone in these waters, he can be forgiven for passing though the Magellan Strait, rather than standing on for the Horn itself. But his life was so outstanding and his voyage around the world (and his earlier voyages) so cleverly and entertainingly recalled that it would be unforgivable not to include his story in this account. Having passed near to the Horn will suffice in his case. Mention is also made of the first four single-handed circumnavigators who were inspired by him and followed in his footsteps. Three of these, however, chose to stay in the warm waters and soft winds of the tropics and took the easier route of traversing the Panama Canal to get past south America. The fourth followed Slocum through the Magellan Strait.

The book then describes the lives and voyages of the eleven men who sailed solo past the Horn before December 1972, the month of the last moon landing. After that, technology and advances in yacht design and materials opened the floodgates and the rounding of the Cape has become almost commonplace. This should not take away from the achievement of these first eleven 'astronauts of Cape Horn'.

Today, yachts of one, two or three hulls emblazoned with sponsors logos (mainly French) looking like Formula One racing cars hurtle past the Horn, some singlehanded and some fully crewed, at speeds unimaginable a few years ago. The single-handed 'rock star' sailors on these boats are a breed apart. They are full time professionals, subsidised by huge amounts of corporate money but they are not really alone. They are in continual shore contact via satellite and internet links to a 'mission control' centre. They have shore teams monitoring their every move (including blood pressure and diet) with weather experts continually telling them which route to follow. They have highly qualified technicians at the end of a satellite phone to help in the event of breakdown or electronic failure or health problems. They transmit regular videos and blogs of their progress and tracking beacons beam their speed and position to the world in real time.

Today, in addition to these passing racing machines, an increasing number of cruising yachts visit the area and a fleet of charter yachts has grown up at Ushuaia in Argentina, the world's furthest south city, where shore facilities for them exist. They take charter parties on trips to the waters of the Horn and Tierra del Fuego and even further south to Antarctica.

It must not be forgotten, however, that before any of these ships, boats and men from the north came to Tierra del Fuego and Patagonia, tribes of native people had populated the area since from around 8,000 years B.C. These Yaghan Indians, some of whom were reputed to be cannibals, lived in the most primitive conditions and adapted so well to the cold and wet to the extent that they did without clothes and often went around naked, even in the depths of winter. They had no written language and paddled their canoes through and around the myriad channels and islands that make up Tierra del Fuego. They were described by Charles Darwin, who studied them in 1833 when HMS *Beagle* was in Tierra del Fuego, as follows:

'These poor wretches were stunted in their growth, their hideous faces bedaubed with white paint, their skins filthy and greasy, their hair entangled, their voices discordant, and their gestures violent. Viewing such men one can hardly make oneself believe that they are fellow creatures and inhabitants of the same world....'

These natives were virtually wiped out in the late nineteenth century by incoming settlers. They are the real heroes of Cape Horn and, amongst their number, there would have been that first man who one day clambered aboard his canoe and, braving the seas in search of food, paddled his way south of Cape Horn.

PART II
SLOCUM AND HIS FOLLOWERS

Before we look at the lives and voyages of the first eleven men who braved Cape Horn alone, we should take a look at the pioneers who came before them, who showed it was possible to sail small boats alone around the world and it was likewise possible (albeit with a crew) to sail south of the Horn in a small yacht. The first and greatest of all single-handers was Joshua Slocum. After him several followed, most keeping to tropical waters far away from the cold and stormy waters of Patagonia and Tierra del Fuego. Then there were three yachts each of which with a full crew braved the waters of the Horn and passed that way before the first single-hander decided that if a crewed yacht could do it, then it could be done solo. We shall examine the lives and voyages of these pioneers in this section.

Chapter 1
Joshua Slocum – The granddaddy of them all

On 24 April 1895, a fifty-one-year-old sea captain set sail alone from Boston on the east coast of North America on a passage which was to take him round the world and into the history books. On his return he wrote what is probably the best and most loved book about a sea voyage ever written. It has never been out of print since its first publication in 1900. Not only did the author write an immortal book but he was the first man ever to sail round the world with nobody but himself as captain, mate and crew. Many have repeated his feat but no-one else can be the first. In an introduction to a 1948 edition of the book Arthur Ransome wrote:-

'His place in history is as secure as Adam's. So long as men sail the seas they will be interested in that first single-handed circumnavigation and will wish to read the book. It has inspired and will inspire many other voyages. It has illumuned and will illumine the dreams of many boat owners. It has been and will be a delight to many who can voyage only in their own armchairs.'

The man was Joshua Slocum.

Early life

Slocum was born in Nova Scotia in 1844 into a seafaring family and as a child spent every minute of his spare time in and out of boats. At the age of sixteen he and a friend sailed before the mast in a fully rigged ship from St John's in New Brunswick to Dublin. Next he sailed as an ordinary seaman from England to China. From there he voyaged through the Malaccas to Australia and back. At the age of eighteen he was promoted to second mate. He twice rounded Cape Horn under sail. His next venture was commercial salmon fishing on the American Pacific coast. Then in 1869, at the age of twenty-five, he was given his first command.

A year later he was in command of a barque sailing from San Francisco to Sydney, where Captain Slocum married his first wife. She sailed with him on the barque *Washington* on a 6,000 mile voyage from Sydney to the Alaskan salmon fisheries. The ship took with it all that was necessary to build the small boats from which they would fish. The crew built them to Slocum's designs as they sailed north. Soon after arrival, the *Washington* dragged anchor in a gale, was driven ashore and wrecked. She could not be refloated. Slocum salvaged everything from the ship, built living quarters and established his fishery. He then built a 35-foot whaler in which, at the end of the season, he, his wife and his crew all reached the nearest port.

He was next given command of the *Constitution*, sailing between San Francisco, Sydney and the South Sea Islands.

In 1873 he was in Manila where the ship of which he was master was sold from under him and he was landed almost penniless, along with his wife and four children. To make ends meet Slocum agreed to build a 150 ton steamship for a friend. First he built a house for his family, between the jungle and the shore. Then he began to turn raw jungle into a boat. All the timber had to be cut on the spot and sawn into planks by hand. Despite many difficulties and the resentment of the local natives, the ship was completed and as part payment for his efforts Slocum was given a 90 ton schooner, the *Pato*.

Thus Slocum became a ship owner for the first time. He had many adventures in this vessel including salvaging a valuable cargo from a sunken British barque on a dangerous reef 400 miles from Manila, sailing to Hong Kong and then 2,900 miles north to the Sea of Okhotsk, where the crew fished for cod out of dories. He then sailed the *Pato* 3,000 miles to Victoria in British Columbia where he sold her 'for a bag of gold' as he put it. He bought a share in an ancient 400 ton barque, the *Amethyst*, planning to use her in the timber trade between the Philippines and China. Later she became a general freighter roaming the Pacific.

Slocum then became part owner and captain of the ship *Northern Light*, which he called 'the finest American sailing vessel afloat'. He then bought a fast barque, the *Aquidneck*, and it was on her that his first wife died in Buenos Aires in 1885. The following year, he took the *Aquidneck* to New York and there married his second wife. After many adventures around the eastern seaboard of South America, the *Aquidneck* sailed from Montevideo up the Bay of Paranagua in Brazil to the village of Guarakasava to load a cargo of timber. Slocum, his second wife and two of their children, Victor and Garfield, spent the Christmas of 1887 on board while the vessel was being loaded. On leaving, and whilst sailing across the Bay to reach open sea, the ship missed stays and ran aground on a dangerous sand bar. The anchor was let go but she dragged broadside on and grounded on the bar. A strong swell pounded her on the hard sand for days until she broke her back. No lives were lost and Slocum managed to sell the wreck. He used the proceeds to pay off the crew, who found passage to Montevideo. Slocum and his family were, once again, left stranded and penniless.

Voyage of the *Liberdade*

No ships came their way, so Slocum, with only his compass, charts and a chronometer to his name, decided, once again, to build a boat to sail himself and his family out of trouble and home. With help from his son Victor, he set out to build a suitable vessel, strong enough to take them up the coast of south America and across the Caribbean. All they had were a few tools saved from the wreck. They had an axe, an adze, two saws, one auger and one bit, two sail needles and a file. They made other tools as they went along. Trees from the neighbouring forest were felled. Metal fastenings were gathered wherever they could be found. Some came from the bulwarks of the wreck, others from the hinges of the doors and skylights, others were made from the wreck's sheathing which the natives melted down and cast into copper nails. Wooden pegs were fashioned to serve as additional fastenings and rope lashings were made from the fibrous bark of trees. Slocum described his craft as *'sufficiently strong and seaworthy to withstand all the buffetings on the main upon which, in due course, she was launched.'*

They started work in January 1888 and she was launched four months later on 13 May. This was the same day on which the slaves of Brazil were liberated. To celebrate this, Slocum named his boat the *Liberdade*, 'Liberty' in Portuguese.

The *Liberdade* was 35 feet long, which seemed to be Slocum's lucky length. The first whaler he built in Alaska to take him and his crew home after the loss of the *Washington* and his famous boat the *Spray*, which took him around the world, were both also the same length.

The Liberdade was 7 feet wide and drew 3 feet. She was modelled from Slocum's recollections of Cape Ann dories and on a photograph of a Japanese Sampan. Her rig was that of a Chinese junk, which he considered the most convenient boat rig in the world. Mrs Slocum made the sails.

A drawing in Slocum's account of the voyage shows the *Liberdade* as a typical double ended flat bottomed dory with a straight overhanging bow, strongly raked stern and lifting rudder, a central cabin built with wooden sides and covered with a lashed down tarpaulin, an aft steering cockpit and a fore hold marked as 'crew'. A cook's stove is shown next to the cockpit by the entrance to the cabin. The ship, or canoe as Slocum preferred to call her, was rigged with three masts from which were set gaff sails with full length bamboo battens and 'lazy-jacks'. Around the full length of the gunwale were fastened a number of bamboo sponsons made from long bamboo poles lashed together. Slocum considered these made the *Liberdade* self righting in the event of a capsize, rather like today's 'RIBs' or rigid inflatables, which have an inflatable collar around the sides. Each joint in the bamboo was an air chamber of several pounds buoyancy and they had thousands of these joints.

Slocum needed permission from the Port Authorities to set sail and leave Brazil. His first request was met by a suggestion that, before they let him go, he should build the Port a new boat, everyone being so impressed by the *Liberdade*. This did not appeal and Slocum came up with a subterfuge. He would merely seek a fishing licence. Thus he set out to equip the *Liberdade* with what would be needed for a fishing voyage. A net was made, hooks and lines were rigged and a ninety-fathom cable made from vines which grew on the sandbanks. Slocum made a wooden anchor out of heavy sinking timber; but then one day a man brought along a proper ship's anchor which his slaves, not knowing what it was, had used as a pot holder! Slocum bartered this for his wife's sewing machine.

The port authorities readily granted him a licence 'to catch fish inside and outside of the bar.'

'And how far outside the bar may this carry us?' Slocum asked.

'Quien sabe?' said the officer – this, in Portuguese, serves for 'Who knows' or 'I don't care.'

'Adieu,' said the official 'we will meet in heaven.'

Slocum wrote '*This meant you can go since you insist on it but I must not officially know of it and you will probably go to the bottom. In this he and many others were mistaken.*'

On 24 June 1888, having loaded all stores, including 100 pounds of dried beef, 120 pounds of sea-biscuits, 120 gallons of water and a musket and a carbine, they crossed the bar and stood out to sea. The wind was from the south-west which brought in a heavy swell that broke and thundered on the bar, keeping other ships inside. *Liberdade* handled the seas 'like a bird' and in the first twenty-four hours made a run of 150 miles and they passed Santos Heads. They put into Santos where they met up with a mail ship, the SS *Finance*, which was bound for Rio de Janeiro. The *Finance* threw a line to the *Liberdade* and took her in tow. They had an exhilarating ride. Mrs Slocum and Garfield took passage on the steamer and Slocum and Victor remained on board, with Victor being given the job of holding an axe to cut the cable if *Liberdade* should take a sudden shear. With spray dashing over them, Slocum sat at the helm for twenty-four hours as they were towed at thirteen knots with waves rising high above the gunwale of the canoe. It was, said Slocum, the most exhilarating ride of his life and proved the boat's seaworthiness. In Rio he met his Excellency the Minister of Marine, who exchanged Slocum's fishing pass for a *'Passe Especial'* and with a clean Bill of Health, they were ready for the next stage of the voyage.

From Rio, which they left on 23 July, they met with head winds and made slow progress to pass Cape Frio. Here they were attacked by a sixty-foot whale which came up under the boat giving them a great scare. In a gale they successfully navigated dangerous coral reefs and they arrived at Bahia after nine days at sea. There they repaired the whale damage.

From Bahia to Pernambuco they were wafted along by constant trade winds with little disturbing their peace for five days. From Pernambuco, they rounded Cape San Roque with a favourable current behind them but ran into a strong gale about half way to the River Amazon. Slocum made the mistake of running for the shore only to find the ship in shallow water with steep breaking waves. They struggled on, sometimes buried in the midst of foaming breakers and at times tossed like a reed on the crest of a wave until little by little they reached deeper water. Slocum was convinced it was the elasticity of his canoe, not its bulk, which saved them from destruction. One night a phantom of their old ship the *Aquidneck* swept past them with all sails set, the skysails seemingly brushing the stars. The sight of this beautiful ship, so like their old steed, left them all bereft and longing for home.

With gaining confidence in their vessel, Slocum pressed on with all sail set until one day the mainmast went overboard followed by the foremast. These were recovered and were soon strengthened by 'fishes' or splints and refitted. They pressed on for Barbados which they reached after nineteen days at sea, a distance of 2,150 miles. There they met many old friends and spent the days resting until 7 October when they set off just after the end of the hurricane season. They glided through the Antilles into the Caribbean. After five days they stopped at Puerto Rico. They then pressed on passing Haiti and Cuba and, on reaching the Bahamas Channel, came to the Lobos Light on a small cay, where they found shelter and anchored to replenish their water supply. On the cay at that time there was a store of some 100,000 gallons of rainwater for use by passing ships. At first the keeper of the light refused them water thinking they were pirates or smugglers but upon seeing Slocum's *Passe Especial* (even though he could not read a word of it) he told them to take all the water they wanted. Two days later they reached Bimini in the Bahamas whereupon they headed on out into the Gulf Stream for America and home.

After a rough crossing they arrived at Cape Roman on the coast of south Carolina. They anchored two miles from the shore in the evening of 28 October, thirteen days from Puerto Rico and twenty-one days from Barbados. They had covered over 5,500 miles in fifty-three sailing days – an average of 103 miles a day, a remarkable effort for a home built 'canoe' which had cost them less than one hundred dollars.

They then set off for Washington DC, taking many inshore passages to avoid the autumn gales. They arrived there on 27 December 1888 where they moored for the winter. Slocum wrote '*After bringing us through the dangers of a tropical voyage....we learned to love the little canoe as well as anything could be loved that is made by hands.*'

The next April they sailed the *Liberdade* to Boston, Slocum's home port, via New York, Newport and Martha's Vineyard. Finally, in 1890 the *Liberdade* was sailed back to Washington DC, where she ended her days as an exhibit in the Smithsonian Institution, '*a haven of honour that many will be glad to know she has won*'.

Whilst this story of the *Liberdade* has little to do with Cape Horn, it is such a marvellous story that it has to be told. It serves as a perfect prelude to the tale of this wonderful and admirable man's voyage alone around the world and demonstrates the qualities that made him such a great seaman.

Chapter 2
Slocum's voyage round the world

The boat - *Spray*

One winter day in 1892, Slocum was in Boston in Massachusetts, wondering what to do with himself, undecided as to whether to apply for a sea command or go to work in a local shipyard. There he met an old friend of his, a whaling captain, who said to Slocum: 'Come to Fairhaven and I'll give you a ship. But,' he added, 'she wants some repairs.'

Slocum went to Fairhaven and found the ship. She was a very antiquated sloop called the *Spray*, propped up ashore in a field some way from the sea. She had been there for seven years. The locals, when seeing Slocum's interest, assumed he had come to break her up. 'No. I'm going to rebuild her,' Slocum said. They were amazed.

Slocum took an axe and felled a nearby tree for a new keel. Saplings were steamed in a steam box until supple and then bent as new ribs. A new stem was fashioned from the butt of an oak tree and was considered strong enough to smash ice; later during Slocum's voyage this piece of oak split a coral patch in two without receiving a blemish.

By March of that year work was well underway. The planks for this new vessel, for this is what she was becoming, were of Georgia pine, one and a half inches thick. A new deck of white pine was fitted. Two cabins were constructed, the aft fitted out with two bunks, a chest for clothing, book cases and a medicine chest. The forward cabin housed the galley.

The *Spray* was 35 feet long, 14 feet wide and 4 feet deep. She was essentially a new boat built over, and to the same shape, as the old one which had been built more than one-hundred years before as an oyster boat on the coast of Delaware. She was extremely beamy and shallow, a shape which today would not be considered at all suitable for the voyage Slocum was about to undertake. She carried her original rig, with a large gaff mainsail, a staysail and a foresail set from the end of a long bowsprit. For light weather she flew a flying jib set from a bamboo stick fastened to the bowsprit. He altered the rig later in his voyage. In Chile, after passing through the Strait of Magellan, Slocum converted her into a yawl by adding a mizzen mast, setting what Slocum called a 'jigger'. He also shortened the bowsprit and boom, cutting down the size of the mainsail, which was then easier to handle.

Slocum maintained that he was always able to get his *Spray* to steer herself on any point of sailing, something which many pundits and cynics have since doubted. Slocum claimed that in the run he made from Thursday Island to the Keeling Cocos Islands, a distance of 2,700 miles in twenty-three days, he was never at the helm, save for about one hour. This all with a following wind, the direction in which it is normally most difficult to get a boat to sail herself.

In all *Spray* cost Slocum US$ 550 plus thirteen months of his own labour.

Slocum spent a season in his new boat fishing along the New England coast but by April 1824 he had decided to make a voyage around the world, alone. On 24 April 1895 with a fair wind, he weighed anchor in Boston harbour, set sail and squared away north for the fishing harbour of Gloucester. He stayed there for two weeks obtaining the supplies he needed. He found an old fishing dory which he cut in half, boarding up the end where it was cut, to use as a tender. He left Gloucester on 7 May and headed south calling in at Westport and Yarmouth on Cape Cod before heading out into the Atlantic. It was in Yarmouth where he acquired, for a single dollar, his famous tin alarm clock, the only time piece he carried on the whole voyage and which at a later stage he boiled in oil to keep it going.

It was a measure of Slocum's outstanding ability as a navigator that he managed without an accurate marine chronometer as carried by most vessels, knowledge of the exact time being necessary for an accurate determination of longitude. However, for an expert like Slocum there was another way which only needed a rough indication of the time. This he proved when he was master of the *Constitution*. After sailing from Honolulu to San Francisco the ship's chronometer broke down. Most masters would have returned to port and waited for a new one. Instead Slocum carried on and made an unusually fast passage for which the ship's owners presented him with a gold watch. Slocum navigated by checking the time from lunar observations with a sextant. These calculations and formulae are extremely complex and tables of lunar distances have long been omitted from Nautical Almanacs, being so little used. All Slocum needed was a clock that roughly indicated the hour.

Thus began the most renowned and successful voyage in all seafaring history. Slocum and *Spray* made a perfect combination. Slocum the consummate seaman, comfortable in his own skin, confident of his abilities, content with his own company but equally at home with the lowly long-shore men he met along the way or in the society salons into which he was invited at his ports of call.

Spray turned out to be the perfect single-hander. Steady on the helm, able to sail herself on all points of sailing for days on end, comfortable in a seaway, capable of handling the heavy weather she met, stable, strong as a rock and no sluggard. Much of this was due to Slocum's superb seamanship but the ship itself had these qualities built into her.

The voyage

Slocum and *Spray* left the harbour of Yarmouth in New England and headed out into the Atlantic on 2 July 1895. On the evening of the first day Slocum wrote that *Spray* was making eight knots in smooth water whilst he had strawberries and tea for his supper. During the first days Slocum suffered some pangs of loneliness but these soon left him never to return.

On 19 July, eighteen days out, he saw land ahead and the next day arrived at Horta on the island of Fayal in the Azores.   Four days later he set sail for Gibraltar. A day out Slocum developed agonising stomach cramps, brought on, he thought, by a surfeit of cheese and plums given to him before he left. He was forced to leave *Spray* sailing herself in a smart breeze whilst he lay in the cabin writhing in agony. Some while later he came too to find *Spray* plunging into a heavy sea. Looking out of the companion-way, he thought he saw a tall man at the helm. His clothes were those of a foreign sailor wearing a large red hat.

'*Senor,*' the apparition said, '*I have come to do you no harm. I am one of Columbus's crew. I am the pilot of the Pinta come to aid you. Lie quiet, senor captain and I will guide your ship tonight. You will be alright tomorrow*'. Slocum made himself comfortable but never took his eyes off this strange guest all night. The next morning Slocum found he was, of course, alone on *Spray* but she was heading just as he had left her having made ninety miles in the night through a rough sea. Slocum wrote '*I felt grateful to the old pilot but I marvelled some that he had not taken in the jib*'.

Spray arrived in Gibraltar on 4 August where he was taken under the wing of the British Royal Navy. He was entertained on three royal naval battleships who were visiting the rock. The Governor of Gibraltar and the United States consul called and visited *Spray*. Such was the novelty of what Slocum was doing that he received this type of reception wherever he went.

From Gibraltar Slocum had been intending to travel 'eastabout' around the world via the Mediterranean and the Suez Canal (which had been opened in 1869) but was dissuaded from this route by alarming tales of piracy in the Mediterranean and the Red Sea. Everyone told Slocum that on his own he would never be able to defend himself. He therefore decided to change his route and go 'westabout' via the south Atlantic and south America.

He left Gibraltar on 25 August 1895 heading south-west only to be chased almost immediately by a pirate felucca. So much for the dangers of the Mediterranean! Slocum piled on all sail but only outran the pirates when they broached on top of a large wave and lost their mast. He passed the Canary Islands and then the Cape Verde Islands, stopping at neither. On he went through the Doldrums, where *Spray* came across much shipping (these waters would be deserted today) and soon met the south-east trade winds which drove him and his ship toward the coast of Brazil. Slocum anchored in the port of Pernambuco on 5 October, forty days out from Gibraltar. There he rested until 24 October.

He continued on to Rio de Janeiro, meeting some rough weather on the way. In early December Slocum tried to avoid a north going current by hugging the shore. Unfortunately he hugged it too close and ran hard and fast onto a beach. He managed to lay out an anchor but in doing so capsized in his small dory and only with difficulty righted it and got back to the *Spray*. Eventually, with the help of some locals, *Spray* was refloated. Next he visited Montevideo and Buenos Aires, where Slocum shortened his mainmast and lopped five feet off his bowsprit.

Slocum set sail from Buenos Aires on 26 January 1896 heading for the Strait of Magellan. He reached Cape Virgin, which marks the start of the Strait, on 11 February. Slocum wrote of this: *'The scene was again real and gloomy; the wind north-east and blowing a gale, sending feather-white spume along the coast; such a sea ran as would swamp an ill-appointed ship.'* A day or two later Slocum was faced with a 180 degree switch in the wind and the sudden onslaught of a ferocious south-west gale, which blew for thirty hours. *Spray* held her own tacking to and fro across the narrow channel. Slocum narrowly avoided being blown right out of the Strait. It was an indication of what was to come.

The Strait of Magellan is 350 miles long but only a little over a mile wide at its narrowest point. It took Magellan thirty-eight days to pass through. Today, this route is hardly used, except by cruise ships exploring the Chilean waters and the occasional yacht. Most passing boats prefer the achievement of making the Horn proper (which sometimes can be an easier route). To use the Strait is considered a bit like a climber reaching the South Col on Everest and then not going on to the summit. The Strait curves and winds between the mainland and the Tierra del Fuego archipelago with many areas of narrows, in which strong tidal streams and eddies can be found. The weather is extremely unpredictable, with frequent short lived gales. The area is famous for its '*williwaws*', sudden strong blasts of wind descending almost vertically from the surrounding mountainous coastline. In other words, it is not a place to linger.

Half way along the Strait is the town of Punta Arenas, where in Slocum's day there was a small coaling station for passing steamships. There were then no facilities for yachtsmen but Slocum found a good anchorage off the settlement. Pretty few facilities will be found there even today and it is acknowledged as a very lumpy and uncomfortable anchorage through which strong tides run.

There he was advised to 'ship hands' with him for the remainder of the passage so as to 'fight the Indians', the Fuegian Yaghan natives, most of whom were hostile, and some of whom were reputed to be cannibals. Slocum could not find anyone to come with him so a kindly ship's captain gave him a bag of carpet tacks saying: '*use with discretion and don't step on them yourself*'. With some trepidation he set sail on 19 February 1896. He anchored the first night in a small bay and there had his first experience of williwaws. Slocum pressed on, anchoring every night in a sheltered bay, but facing strong headwinds on much of his passage. Eventually he reached Port Tamar from where he sailed, without incident or attack by natives, to Cape Pilar at the westernmost end of the Strait and then out into the Pacific Ocean. There he faced the fiercest gale he had yet met. He left *Spray* under bare poles and they drifted before the wind for four days. He was lucky in that the wind drove her south along the coast toward Cape Horn itself. He could well have met a wind with much west in it, in which case he would have been blown ashore, On the fifth morning he found *Spray* being blown toward some ferocious looking rocks and breakers. These rocks were known as the Milky Way and lay north-west of a channel, the Cockburn Channel, which led back into the Magellan Strait. Somehow Slocum conned *Spray* through these rocks into the channel and he was soon back in smooth water, near where he had started some six days before. That night he anchored in a snug anchorage in Froward Reach. Before he turned in he sprinkled the decks with the carpet tacks. He was woken by a crowd of savages clambering onto his deck and then howling like a pack of hounds, clawing the air with rage, as their bare feet discovered the carpet tacks. They jumped pell-mell into the sea or into their canoes and fled. Slocum fired his gun at them as they retreated.

Now Slocum was forced to retrace his steps through the Strait back to

Sandy Point and on to Cape Pilar again. He had the same fight against head winds and adverse currents. Having made six attempts to get past Cape Pilar, the *Spray* eventually broke free on 23 April 1986 and headed north-west into the Pacific with a favourable south-east wind. Fifteen days later, he reached Juan Fernandez Island, the island on which Alexander Selkirk had been marooned and which was the model for Daniel Defoe's 'Robinson Crusoe'.

Slocum continued across the Pacific, stopping often amongst the Polynesian islands. He visited Australia, sailed across the Indian Ocean and rounded the Cape of Good Hope. In Cape Town, Slocum met President Kruger, who as a believer that the world was flat, told Slocum it was impossible for him to be sailing round the world but rather that he was merely sailing in the world.

Slocum then sailed up the length of the Atlantic Ocean to arrive back in Boston on 3 July 1898, just over three years after he had left. He sailed *Spray* round the coast to her birthplace in Fairhaven and tied her up to the same old stake that had held her when she was launched.

Slocum went on sailing *Spray* for the rest of his life and in 1909 at the age of sixty-five set out on his 'last voyage'. He left Bristol on Rhode Island bound for the Orinoco River in Venezuela. Neither Slocum nor *Spray* were ever seen again.

It was not until 1959 that a story emerged making it likely that *Spray* had been run down and sunk by a mail ship two nights after Slocum had left Turtle Island in the Lesser Antilles. The captain of a mail ship later revealed that on one dark night they had hit what the captain claimed was a 'native boat'. The second mate of the ship, who witnessed the collision, reported that the boat they hit was definitely not a native one and that there was no-one at the wheel. A long deep gash in the stem of the mail ship was apparent when it put into port. The steamer's officers decided to keep quiet about the collision and nothing was said at the time. This story can never be proved but it has the ring of truth about it.

Chapter 3
The next three to go

The next three single-handers to circumnavigate the world set off in 1921, 1924 and 1928 respectively. However, these sailors preferred the steady trade winds and warm waters of the tropics and sub-tropics. They all passed through the Panama Canal, thus avoiding the cold, storms and big seas of the Southern Ocean. These sailors merit mention for their pioneering exploits, opening up as they did the various routes which thousands have followed in subsequent years. They were also the first to describe the pleasures and wonders to be found in travelling in and wandering amongst the Polynesian islands of the Pacific.

Harry Pidgeon

Born in 1874 on a farm in Iowa, Pidgeon did not set eyes on the sea until he was eight. His first experience of water was as a canoeist in Alaska, where he and a friend built a canoe and 'shot' the rapids on a descent of the Yukon River. Back on his home farm Pidgeon could not settle down so returned to Alaska looking for adventure. He went exploring and hunting. He turned to photography as a hobby which he later turned into a business. Next he went to Minneapolis where he built a houseboat on which he spent a year gently floating down the Mississippi to New Orleans. Reluctantly he returned to the plains of Iowa, where he took up farming and ran a photography business.

But he had tasted adventure and he wanted more. He wanted to see the world. One day he realized he could do this in a boat of his own, if he could find the money to build one.

He found what he wanted in the pages of the American yachting magazine *Rudder*. It was a design by its famous editor, Thomas Fleming Day, for a 34-foot yacht which Day called the *Sea Bird*. The design was for a 'V' bottom boat with a single chine, easy to build and specifically aimed at amateur builders. Pidgeon sent for a set of plans which came in a book entitled *How to Build a Cruising Yawl*. This book contained the plans and offsets for three different designs. Pidgeon took ideas from all three, adding a few of his own. In 1917 on the shore of Los Angeles Harbour he started building his dream boat. It took him a year to complete and cost him US$ 1,000. He called the boat the *Islander.* In 1918, after the First World War had ended, Pidgeon went on a shakedown cruise to Hawaii, taking a companion for the return leg.

On 18 November 1921 he set off alone from Los Angeles bound for the South Seas. As to the perils of sailing alone he said 'It is only the starting that is hard.' His voyage is wonderfully described in his book *Around the World Single-Handed* and he pioneered the route which has been taken by yachtsmen ever since – west across the Pacific to the Polynesian Islands, including the Marquesas, Tahiti, Moorea, Samoa, Fiji and the New Hebrides, then across the Timor Sea north of Australia, across the Indian Ocean to Cape Town, up the Atlantic to the Caribbean, then west to the Panama Canal, (which he was the first to transit solo) and finally north back to Los Angeles. The voyage lasted from 1921 to 1925. He repeated the voyage in the years between 1932 and 1937, becoming the first man to sail twice around the world alone. He had adventures everywhere he went, was warmly welcomed at each stop he made, was fascinated by the Marquesas islanders and became enamoured with Tahiti. On the first voyage he suffered many groundings, often having no up to date charts, and he was forced to make a lengthy stop to repair his boat on Prince of Wales Island, off the northern tip of Australia. Christmas was spent in Durban and later he met the worst seas of his voyage off the Cape of Good Hope. Soon after leaving Cape Town he was embayed and driven ashore on a sandy beach. Nearby farmers helped him get *Islander* afloat. They couldn't understand what Pidgeon was doing - like their President Kruger, they believed the world was flat and how could anyone sail 'round it'.

He stopped at St Helena and Ascension Island on his way up the Atlantic and then called in at Port of Spain in Trinidad before making for the Panama Canal. There he met Alain Gerbault (see later in this chapter) who was also passing through the canal on board his yacht *Firecrest*. Pidgeon did not like *Firecrest* as she was a hard-to-handle racing yacht and Gerbault did not like *Islander;* he thought her ugly, offending his aesthetic sensibilities. For passage through the canal, Pidgeon had to pay three and three quarter dollars for the toll and five dollars for his boat to be measured.

It took Pidgeon eighty-five days for the passage from Balboa, at the exit of the canal, to Los Angeles. He drifted for many weeks in the Doldrums. He arrived on 31 October 1925, just under four years since he departed. He was awarded the third Blue Water Medal by the Cruising Club of America. *Islander* was shipped across America, free of charge, to be displayed in New

York. Pidgeon stayed on the east coast for four years, living on board whilst he wrote a book about his voyage.

In 1932 Pidgeon set off on his second circumnavigation, which took him five years, following a similar route. Later during World War II he married and in 1947, at the age of seventy-three, he and his bride departed from Hawaii on a third round the world voyage. They got caught in a typhoon in the New Hebrides and the *Islander*, by then old and tired, was driven ashore and wrecked. Back home again he started building another *Sea Bird* design, a little smaller than *Islander*, but Pidgeon died at the age of eighty-one before the vessel was finished.

Pidgeon said he loved every minute of his voyages, which were made not simply for the joy of sailing but because it was his way of seeing something of the world. He added that the days he spent on them were the freest and happiest of his life. Pidgeon asked little from life, never accumulated much wealth, but just wanted to go on his way alone. He had that estimable quality of getting a huge amount out of life with the minimum of fuss and without being any trouble to anyone. He was remembered fondly by all the people he met around the world, from lowly natives to the highest officials. In this he shared with Joshua Slocum many of the same qualities. They were two extraordinary men.

Alain Gerbault

Two years after Pidgeon had set off on his voyage, a Frenchman called Alain Gerbault left New York headed for the Panama Canal. He followed in Pidgeon's footsteps, meeting him at the entrance to the Panama Canal, and ended his circumnavigation in France in 1929. He was the third man to sail around the world alone and the first Frenchman. He arrived back a hero.

Alain Gerbault was very much a loner and a dreamer. He came from an aristocratic French family, was a flying ace in the First World War, became a tennis champion, an international bridge player and a top football player. In between all this, he worked as a civil engineer. Despite all the acclaim these achievements brought him, Gerbault always felt his life was hollow and constantly strove to find something more, something deeper.

In an attempt to escape and find what he was seeking Gerbault took up sailing and bought a yacht. She was called *Firecrest* and in many ways was totally unsuitable for his intended solo voyaging. Built in England in 1892 of teak and oak she was a fast racing yacht designed by the famous naval architect Dixon Kemp. She was exceedingly narrow and deep, a type known as 'plank on edge' (the result of an idiosyncratic rating rule in force at the time), had an extremely narrow beam of only 8 feet and a draft of 7 feet on an overall length of 39 feet. She was flush decked, very fast but very wet and sailed at an extreme angle of heel, cutting through oncoming seas instead of rising to them. Rigged at first as a gaff cutter with a long overhanging boom and a 12-foot bowsprit, she was a real handful for one man to handle. To get to know *Firecrest*, Gerbault sailed her in the Mediterranean for two years. During this time he also became French tennis champion.

It is almost impossible for yachtsmen today to understand just how hard it was in those days to sail a boat like *Firecrest* across an ocean, with or without a crew. Ropes were cotton, sisal or hemp, all of which rotted and became rock hard when wet. Sails were made from cotton or flax which were subject to rot, were easily stretched out of shape and became as hard as a board when wet with rain, spray or sea water. Standing rigging was galvanised wire which needed splicing by hand. Foresails were hanked on with bronze piston hanks.

To balance properly, the boat needed both a staysail and a foresail, set from the end of her 12-foot bowsprit,. Headsails had to be constantly changed on a heaving pitching deck with the bow frequently underwater. There were no bow pulpits or guardrails to keep one on board. There was no engine and no electricity. There were no winches. Running backstays, necessary to keep the mast standing, had to be let go or set up with tackles on each tack or gybe. Lights were flickering paraffin lamps and all navigation had to be done with sextant and chronometer. The sails had to be balanced so that the boat could be made to sail herself to allow the skipper to sleep, cook meals and perform the never ending repairs of sails and rigging. Foul weather gear comprised leaky oilskin trousers, a fisherman's smock and a sou'wester, none of which were particularly effective. The boats had no radios, flares, liferafts, lifejackets or safety harnesses. And yet, these early sailors, knowing nothing else, never complained and performed amazing feats.

Without telling anyone of his plans, and turning his back on his brilliant career, Gerbault set sail alone from Cannes on 5 April 1924 and, after stopping in Gibraltar, to repair a broken goose-neck on his boom, sailed *Firecrest* to New York.

On leaving Gibraltar, he was immediately faced by two weeks of incessant westerly gales. His old sails and tired rigging gave him trouble from the start. Gerbault described in his book, *The Fight of the Firecrest,* how on 20 August, with the wind at hurricane strength, he was hit by a massive wave, *'a thing of beauty as well as awe as it came roaring down upon us'*, which buried the boat under tons of solid water. Gerbault leapt into the rigging to save himself. In time the *Firecrest* emerged, partially disabled, and the great wave roared away to leeward. The 12-foot bowsprit was broken halfway along held on only by the jib stay. It lay in a maze of rigging and sail canvas under the lee rail, where the sea was using it as a battering ram against the planking threatening at every blow to stave a hole in the hull. The mast was swaying dangerously. Gerbault managed to get the wreckage aboard, secure the mast and set a trysail. He continued, plagued by rigging and sail problems, until he reached New York after 101 days at sea. Despite having left France quietly and with no announcement he was besieged and wildly acclaimed as the first single-hander ever to sail across the north Atlantic from Europe to north America. He became a hero in France, was awarded the Legion d'Honneur and was the first man to be awarded the Blue Water Medal of the Cruising Club of America. That year he also won the tennis Davis Cup for France.

In New York, Gerbault got rid of *Firecrest's* gaff rig and replaced it with a bermudan mainsail hoisted on a new hollow 46-foot mast. He had a new boom made and he shortened the bowsprit by three feet.

Gerbault set off in *Firecrest*, again alone, from City Island in New York on 2 November 1924 this time bound around the world. He was determined to prove that life could be lived simply, honestly and in contact with the things which he thought really mattered.

He made a three month stop in Bermuda, where he had the underwater copper sheathing removed and the whole hull re-caulked. At Panama he anchored for two months making preparations for his long cruise through the Pacific.

Sailing was never the whole thing with Gerbault. It was merely part of his need for remote islands, secluded anchorages and simple people, wandering and savouring new experiences as he went. Over the coming months he sailed slowly through the island chains of Polynesia. He fell in love with Mangareva and its people and nearly gave up the venture then and there. However, despite all the attractions on offer in those islands, Gerbault always refused to have any physical relationship with, or have a child by, any Polynesian girl as he felt this would defile the purity and beauty of these island races.

He went on to Tahiti, Bora Bora, Samoa and the Wallis Islands. There he experienced his worst moment in the Pacific. One night a gale got up and *Firecrest* broke her anchor chain. She dragged across the lagoon onto a reef where she grounded and lay battered against the coral. She heeled right over until water began to pour below through the skylight. Gerbault could do nothing but swim for shore. To his amazement, when half way there, he saw *Firecrest* float off the reef and seemingly follow him. At the same time as he reached the beach, the boat drove into the sand beside him.

By daybreak the gale had passed and Gerbault, who had become convinced his voyage was over, saw that *Firecrest's* lead keel and the ten bronze bolts which secured it were missing. Relieved of the weight of four tons of lead, she had floated free of the reef. Gerbault found the keel and, with lots of help, dragged it off the reef and floated it back. He now needed ten new bronze bolts on an island which had no forge and was very rarely visited from outside. Eventually, after a failed attempt using a forge on a passing tramp steamer, a French Naval sloop arrived. The navy crew forged new bolts for him and refastened the keel to the hull. It was four months before he was able to leave the island.

He then ventured slowly through the rest of the Pacific before passing north of Australia. He followed Pidgeon's route back into the Atlantic and sailed into Cherbourg in Normandy on 21 July 1929, five years after he had left New York. He had spent 700 days at sea and covered over 40,000 miles. His was the third solo circumnavigation.

The titles of the two books Gerbault wrote on his return reflected what he was seeking. The first, a simple account of his circumnavigation, was published in November 1929 titled *'In Quest of the Sun'* and the second, an impression of life in the Polynesian islands, was published in August 1933 and called *'The Gospel of the Sun'.* This book was dedicated to Marao Taaora, Queen of Tahiti, with the words: *'with a pleasant memory of our tales and all my feelings of admiration and love for all that belongs to Tahiti.'*

As soon as he could escape from the acclaim and publicity that greeted him, Gerbault immersed himself in building a new 34 foot long cutter which he called simply *Alain Gerbault*. When asked his destination he merely said 'toward the South Seas'. Back in the Pacific he spent many years on a solitary tour of Polynesia, shunning all officials and Europeans. Like Robert Louis Stevenson and Paul Gauguin before him he sensed and understood the unique culture of the Pacific natives and lamented their disappearing civilisation amid contamination by European and American influences. At the end he was found suffering from malaria aboard his boat at Dili, in Portuguese Timor, where he died on 16 December 1941. He was only 47. In 1946 his body was transferred back to Bora Bora by the French navy where he was buried with full naval honours.

Edward Miles

The fourth man to sail round the world alone was a strange and almost forgotten figure, the American sailor Edward Miles. He set off from New York in August 1928, whilst Alain Gerbault was still at sea. Miles was the first man to sail around the world 'eastabout' via the Mediterranean and the Suez Canal. His voyage was unusual and eventful, but is hardly remembered today, if at all. He wrote an account of his voyage in his book '*Miles and Knots, a Voyage Alone with One Man Boat Sturdy*', which is now virtually unobtainable.

After a career at sea as a young man, Miles settled in Memphis where he became a successful house builder. He made sufficient money to build a yacht, which enabled him to sail the world's oceans so as to promote his own personal message of hope and reconciliation. He believed that fundamentally people were friendly and kind who, if left to themselves, desired peace not war. In the 1930s he wanted to spread this message in an attempt to prevent another world war. He is reported as saying *'Prejudices are unnatural and are stirred up by so-called patriots who thrive on racial prejudice'*, a sentiment which has much resonance today.

Miles single-handedly built the *Sturdy*, a schooner-rigged yacht 37 feet long and 11 feet wide. He completed her in 1928 after two years of hard work, doing everything himself including the casting of a 5,000 pound lead keel. Miles refused all offers of help from friends. His long suffering wife left him when she learnt of his plans.

Aged forty-nine, he and *Sturdy* left New York in 1928 and arrived in Gibraltar after forty-five days at sea. During his voyaging Miles wrote little about the trip itself preferring to write about his quest to bring goodwill and peace to the people of other countries.

He next sailed across the Mediterranean calling in at Tangier, Algiers, Tunis and Malta. He then made a detour to Greece and Istanbul, ending up in Alexandria in Egypt. He visited officials in each of these countries to talk brotherhood and reconciliation. He laid up the yacht in Alexandria and returned to America.

Nine months later he returned and passed through the Suez Canal. Three days out into the Red Sea, in blistering heat, Miles spilled some petrol which caught fire and the *Sturdy* was burnt to the waterline. Miles escaped and managed to reach a nearby lighthouse. He was taken back to the Suez Canal.

Miles returned to the USA by steamer, drawing up as he went a set of plans for a new boat. Back in Memphis he started all over again and built a somewhat altered version of the original. *Sturdy II* was a foot shorter than the original with a twenty horse-power auxiliary engine, a diesel this time. Whilst building this boat he divorced his first wife (who had left him some time before) and promptly re-married (this wife stayed at home during his travels).

On completion, the new vessel was shipped to Egypt on the deck of a steamer and launched at a port near Suez. In September 1930, he once more entered the Red Sea. Miles described his passage down the Red Sea as 'pure hell'. He experienced extreme heat, calms and light winds and had to run the engine almost continually to make any progress. To try to keep cool he rigged up a pump to spray sea water over a canopy spread above the cockpit. Next he sailed across the Indian Ocean to India where he spent much time promoting his cause. Passing down the Malabar coast, he crossed to Ceylon where he promptly went aground on a coral reef when entering the port of Galle. Local fishermen helped him to get *Sturdy II* afloat and to repair the damage. Miles reflected later that this example of Christians, Buddhists and Muslims all working together to help an unknown human being reinforced his conviction that he was on the right course toward a better world.

He crossed the Bay of Bengal and sailed through the Malacca Strait to Singapore. From there he went on to Manila, Hong Kong and Japan. He crossed the Pacific to Honolulu in a time of fifty-two days, the longest passage of his trip, *Sturdy II* being the first small boat to sail this route. He spent a month there delivering his message to the mixed race population. Next he crossed the remainder of the Pacific to San Francisco in eighteen days and then, stopping often, sailed down the western seaboard of America and Mexico to the Panama Canal. From Panama he sailed to Cuba and on up the Atlantic coast to New York arriving there on 17 June 1932, some six years after he had started to build the original *Sturdy*. He arrived back broke and penniless.

He could not find a publisher or magazine interested in his writings, or in his account of his voyage. In order to live and to continue his mission, he was forced to sell first his navigation instruments, then his tools and sails and finally the *Sturdy II* itself. He received US$ 1,000 for her, less than a fifth of the cost of the materials that had gone into building her.

In 1933, Miles formed an organisation to fight against religious and racial prejudice. But at that time, with the likelihood of world war looming and America deep in recession, no-one was interested in his ideas and Miles was considered an impractical dreamer. Despite having no funds (sometimes not even enough to eat) he never became embittered but put people's response to his message down to ignorance. Amazingly, in 1944 Miles ran for president of the USA as an independent. He was defeated by Franklin D Roosevelt. To the end he never regretted sailing 32,000 miles alone to try to bring friendship and understanding to the world.

Interestingly, the route taken by Miles was the route Slocum had intended to take until the British Royal Navy warned Slocum off a passage across the Mediterranean on account of pirates. Thus, on leaving Gibraltar, Slocum turned west, instead of east, and into the history books. Miles received no such warning, went east, and is now all but forgotten.

Chapter 4
Louis Bernicot follows in Slocum's wake

S ome four years after Edward Miles arrived back in New York a Frenchman, Jean Louis Bernicot, set off on a solo circumnavigation in his yacht *Anahita*. He was inspired by Slocum, but unlike the first three of Slocum's followers described above, Bernicot shunned the easy passage though the Panama Canal. Instead he headed south to follow Slocum through the Magellan Strait.

Bernicot is a bit of an enigma for whilst he made a very efficient and seamanlike voyage, it is difficult to work out a real motive for what he did. Unlike Harry Pidgeon, he was not a wide-eyed wanderer intent on seeing and experiencing as much of the world as possible, with the sailing merely a means of travel. Unlike Gerbault, he was not a romantic seduced by the Polynesian islanders who, after his voyage, went back to live amongst them, promoting their cause and helping them survive in a hostile world. Unlike Miles he had no message to impart to the world. Captain Bernicot, as he was called, was simply a loner, a very competent seaman and navigator, who liked the solitary life at sea without having much interest in the lands he passed by.

Like Slocum on the other hand, Bernicot was a retired sea Captain but without much of Slocum's *joie de vivre*. The book Bernicot wrote about his voyage is somewhat pedestrian and contains little insight as to Bernicot's real thoughts as he crossed the oceans of the world. This book, originally written in French, was later translated into English by Edward Allcard (see chapter 10 below), himself a renowned author and world girdling sailor, who tried to enliven Bernicot's account as best he could.

As a reason for his voyage, Bernicot quoted some words from a poem by the Reunion poet Leon Dierx,:-

> *'To be alone, to be happy, to forget the universe...*
> *To let the pure breeze blow through the hair,*
> *Far from the sinful men and a deceitful world*
> *To intoxicate oneself with silence and shade and whispers.'*

These words do not really connect with what Bernicot actually achieved or recorded. He stopped only twelve times during the whole trip and hurried back to France after a voyage lasting only twenty-one months, involving less than twelve months actual sailing time. This was in fact a very fast time for those early days. His few short sightseeing trips ashore were mostly provided by local influential people and do not suggest a man inquisitive about the nature and beauty of the rest of the world. He later told Edward Allcard that he only went alone as he could not persuade anybody in his family to accompany him.

Bernicot, unlike Slocum, clearly stood on ceremony and never forgot who he was - a Captain of the old school, who only spoke to his crew through his junior officers. Slocum would speak to and mingle with every-one he met of whatever rank and standing, including lowly members of his ships' crews, and he relished their company. Bernicot on the other hand confined himself to meeting and talking to people of his own rank. In a telling piece in his book, when two Spanish fishing boats with enthusiastic waving crews circled his boat he records *without concerning myself with them any more I returned to my interrupted work....*. They were merely Spanish fisherman but he was the French Captain Bernicot. The Polish yachtsman, Richard Konkolski, in a short piece he wrote about Bernicot, records how Bernicot never failed to list the full names and titles of all officials he met but did not once mention even the first names of the many people who really helped him and often shared with him all they possessed. He never scrubbed or painted his boat in port – that was not Captain's work.

Louis Bernicot was born on 13 December 1883 at L'Aber-Wrac'h on the north coast of Brittany. He studied at Brest and joined the French Merchant Navy. He then spent nine months aboard the four masted barque *President Felix Faure* and obtained his Junior Officer's certificate. Two years later in 1908 he received his Masters Certificate at Bordeaux and joined the Compagnie Generale Transatlantique, with which company he stayed until his retirement in 1934 at the age of fifty-five. He moved to a small estate he had in the Dordogne area of SW France and became a gentleman farmer. After a year or two he decided it was not the life for him. Instead he would build a boat and sail round the world. He knew that his fellow Frenchman Gerbault had already done this in the *Firecrest* but admitted he had not read his book. He was quite ignorant of Joshua Slocum and the *Spray* until he saw his name mentioned in a magazine. Bernicot thought this an odd coincidence as he said he had already made up his mind to go through the Magellan Strait before learning of Slocum's route.

51

The boat - *Anahita*

After studying Slocum's book, Bernicot decided on the type of boat he wanted. She was to be quite different from the *Spray*, being much more conventional for her day - long and narrow with a deep draft. He commissioned a design from the French naval architect, Talma Bertrand. She was to be 41 feet long, 11 feet wide with a draft of 5 feet and 7 inches.

When ordering her from boatbuilders in Carantec in Brittany he insisted on two things which in those days would have been considered peculiar – namely, no internal ballast and a dog-house at the end of the coachroof, rising about three feet above the deck. There was much shaking of heads from the builders who thought this served no useful purpose and would be vulnerable to sweeping seas. The boat was rigged as a Bermudan cutter with roller reefing on the main boom. Another innovation was that Bernicot had a steering wheel fitted inside the dog-house, under the floor of which there was a small auxiliary petrol engine.

The voyage

Bernicot took delivery of the *Anahita*, in August 1936. Upon seeing her for the first time he had the mast shortened by three feet. With no sea trials he filled up his one hundred gallon water tank, took on his food supplies and set off on 22 August 1936 bound for Argentina. He crossed the Bay of Biscay in good conditions and set a course to pass twenty miles clear of the Spanish and Portuguese coasts. On 28 August he experienced his first spell of bad weather and found the boat very hard on the helm and difficult to keep on course. The rudder became increasingly stiff to turn and he decided to put into Funchal on Madeira, which he reached on 5 September. The shipyard could not find anything wrong but merely poured molten tallow down the rudder trunk telling him it would ease with use.. He stocked up with fresh fruit and vegetables and left three days later, planning to sail non-stop to Mar del Plata in Argentina.

After passing the Canaries and Cape Verde Islands (likeSlocum he did not stop at either) he experienced fresh head winds rather than the to be expected north-east trades. On 1 October he reached the Doldrums which he passed through quickly, with the help of his engine. He crossed the Equator on 13 October, further west than was advisable. Square rigged sailing ships of old would often have difficulty in doubling Cape San Roque on the western tip of Brazil. If they hit the coast north of the Cape, these ships, not being able to make much progress to windward against an ever present northerly current, would have to turn back north-east and take a huge clockwise circular route far out into the north Atlantic until they met the north-east trade winds when they would try again, crossing the equator further to the east. This could add weeks or even months for a trip to Argentina or Cape Horn.

Bernicot recorded pleasant sailing down to the Tropic of Capricorn, where he lost his watch overboard, his only accurate timepiece. He was then left with only a small dashboard clock of unknown accuracy and he had to navigate by dead reckoning from there on, with no real knowledge of his longitude. He was also finding it very difficult to get his boat to steer herself with the wind abaft the beam. *Anahita's* bottom was fouling badly and on one calm day, whilst trying to scrape off the weeds with a scraper attached to his boat hook, Bernicot lent out too far and slid head first into the water. Dropping the scraper he managed to grab the boat's rail and haul himself back aboard. He had a lucky escape.

In early November, on approaching the coast, he was hit by a violent *pampero*. These warm strong dry winds blowing off the land are at their strongest between the months of October and January. On 11 December he sighted the heights of Mar del Plata in Argentina and by the evening passed between the massive breakwaters protecting this artificial harbour. *Anahita* was dried out for a bottom paint and, following a few dinners with local dignitaries, Bernicot left on 22 December.

He had a hard passage to the entrance to the Magellan Strait, far to the south, and progress was slow. On 7 January the barometer fell steeply and by the next morning Bernicot got his first introduction to the waters and winds of the 'Roaring Forties'. In the teeth of a full gale, a real Cape Horner, he struggled to lower all sail whilst facing the biggest seas he had ever experienced. At one- thirty in the morning he went below to get some sleep but it was no more than thirty minutes before he was flung violently against the adjacent bulkhead. After a pause *Anahita* righted herself, having been hit beam on by a huge sea which nearly rolled her over. Bernicot sorted out the mess both on deck and below, where the cabin was in total disorder with his navigation books, charts and much food floating about in oily bilge water. His sextant was badly damaged and the engine had filled with sea water. At daybreak on 16 January he sighted the Patagonian coast to the north of Cape Virgin, which marks the entrance to the Magellan Strait.

Square rigged sailing ships were advised not to attempt the east to west passage of the Magellan Strait, as the prevailing winds would force them to tack back and forth in the channels, which are between two and ten miles wide. Logs of navigators from those days record passages through the Strait lasting for up to eighty days, i.e. no more than an average of four miles a day! As far west as Punta Arenas the weather can be moderate but further to the west the weather is nearly always very bad and is probably the worst to be found in any inhabited region of the world.

The Strait, which Bernicot now entered, is fifteen miles wide at its entrance until the first narrows are met forty miles westward, where the tides run at up to eight knots. After the second narrows there is an inland sea called Broad Reach with the port of Punta Arenas on the west bank. Forty miles south of this the Strait bends round to the west and then leads almost straight toward the Pacific in a north-west direction. This last part is subject to fierce tidal streams coming from both the Pacific and the Atlantic. Although there are many possible anchorages, they are difficult to reach and offer only minimal shelter. All are subject to strong winds and *williwaws,* sudden violent, cold, katabatic gusts of wind descending from the surrounding mountains.

Bernicot remarked in his book that the seas he met were not big but were very short and steep putting great strain on the boat. He wrote that the winds he found would have been ideal for *Anahita* to have headed south through the Le Maire Strait (which lies between the mainland and Staten Island to the east) and then on to Cape Horn. Instead *Anahita* found herself pitching and plunging into a steep sea, making little or no headway.

No one had yet sailed alone south of Cape Horn and Bernicot probably did not believe it was possible. Had he done so he would have sailed into the history books.

Eventually he arrived at Punta Arenas and on the morning of 23 January, Bernicot dropped anchor where Slocum had anchored *Spray* some forty years before. Little had changed. The next day *Anahita* was towed to the naval quay and moored alongside a warship where he met various local dignitaries. He told the French military attaché to Chile, who was visiting the area, that he did not have time to join him in an expedition to Tierra del Fuego, an opportunity most passing seamen would have jumped at. Bernicot just did not seem interested in these things.

On 26 January, he set sail to a light breeze in fair weather and at first made good progress. Later he ran into strong south-westerly squalls which produced yet another steep choppy sea into which *Anahita* pitched badly. In one of these plunges the stemhead fitting, which he had recently repaired, pulled off putting the mast in danger. He carried on looking for calmer water. By ten o'clock that evening he had Cape Froward abeam, the turning point and most southerly point of the mainland of south America, Tierra del Fuego to the south being an island. He continued, fearing for his mast, until he reached Playa Parda, a perfectly sheltered bay with a very narrow entrance. At first he anchored outside then plucked up courage to try the narrow entrance, which his chart showed was no more than 200 feet wide with deep water close to on the starboard side. As he approached, Bernicot could not see the entrance until nearly touching the rocks. Bernicot trusted himself to his chart, which was based on an English survey dated 1868 and which he found absolutely correct. On entering the basin Bernicot was startled by the beauty of the place. He anchored in the middle of a sheet of perfectly calm water with gigantic rocky masses overhanging on every side. Two waterfalls poured fresh water into the pool. Looking back from where he had come Bernicot could not see any entrance and he was quite enclosed in total isolation. He rowed ashore, filled his cans with fresh water and collected a bucket full of mussels. Back on board he repaired the fitting which fastened the forestays to the stemhead. The next morning Bernicot with regret headed out of his splendid isolation to continue his struggle to get out of the Strait.

Just before dawn, two days later, Bernicot sighted the flash from the lighthouse Felix, being the last light on the southern side of the Strait before the open sea. He pressed on with a following wind taking advantage of these exceptional conditions. Bernicot recalled that Slocum only succeeded in passing Cape Pilar at his seventh attempt. Bernicot was having it easy.

On 29 January 1937, Bernicot and *Anahita* passed Cape Pilar where-upon they met a huge Pacific swell from the south-west. The strengthening easterly wind blew the crests off the tops off the on-coming waves in an impressive fashion. Bernicot reflected that there was nothing 'pacific' about the ocean he had just entered. He passed near to a wreck with its masts sticking vertically out of the water. Later he nearly hit a mass of wreckage with loose rigging hanging from it. The whole scene had a demoralising effect on the old mariner who was fearful of the long voyage ahead, despite his having successfully navigated the Magellan Strait in exemplary fashion.

Soon after noon he passed a lighthouse, built on isolated rocks far from the shore, which was Bernicot's last sighting of the coast of south America.

The wind soon increased and backed to the north-west, the sky turned dark and Bernicot struggled to get away from a lee shore. Soon he was beating into a full gale and was forced to heave to. He was driven far to the south but there was enough north in the wind to prevent him from being blown ashore. He was lucky. The gale lasted for seven days with Bernicot getting very tired and suffering an attack of lumbago. For days afterwards he was only able to crawl about the deck.

Gradually Bernicot coaxed *Anahita* to the north but ran into another gale three days later and hove to for thirty-six hours. Once again Bernicot was uncertain of his longitude. He had two watches on board and found a difference of five minutes between them. Foolishly, he had not checked or rated either before leaving Punta Arenas and therefore had no way of knowing which was correct. Any sextant sight he took could therefore give him a position many miles out. Later he passed Juan Fernandez Island which lies on the 35° South parallel but he had no way of calculating how far off he was.

The wind now settled in the south-east. He had reached the trade winds at last. On 16 March, Easter Island appeared on his port bow. There being no safe anchorage on the island, Bernicot sailed onward but he was now sure of his position. He became impatient to reach his destination of Tahiti but as he was running short of fresh water, he decided to call in at the legendary Mangareva. There, like all incoming sailors arriving from the cold and damp rocky coasts of south America, he was amazed by the startlingly white sandy tropical beach off which he dropped his anchor. He was invited by the Governor to stay at the Residency and take his meals there, even though he was told that the islands were short of supplies as no ship had called for over five months. Bernicot carried out various repairs and had *Anahita* dried out so as to check the rudder which was still giving trouble. Natives cleaned her bottom using coconut fibres instead of brushes.

On 13 April Bernicot set off with filled water tanks and, demonstrating the generosity of the natives, he was given an ample supply of bananas, oranges, mangoes and coconuts. Late on the evening of 29 April he reached Tahiti, sailed round Venus Point and dropped anchor in the placid waters of a sleeping Papeete.

Bernicot's stay in Papeete followed his usual pattern. He saw little of the town, the island or the local people. He visited and was entertained by the local dignitaries, including the Governor, carried out various repairs and had the bottom of the boat cleaned and repainted. He remarked in his book: '...*as for the natives themselves, I cannot say much about them; one sees so little of them...*'. He had a new mainsail made and a local boat builder moved the mast forward by six inches to improve balance and to stop the boom hitting the backstay. Then it was time to leave.

Most voyagers, having sailed half the way round the world to get to the island paradise of Tahiti and the Society Islands, linger there for a while or maybe even for a whole season. These islands are amongst the most beautiful in the world and the natives most welcoming (as the sailors on HMS *Bounty* under Captain William Bligh found to their cost). Most circumnavigators would visit the lovely nearby island of Moorea before setting off for home. Not so for Bernicot, with 20,000 miles still to go he wanted to press on and he left Tahiti on 26 May 1937, twenty-five days after arriving.

He soon passed the island of Moorea and later that night Maiao, the last land he would see until the New Hebrides. On 14 June he crossed the 180° meridian, the International Date Line, and jumped straight into 16 June having had no 15 June. He passed the New Hebrides on 22 June after an uneventful passage with much calm weather.

A few days later as he neared the entrance to the Torres Strait, the narrow pass between the northern tip of Australia and New Guinea, the weather became threatening and he became uncertain of his position. Eventually he sighted the beacon on Bramble Cay, which marks the start of the Bligh Channel, named after Captain Bligh of HMS *Bounty* fame. Bligh passed this way with his eighteen men in the 20-foot ship's boat having been set adrift by the mutineers. The Torres Strait passes through a maze of coral reefs and islands with shifting underwater sand dunes, through which strong tidal streams flow. It is very shallow with depths of only between four and eight fathoms. Bernicot met squally weather and was forced to spend the first night tacking back and forth in in the narrow channel as he could not find a suitable anchorage. The next day he anchored in some rough unprotected shallows off Coconut Island, which Gerbault had visited on his voyage in the *Firecrest* (described in his book *In Quest of the Sun*).

Two days later he sailed south-west to Thursday Island, which marks the end of the Torres Strait and which is only twenty-four kilometres north of mainland Australia. He then passed through the Arafura Sea in six days of good weather after which he entered the Timor Sea. On 26 July Bernicot sighted Roti Island near Timor. This island was where Bligh made his land-fall at the end of his voyage. Bligh's men were exhausted and near death and were taken in at a Dutch trading post. They all recovered their health and not one man was lost on their incredible voyage, something which did much to help Bligh regain his reputation as a fine seaman.

After a rough crossing of the Timor Sea, Bernicot passed Christmas Island on 3 August, without stopping. Four days later he anchored off Direction Island in the Keeling or Cocos islands, where he was met by the usual assortment of dignitaries and staff from the Eastern Telegraph Company. He then moved *Anahita* to Home Island, to the same place where Slocum had beached *Spray* to paint her bottom. Bernicot did the same. On 22 August, exactly one year to the day after he had departed from Carantec, he set sail for the 2,300 mile passage to Mauritius, his next port of call.

Here, Bernicot did actually show some interest in his surroundings, made several outings over the island and described some of the people he met. Maybe this was because from the moment he arrived in this French island he became the centre of attention and much talked and written about. Perhaps he actually liked his moment of fame. Bernicot related in his book how one journalist in a newspaper article about him 'artlessly' expressed his disappointment at not finding a character more in keeping with his expectations.

A ship repair yard offered Bernicot a free lift-out for *Anahita*, the same offer they had made to Harry Pidgeon on his second round the world trip on the *Islander*. Bernicot refused this as he was keen to press on and he left Port Louis on 16 September.

He headed for Reunion, which he reached late in the evening on the next day. Again he received invitations from all quarters, lunched with the Governor, was taken on a tour of the island and visited Cilaos, a picturesque caldera in the centre of the island. Bernicot was now enjoying his celebrity status and his old aloofness from his days as a ship's captain appeared to be dropping away. He was actually becoming approachable. In his book he now starts to write more freely about his exploits ashore. Back at the port, *Anahita* was hauled out and the whole boat repainted. Repairs were carried out to the deck to cure leaks and the rigging was treated for rust.

With the start of the hurricane season drawing near Bernicot left Reunion on 20 October. After five good days with a fair wind he was within 300 miles of Durban when he was forced to heave to for two days to allow a north-east gale to pass. He ended up being towed into Pot Natal in a flat calm.

The distance from Durban to Cape Town is 840 miles and is often a difficult passage. By standing out to sea one can gain advantage from the strong south-west flowing Agulhas current but can then run into frequent fierce westerly gales. These blowing against the current produce some of the worst seas found anywhere in the world. Large crude carriers and container ships have broken their backs and been sunk by giant rogue waves which develop here, especially over the shallows of the Agulhas Bank.

Bernicot left Port Natal on 2 December and had an easy passage until he approached the entrance to Cape Town, where the wind went round to the south-east and blew up to a Force 10 gale. He could not make it past the mole at the entrance of the harbour and was forced to anchor in its lee. A powerful launch came out from the Royal Cape Yacht Club and towed him in. Bernicot cannot have been too happy having had to be towed into both the ports he visited in South Africa.

Originally Bernicot had planned to sail from Cape Town to St. Helena and Ascension Island but decided instead to sail direct to Gabon so as to meet up with one of his sons who was working in west Africa. Bernicot left Cape Town on 4 January 1938. Sailors usually avoid the seas off the west coast of Africa as winds are generally very light and a permanent area of high pressure persists in this area. The preferred route is out into the Atlantic where the south-east trades can be picked up. Bernicot however kept close to the coast and experienced persistent light winds, but he was helped by the Benguela current which flows up the African coast toward Namibia. As Bernicot passed the mouth of the Congo River the sea took on a dark olive colour, caused by silt and vegetation driven seaward by the current. This can be seen up to 300 miles out to sea. On 26 January he raised the coast to the south of Pointe Noire in the Congo, his destination.

Bernicot never met up with his son who, he learnt on arrival, had actually been in the port a few weeks before on his way to a new job in the interior of Gabon. There was no way of communicating and Bernicot was not prepared to leave his boat for the three weeks it would take him to get Gabon and back. Bernicot therefore put in hand various repairs, including replacing much of the rigging and having the mainsail re-cut. Once more the boat was hauled out and the bottom painted.

Bernicot, judging his boat to be in good shape to face the north Atlantic, set sail on 2 March on one of the longest legs of his voyage. He had provisioned the ship for a non-stop 6,000 mile passage to France. He had worked out that this was quite feasible as for most of the way he should benefit from favourable conditions provided he took the route of the old sailing ships. He would take a long detour westward out into the Atlantic, going outside the Cape Verde and Canary Islands, aiming to cross the equator at 20° West (Pointe-Noire lay 15° East). Then he would take a curve north into the Atlantic until he reached the westerlies which would blow him home.

The passage started well but then he had to endure two weeks of calms and light winds. On 28 March *Anahita* crossed the Equator at 19° 15' West and two days later he crossed his outward path after nineteen months away and after less then twelve months of actual sailing. He made slow progress through the Doldrums and the area known as the 'Horse Latitudes', where a large area of high pressure persists. Bernicot decided to replenish his supplies by calling in at Horta in the Azores, which he reached after sixty-seven days at sea. On 14 May he set off heading for the Gironde estuary and Bordeaux in France.

As he entered the Bay of Biscay he crossed the 'line of fire', the name given by sailors to the busy shipping route between Ushant and Cape

Finisterre (so named because as you approach the area at night all you see is a line of lights stretching all along the horizon from ships steaming north or south in a steady procession.) Bernicot met typical squally Biscay weather, At nightfall on 29 May 1938 Bernicot sighted the glow of the Coubre lighthouse which marks the northern side of the entrance to the Gironde estuary. As it got darker the wind increased, heavy rain started to fall, the seas became short and steep and the visibility became very thick. At two o'clock in the morning and not really knowing where he was, he felt his way into the mouth of the estuary. He saw no lights. Eventually he decided he was off the town of Le Verdon-sur-Mer where he anchored, having sailed 31,010 nautical miles since leaving France. A year later the Second World War started.

Bernicot ends his book with the following words:

At four o'clock on the morning of May 30th 1938, Anahita, with her wings folded, lay at anchor, rolling to the short swell coming round Pointe de Grave.

Bernicot was the second Frenchman to sail alone around the world and only the fourth man in history. It was an exemplary voyage carried out in a fast time and with no fuss or drama and probably for the first time (but not the last) it was the sailing which was the most important factor and not the visiting of strange lands or the meeting of new people. Bernicot returned to his farm for the duration of the Second World War, in which he played no part.

Later life

Miraculously, *Anahita* survived the war intact. Many yachts in France were requisitioned or destroyed by the Germans or had their lead or iron keels and all metalwork removed to aid the war effort. However, she did suffer from five years of neglect which Bernicot soon put right after the Liberation.

The first voyage Bernicot made once the war was over was in September 1945 when he sailed *Anahita* to Pointe Noire in west Africa to take his son back to Gabon to resume his employment there. They sailed from La Trinité in Brittany via Casablanca, the Canary Islands and Dakar. They arrived in the Congo in January 1946. This voyage must have been one of the first long distance voyages to have taken place only four months after the end of the Second World War in Europe. He arrived back in France in June 1946.

Bernicot continued to sail *Anahita,* often with his family and friends. He sailed alone to Casablanca in 1951 and made his last voyage, also to Morocco, in 1952. He died at his home in the Dordogne on 29 November 1952 aged sixty- eight.

There are a number of differing accounts about the circumstances of his death. Edward Allcard, in the foreword to his translation of Bernicot's book, states that on the way to Casablanca on his last voyage, Bernicot had to go aloft in bad weather. Whilst aloft a wire shroud parted and struck him hard on the head causing him severe injury. Bernicot told no-one of the accident when he reached port. Allcard then says that he developed a tumour and six weeks after his return to France he died.

Don Holm, the American writer, in his book 'The Circumnavigators' says that in the autumn of 1952 while Bernicot was working atop the mast, a stay snapped and knocked Bernicot to the deck, killing him.

An entry in Wikipedia France states that in 1952 Bernicot had an accident whilst moored in the island of St Martin de Ré, and suffered pain to his groin. In August of that year, back in the Dordogne, he was diagnosed with untreatable oesophagus cancer. The truth probably lies somewhere between the first and third account. Bernicot was buried at St Nexans near his farm.

Despite his achievements Bernicot is hardly remembered today, if at all. Had he made that fateful decision and continued south instead of turning west when he reached the entrance to the Magellan Strait, and had he carried on to pass south of Cape Horn, he would today be lionised as the first person to have successfully circumnavigated the world alone around Cape Horn. Instead he has been largely ignored. Most ignominiously of all, Edward Allcard at the age of 102, when his memory was perhaps not what it used to be, could not even remember having translated Bernicot's book into English, until I showed him a copy of it.

After Bernicot's death, *Anahita* continued to sail for many years under different owners, sailing for several seasons under the Swedish flag. In 1982 she was acquired by the Association Amerami which maintained a museum in Brest for the preservation of the maritime heritage of the Atlantic and undertook the restoration of famous vessels. Unhappily the restoration of *Anahita* never proceeded and she ended up in 2000 stored ashore in a boatyard in Honfleur in Normandy, where she deteriorated badly until she was beyond repair. Later she was destroyed and is now no more.

Chapter 5
The first yachts to pass south of the Horn

Before Slocum navigated the Magellan Strait and before Pidgeon, Gerbault and Miles had completed their solo circumnavigations via the Panama Canal, three yachts did actually sail south of Cape Horn through the Drake Strait, but all of them carried a crew - none were sailed single-handed. These three vessels and their voyages are described briefly below.

The Schooner *Coronet*

In 1888, eight years before Slocum sailed through the Magellan Strait, a magnificent fully crewed 133 foot long schooner, the *Coronet,* sailed from New York on a circumnavigation. After sailing south down the Atlantic Ocean she passed south of Cape Horn from east to west and then called at ports in Honolulu, Yokohama, Hong Kong, Ceylon, India, Aden and Malta before returning to America, arriving back in April 1889. The *Coronet* is thus the first recorded 'pleasure' vessel to have actually sailed south of Cape Horn and through the Drake Passage.

The *Coronet* had been launched in 1885 and was one of the most beautiful and elegant sailing yachts of her day (and probably of all time). She had been built with no regard to cost in a boatyard in Brooklyn for an industrialist named Rufus T Bush. She was built to cruise the world's oceans in comfort and style. She was 133 feet on deck and 190 feet from the tip of her bowsprit to the end of her mizzen boom. She was 27 feet wide, drew 12 feet, carried 75 tons of ballast and set 8,500 square-feet of sail. She shipped a crew of twelve and could take up to ten guests in sumptuous surroundings. The interior included mahogany panelled staterooms, a grand marble staircase, stained glass doors and a main saloon that featured etched mirrors with gilded mouldings, a tiled fireplace and a piano.

As mentioned in chapter 2, it was on 11 February1896 that Slocum entered the Magellan Strait to pass from the Atlantic Ocean into the Pacific. Remarkably, just eight days before that the *Coronet* had for a second time rounded Cape Horn from east to west on a second long voyage. Possibly the two vessels had met and spoken somewhere on their way down the

Atlantic. For this second passage of the Horn, the *Coronet* had left New York in December 1895 to sail to San Francisco. On 2 February they were off Staten Island and the next day passed Cape Horn in good weather with a moderate south-east wind, missing all the bad weather which Slocum experienced in the Magellan Strait. The *Coronet* drove on and arrived in San Francisco on 1 April 1896.

The *Coronet* has survived to this day and is currently undergoing a major and hugely expensive restoration in Rhode Island in the USA. Once sailing again she will be a magnificent example of America's gilded age when such a grand yacht was a symbol of great fortune and success and she will undoubtedly outshine many of today's outlandishly expensive super-yachts owned by Russian oligarchs and internet magnates.

George Blyth and *Pandora*

It was not until 1911 that a second yacht sailed south of Cape Horn, this time from west to east. She was the little known *Pandora,* built in Perth in Australia in 1910 by a British sea captain George Blyth assisted by his crew, the Australian Peter Arapakis. The *Pandora* was 37 feet long with a 14 feet beam and a draft of 6 feet. She was a rough copy of Slocum's *Spray*, one of many to be built over the coming years. She was rigged, like *Spray*, as a gaff yawl.

They left Bunbury, a port in West Australia south of Perth, on 3 May 1910 intending to sail round the world via Cape Horn and the Cape of Good Hope. *Pandora* called in at Melbourne and almost immediately after that ran into a hurricane in the Tasman Sea. She ran before the wind under bare poles, was pooped and knocked onto her beam ends. *Pandora* lost much of her deck gear and suffered damage to her bulwarks. They stopped for a month in Bluff in New Zealand to carry out repairs. Rather than take the direct course to Cape Horn, *Pandora* headed north-east and made a fast passage to the isolated and infrequently visited Pitcairn Island, which lies in latitude 25º South and is where the survivors of the mutiny on HMS *Bounty* ended up. They then stopped for a week at Easter Island, despite there being no real safe anchorage. They departed for passage round Cape Horn aiming to sail non-stop to the Falkland Islands.

On 16 January 1911, Cape Horn was some three miles on their port beam. Visibility was poor with flying scud and sleet. Blyth later wrote to a friend '*We had bad days in the Tasman but I never knew what the sea was until I came here. Off that gloomy southern end of the Fuegian archipelago there came on me a sense of foreboding'.* Despite this they sailed passed the Horn without incident.

On 22 January they were caught in a bad storm south of the Falkland Islands. *Pandora* was lying beam on to the seas under bare poles, making heavy weather of it, with the crew below and her wheel lashed. *Pandora* was hit by a huge wave which laid her on her beam ends. She capsized and was dismasted. A second wave then hit the port quarter and *Pandora* was rolled completely over. When the *Pandora* righted herself, the crew hastened on deck to find the dinghy had been washed overboard and the main mast broken. They cut away the wreckage with an axe, leaving the boat to the mercy of the waves. The next morning they were able to spread a small sail from the remaining stump of the mast and they made slow progress toward the Falkland Islands. They were sighted by a Norwegian whaler which towed them 10 miles to a whaling station on New Island, one of the most westerly islands in the Falkland archipelago.

With help from the Norwegians, the *Pandora* was repaired, given new masts and refitted for sea. On 4 March 1911 they left and sailed to St Helena and Ascension Island. They then sailed non-stop to New York in forty-six days, a distance of 4,850 miles.

Despite all their problems the crew were determined to continue round the world. They left New York bound for England but were never seen or heard from again. No wreckage was ever found. *Pandora's* voyage is, like those of the *Sturdy I* and *Sturdy II*, now largely forgotten.

Conor O'Brien and *Saoirse*

The next recorded voyage of a small yacht to sail round Cape Horn through the Drake Passage was that of the *Saoirse,* one of the very first boats to sail under the tricolour of then new Irish Free State. She was designed, built and owned by a wealthy yachtsman, Conor O'Brien, an Irish intellectual, aristocrat, patriot and ardent Irish nationalist. During the Irish rebellion O'Brien had smuggled guns to Ireland under the eyes of the British in his own yacht *Kelpie* and in the yacht *Asgard*, then owned by the well known writer and Irish nationalist, Erskine Childers (the author of the famous book *The Riddle of the Sands*). The *Asgard* is now housed in the National Museum of Ireland.

Saoirse (Gaelic for 'freedom') was 42 feet long and an exceptionally well thought out and well equipped yacht. She was designed by O'Brien himself, who was an experienced yachtsman with very definite ideas of what an ocean cruising yacht should be. *Saoirse* was built for him in Baltimore in

County Cork. She was rigged as a gaff ketch and carried a large square sail on the main mast. Below decks her accommodation was commodious and included a separate captain's cabin for O'Brien and a spacious galley with a large coal burning stove, *'the comforter of our stormy hours off the Horn'* as O'Brien put it. On deck there was a chart room in a deck house which contained an additional berth for the off watch crew.

She was sailed by the owner with three paid hands (who changed regularly and with some rapidity, some only doing short legs) in a very efficient circumnavigation. They left Dublin on 20 June 1923, passed down the Atlantic Ocean, stopping at Pernambuco in Brazil and then on to the Cape of Good Hope and Cape Town. Next they sailed south of Cape Leeuwin to Melbourne and on to Auckland in New Zealand. From there O'Brien ran *Saoirse* along the 40° South line of latitude until near the Horn, where he ducked down to 56° South.

Until he arrived off Tierra del Fuego, O'Brien was uncertain whether to pass through the Magellan Strait or go south round the Horn itself, still very much an unknown quantity. In the event as they approached land, a strong north-westerly wind drove them to the south and O'Brien thought it too rough to enter the Magellan Strait at Cape Pilar. This was where Slocum had such a struggle to escape its clutches. As they approached the Horn at the end of November 1924, the wind unexpectedly died and they drifted past the Cape and toward Staten Island. This lack of wind meant they could not get through the Le Maire Strait, which lies between Staten Island and the mainland, from where they intended to head north to Montevideo. Instead in a continuing calm, they drifted past the east of Staten Island and then made for the Falkland Islands, where they arrived on 6 December 1924, forty-six days out of Auckland, a distance of 5,800 miles. Whilst in the Falklands, O'Brien shipped on board a passing trawler and made a visit to Antarctica.

They arrived back in Dublin on 20 June 1925, exactly two years to the day from their departure. They were met by cheering crowds and O'Brien was celebrated as a hero, being the first Irishman to circumnavigate in a yacht. O'Brien wrote a very well written account of his voyage titled *Across Three Oceans,*which became a best seller.

Later that year O'Brien was commissioned to build and design a ship for the Falkland Island Company to be used to ferry people, live animals and stores between the islands. O'Brien came up with a 56-foot ketch-rigged vessel, similar in form to *Saorsie* but narrower, shallower and more elegant. She was built in Baltimore and christened the *Ilen*. She set off for the Falklands in October 1926 with O'Brien and two hands on board. She served the Falkland islanders well for nearly sixty years. The *Ilen* is now back in Baltimore undergoing a major re-fit and it is planned for her to be re-launched in 2018.

On his return to Ireland in 1927, O'Brien settled into a self sufficient life on his family owned Foynes Island on the south shore of the Shannon Estuary in County Limerick, sailing *Saorsie* whenever he could.

In 1928 he married the artist Kitty Clausen and in 1931 the couple sailed *Saorsie* to the Mediterranean, where they spent the next two years. On their return O'Brien wrote, and Kitty illustrated, a well received book describing their voyaging titled *Voyage and Discovery*. They were back in the Mediterranean in 1934 sailing amongst the Greek Islands. The next year when sailing *Saorsie* back to Ireland Kitty died suddenly when they were in Vigo in Spain.

O'Brien made no more voyages in his beloved *Saorsie* but remained in Ireland until his death sixteen years later. He produced a steady stream of books, some on sailing, together with a number of adventure stories with a nautical theme (benefiting from the huge success of Arthur Ransome's sailing stories for children). During the Second World War he joined the Small Vessels Pool, a voluntary organisation which delivered small naval vessels around the coast of the British Islands and even across the Atlantic. He sold *Saorsie* in 1941.

O'Brien died on his island in April 1952 and his coffin was rowed to the mainland to Loghill Church where he was buried. His books on seafaring and the design and handling of ocean going yachts were his legacy and influenced a whole generation of yachtsmen who came after him. For many years after O'Brien's death *Saorsie* was a well known sight, cruising extensively amongst the waters and harbours of southern England. The author remembers going on board her in the late 1950s and being impressed by the strength of her build and comfort of her cabins.

Part III
THE ELEVEN CAPE HORN
'ASTRONAUTS'

Chapter 6
Alfon Hansen – The first to go alone

Once news of Slocum's successful voyage into the stormy Southern Ocean had became known it was only a matter of time before others would try to emulate him. Pidgeon, Gerbault and Miles had shown it was possible for one man to sail a yacht solo around the world. The voyages of the *Pandora* and Conor O'Brien in *Saoirse* had shown that a small well found yacht could sail round Cape Horn, albeit fully crewed and from west to east. Nobody had as yet sailed a small yacht (the *Coronet* cannot be so described) south of Cape Horn from east to west, either fully crewed or alone.

Donald Holm in his book '*The Circumnavigators*' makes mention of a possible rounding of Cape Horn in 1849, forty-seven years before Slocum's voyage, by an American, J M Crenston, who Holm says sailed a 40-foot cutter called *Tocca* from New Bedford in Massachusetts to San Francisco via the Horn. Holm states that the trip took 226 days and the *Tocca* sailed 13,000 miles. However, the records are vague and do not say whether Crenston actually doubled the Horn itself and it is considered by others (including the nautical author and historian Commander Errol Bruce) that he actually sailed through the Magellan Straight and that he probably had a crew with him.

The first yachtsman known to have achieved a solo passage south of the Cape was a Norwegian sailor called Alfon Hansen. He set off alone from Norway in 1932 in a 36-foot gaff cutter called *Mary Jane*. Hansen was a good looking muscular man in his middle thirties. He is reputed to have had enormous hands and a shock of black hair tumbled over his forehead. He always sailed with a dog and a cat as his mascots and was proud of his library of over 100 books which he carried on board. He was a lady's man and it is said that there was mounted in his cabin a photograph of a bathing beauty autographed by Miss France, Miss Germany, Miss Russia, Miss Romania, Miss Hungary and Miss Tunisia. He had been a sailor all his life and had worked as a pilot in the Norwegian merchant marine. As a young seaman he was a member of the crew of a large luxury schooner called the *Zaca* when she called in at Nuku Hiva in the Marquesas Islands.

There Hansen met the well known Norwegian yachtsman Erling Tambs and his family who were cruising the Pacific in their yacht the *Teddy*. This meeting may have been the inspiration Hansen needed to take off to see the world from the deck of a small yacht. Whatever happened, Hansen returned to Norway and bought his own little ship.

The boat

His boat, the *Mary Jane*, had been designed by the famous Norwegian naval architect and boat builder Colin Archer, who was renowned around the world for the seaworthiness and safety of his designs. Archer designed and built a number of sailing lifeboats for the Norwegian Society for Sea Rescue, one of which now named *Colin Archer RS1* still survives as a floating museum. All his boats, of which he designed over 200, were strongly built, beamy, durable, double-enders usually rigged as gaff cutters. Many of his boats came to be converted for or used as pleasure yachts in the 20th century. His most famous vessel was the *Fram*, which was used for Nansen's expeditions to the north Pole and by Roald Amundsen on his historic expedition to Antarctica, when Amundsen and his team became the first men to reach the south Pole. The *Fram* is now housed in a museum in Oslo.

It is thought that Hansen's boat had previously been a pilot cutter. He renamed her *Mary Jane*. She was 36 feet long, 12 feet wide and drew 6 feet. She was rigged as a gaff cutter and had no engine. When there was no wind Hansen propelled her with a large oar. She was in Hansen's opinion the best possible boat for a world cruise.

The voyage

Hansen set sail from Oslo on 15 July 1932, alone save for his dog and cat, which he called Mate and Sailor. His first stop was in Weymouth in England. He sailed south across the Bay of Biscay, stopping in Gijon on the north coast of Spain. He then called in at Oporto and Lisbon. When leaving Lisbon he was well down the River Tagus before he realised his cat, Sailor, was missing. He returned and a search found her on a nearby tugboat.

Setting off again he made for Las Palmas in the Canaries. He then crossed the Atlantic to Miami in Florida, in a time of forty-three days. Rather than heading south from there, Hansen instead sailed north up the Mississippi, cruised the Great Lakes and worked his way out to sea along the St Lawrence seaway in Canada. This circuitous route, much of it on inland waterways, would have called for much use of his oar to propel the boat. When they were at Detroit, Sailor, his cat now with over 8,000 miles of cruising under her belt, was run over by a car and her place was taken by one of her kittens, who Hansen named Sailor Jr. In Chicago, Hansen visited the Century of Progress Exposition, part of the Chicago World Fair to celebrate the city's centennial.

On reaching the north Atlantic, Hansen sailed slowly south once more and eventually reached Buenos Aires in the spring of 1934, two years after he had left Norway. Hansen remarked that on long passages he hove to whenever he got tired and that his voyaging was not made in search of anything but contentment.

In Buenos Aires he moored up at the Yacht Club of Argentina where he met Vito Dumas, whose yacht *Lehg II* (a similar type to *Mary Jane*) was being built nearby. Dumas, whose remarkable story is told in chapter 7, later made his own single-handed voyage round the world via Cape Horn becoming the first man to sail solo past the Horn from west to east. Dumas and Hansen found they had much in common and soon became firm friends. At first it was their boats which bought them together but they saw in each other the same characteristics - the sharing of a sense of self reliance, a liking for loneliness and a deep feeling of restlessness. Despite this they were both somewhat larger than life outgoing characters. According to the author Donald Holm, they both retained unusually strong ties to their mothers, even when grown men (perhaps, he says, psychologists would relate this to their passion for the mother sea).

The two spent many enjoyable hours together at the yacht club where *Mary Jane* lay and where *Lehg II* was being built. Dumas was later to write: *'it was a joy that day in 1934 when Hansen came on board Lehg II, signed his name on a panel of the uncompleted cabin and expressed his approval of the boat's design'*.

Alone, save for his cat and dog, Hansen left Buenos Aires for Cape Horn in June 1934, mid winter in the southern hemisphere. Today the decision to take this route in the middle of the southern winter would be considered the height of folly. Current thinking is that mid-summer (i.e. December or January) is the right time to pass Cape Horn, when winds are thought to be at their lightest, or at their least strong, when nights are at their shortest and when the risk of meeting ice is at its least. But in 1934 the thinking was quite the reverse. Dumas, who made his passage of Cape Horn in 1943, recorded in his book *'Alone Through the Roaring Forties'* that according to the Argentine Nautical Instructions the best time for naviga-tion in Cape Horn waters was when the sun was lowest in the north. That is between the beginning of June and 15 July – midwinter in the southern hemisphere. Regardless of the wind strength, midwinter is the time when temperatures are at their lowest, when daylight is very short (Cape Horn is at 56° South, as far south as Edinburgh is north and anyone who has lived in Scotland will know how short the days are in midwinter) and when the risk of running into ice is at its highest (in mid winter ice can be found as far north as 40° South).

Hansen sailed 300 miles south and called in at Mar del Plata. He then left bound for Chile and at some time along the route became the first man to pass south of Cape Horn alone in a small yacht. After passing the Horn from east to west he arrived in Ancud in Chile 110 days out from Mar del Plata. Ancud is located on the island of Chiloe which lies off the west coast of Chile in latitude 41° South, Hansen can therefore truly claim to have 'doubled the Horn' generally defined as travelling from 50° South on one side of south America to 50° South on the other side. After a stop in Ancud to recover, Hansen set out to sail north to Puerto Corral some 200 miles away, near the port of Valdivia. He never arrived. For a long time his friends could not believe that he had been lost at sea. Months later some wreckage from the *Mary Jane* was found. There was no sign of Hansen. In all probability he was embayed and driven ashore, unable to claw off a lee shore, in one of the ever present westerly gales which batter the Chilean coast, especially in winter time.

Hansen is barely remembered today as no writings and few accounts of his voyage have survived. Had it not been for his meeting with Vito Dumas in Buenos Aires before he departed for the Horn, his voyage and achievements may never have come to light. Later Dumas wrote '*What a loss that Al Hansen with all his determination and enthusiasm should not have lived to round other capes and other seas*'.

After Hansen's voyage had ended on the wild and rocky coast of Chile, the only other lone voyager who came south to the waters of south America before the start of World War II, was Louis Bernicot in *Anahita*. He passed through the Magellan Strait, as recounted in chapter 4 above.

Chapter 7
Vito Dumas – The first man west to east

In the late 1930s with the threat of war looming, the waters of the south Atlantic and south Pacific were a place best avoided. Both Germany and Great Britain had large naval fleets stationed in these waters and pleasure yachts were not welcome. However, one man decided he could not wait for hostilities to cease before he took off on what has come to be remembered as one of the most renowned voyages of all time - to sail alone around the world through the Roaring Forties and south of Cape Horn.

The man

Unlike Slocum, Hansen and Bernicot, all of whom had been professional merchant seamen, Vito Dumas had no seafaring background and spent most of his life as a cattle rancher and farmer in the Argentine.

Dumas was born in Buenos Aires on 26 September 1900 into a family of Italian immigrants. He was strong and healthy and became a strong swimmer. At the age of twenty-three he won a River Plate championship by swimming across forty-two kilometres of the Plate estuary from Colonia in Uruguay to the Argentine. He was in the water for twenty-five and a half hours. He also began to sail small boats in the same waters.

Home life was difficult. As he grew up his parents' finances steadily deteriorated. In order to help out, Dumas was forced to leave school at fourteen and he started on a range of menial jobs, whilst continuing to study drawing and sculpture at the Academy of Art in the evenings. In his twenties he went into the cattle business where he prospered. He joined the local yacht club, sailing whenever possible.

In 1931, at the age of thirty-one, Dumas travelled to France where he bought an ancient International Eight Metre Class racing yacht, intending to sail her back to Buenos Aires. It was a most unsuitable vessel for a voyage of this type.

These boats were built to an International rating rule and were intended for inshore racing 'round the buoys'. They were smaller sisters to the Twelve Metre Class yachts which were used for a time for the America's Cup. Until

1936 the 'Eights' were the most prestigious class in the sailing Olympics. They were around 50 feet long, narrow, extremely elegant with long overhangs and carried a tall mast and large sail area They were normally raced with a crew of six. Blisteringly fast and difficult to sail well, they were open boats with large cockpits and small cabins with only minimal accommodation. They had very low freeboard and gave a very wet ride with the boats slicing through waves rather than riding over them. When raced hard in bad weather they could fill and sink and it was usual to have one crew member pumping or bailing full time. They were not at all an ideal boat for one man to sail on a long ocean voyage but Dumas chose one of these nevertheless. As far as is known, before his trip none of these boats had sailed across an ocean.

So in 1931 Dumas arrived at the inland sea of Arcachon on the west coast of France just south of Bordeaux and bought one of these beautiful boats. She was twenty years old and he called her *Lehg I*. It is said the name is an acronym of four names which marked Dumas's life. Dumas re-rigged her as a gaff yawl with smaller masts and a shortened bowsprit. Otherwise he set off in her much as she was. He left alone from Arcachon sailing out of the estuary, past the large sand dunes that guard the narrow entrance, heading for Buenos Aires, some 6,300 miles away. Dumas called in at Vigo in northern Spain, the Canaries and Rio Grande do Sul in the southernmost part of Brazil. From there he sailed on to Montevideo and then across the mouth of the River Plate home to Buenos Aires. It was an incredible voyage which was hailed in Argentina as a triumph and the boat *Lehg I* was exhibited in the Provincial Museum 'Enrique Udaondo' at Lujan in Buenos Aires where she remains to this day.

Dumas went back to his ranch and his cattle, whilst dreaming all the time of further sea voyages. Life on the Argentinian pampas satisfied him for a while but he missed the solitude, peace and freedom he found afloat and for which he had been craving all his life. In 1933 Dumas first came up with the idea of what he termed his 'impossible voyage' - to sail around the world on the 40° South line of latitude alone through the Roaring Forties. For this he needed a suitable boat.

It is extremely hard today to understand just how extraordinary even the idea of such an undertaking was in the 1930s, let alone actually setting out to do it. Prior to 1930 only two yachts had ever sailed across the Southern Ocean from Australia and then round Cape Horn and both of these had two or more people on board. Only one man had sailed alone south of Cape Horn and no man had ever sailed alone around the world south of the three most southerly capes, the Cape of Good Hope, Cape Leeuwin in Australia and Cape Horn. Dumas became convinced he could do it.

The boat *Lehg II*

Dumas approached the Argentinian naval architect, Manuel Campos, to design him something suitable. Discussions between the two men led Campos to choose the 'Norwegian' type as being ideal for sailing before the wind in bad weather. This type of double-ender can be found all round the world in varying forms. Campos knew of them in the Argentine, called 'boats with double stems' which had been developed for use in open anchorages and for launching off open beaches. In south America they were known as 'whale-boats' and were of Spanish or Mediterranean origin. In the late 1920s yachtsmen began to appreciate the excellent qualities of these boats, especially those built from the designs of the Norwegian Colin Archer. (As seen in the previous chapter, Alfon Hansen had one of his designs).

Campos investigated this type but decided that built as they were for fishing or as pilot and life boats, they were too heavily built with old fashioned gaff rigs, had too much displacement and too much interior ballast to make them suitable for the venture Dumas was planning. But Campos liked the hull form. He therefore came up with a modernised version of the classical Colin Archer – a little over 31 feet long, 11 feet wide with a draft of 5 feet and 7 inches. She was to be a Bermudan ketch with a mainsail of 215 square -feet and a mizzen of 77 square-feet. All ballast was carried in a three and a half ton external iron keel and the whole boat was simply and strongly constructed so as to keep weight to a minimum. Down below she was simply laid out comprising a galley to one side of the main companion way, two berths, a toilet compartment and a large forecastle for stowage. It was more than coincidence that this boat was very similar, although a little smaller narrower and deeper, than Al Hansen's *Mary Jane*.

The boat, christened *Lehg II*, was launched in 1934. Dumas had a few trial sails and short cruises in her. But the world was then in recession and the difficulties on his ranch and farm escalated. He had to give up his plans for a long voyage. He was forced to remain on his land and he even had to sell his lovely new boat to raise money to buy a tractor and some cattle.

He made real efforts to forget the sea, his planned voyage and his ship. Yet still, he said, he smelled the sea in the wind when it blew off the estuary of the River Plate and he could not entirely forget his wild idea.

War came in 1939. Dumas could have stayed quietly on his ranch and 'let the madness pass', but he became restless believing life had more to offer.

In the evenings he pored over his charts wishing to be back at sea again. He studied the Roaring Forties and considered his 'impossible route'. He was torn as to what to do. Either he could remain at home or he could cut loose and respond to his sea fever. Eventually he decided, despite the war, to go back to sea, to his voyage and to Cape Horn. All he needed now was a boat and for him the only possible one was his old *Lehg II*.

The voyage

One day in 1942, with the world still engulfed in a seemingly never ending war, Dumas loaded up his car with his kitbag, charts, navigation instruments and tables, chronometer and compass, said good bye to everyone on his ranch and went in search of his boat, which he referred to as his 'old mate'.

With his brother accompanying him, Dumas discovered that *Lehg II* was still owned by the doctor to whom he had sold her eight years before. The doctor agreed to sell her back to Dumas. Promising to find the money somehow, *Lehg II* was put on a slipway for repairs. Manuel Campos, who had designed her, came up with a new rig and sail plan to stand up to the terrible weather Dumas could expect. New sails were made by some old friends of Dumas who had no idea when or whether they would get paid. Other friends clubbed together and eventually Dumas raised enough money to pay for the boat. People from his yacht club worked on the boat for free, whilst others produced supplies, equipment and clothing. He set the date for his departure as 26 June 1942.

What Dumas was setting out to do was extraordinary but he was an extraordinary man. A tough loner he had already proved his mettle in his voyage in *Lehg I* but setting off to sail round the world alone through the Southern Ocean was something else. And he was going to do this in wartime. And, as we shall see later, in the heart of the southern winter. Whilst Argentina was neutral during most of the Second World War, there were German and British warships and submarines in the south Atlantic, seeking out and destroying each other and each others merchant ships. Only three years before, in December 1939, the Battle of the River Plate had taken place when three British warships battered into submission the huge German battleship the *Graf Spee*, which the Germans then scuttled in the mouth of the River Plate in preference to seeing it captured by the British. The Southern Ocean was hardly a safe place for a yacht on a private venture at that time, but Dumas felt time was running out and the war could go on for ever.

On 27 June 1942, after an emotional and tearful farewell from his mother and brother, Dumas set off. First he took a friend on board for a short shakedown trip to Montevideo. All went well but much on board needed attention. Dumas was stormbound there for a few days with the port closed. A strong pampero was blowing.

By the standards of today Dumas was woefully unprepared for what he was taking on. He had no safety equipment, no radio, no liferaft, no lifejacket, safety harness or flares, precious few tools (he claims in his book that he had only one screwdriver on board) and not even a bilge pump (on the basis that his boat made no water and he preferred to rely on a bucket). But his boat was as simple as it could be with very little that could go wrong. He had no engine, instruments, winches or other mechanical aids. However, he did have tough 'bullet proof' sails and he even lashed down a heavy canvas tarpaulin over the whole of the boat's cabin top to stop leaks or large seas damaging it. This remained for the whole voyage and as a result the cabin below was in perpetual darkness. There was no heating save for a kerosene galley cooker.

Despite the port's closure, Dumas sailed on 1 July and was soon out of the harbour facing heavy seas and a south-westerly wind blowing at over thirty knots. His crossing to Africa had begun, a distance of 4,000 sea miles. He was the first person ever to venture into these waters alone in a small yacht. He had a hard time of it and soon the wind increased to sixty knots. He hove to for some rest, letting the boat look after herself.

That night he woke to find the floor boards in the cabin awash and the bilges full. Having no bilge pump he baled the boat dry with his one and only bucket. The boat had never made a drop of water before and Dumas tried to find the source of the leak. Eventually he traced this to a shake in one of the underwater planks in the forward part of the hull. He got together some canvas, red lead, putty, a piece of planking, nails and a hammer. After a struggle he managed to stem the leak to a trickle.

He was now 480 miles east of Montevideo. All went well for a few more days until Dumas' right arm became infected, rendering it virtually useless. He also had open wounds on both his hands which he had to bandage. As the days progressed his arm got worse and swelled alarmingly, leaving Dumas lying feverishly in his bunk. The leak he had stemmed began to get worse again. He gave himself an injection to try to lessen the pain which was becoming unbearable. Dumas got to the stage where he could not care whether his boat carried on or sank. Not getting any better and realising that he could not reach land as he was, he decided to amputate his infected arm. He lay in his bunk, feeble, feverish, depressed, often praying and tormented by the boat's endless rolling and pitching. On the morning of 13 July Dumas awoke to find a gaping hole in his arm three inches wide with pus flowing from it. He used a marlinespike to get to the core of the abscess. He dressed his arm, gave himself another injection and for the first time in days went back to the tiller.

He ran on under trysail, mizzen and staysail with a strong westerly wind behind him. His arm recovered and he spent many hours at the tiller making only slow progress. Gale followed gale and Dumas had to bale the boat dry twice a day. Recovering gradually, Dumas made a better repair of the leak and set a storm jib which meant working on the end of the bowsprit. This sail balanced the boat better and progress began to improve. On 13 August he crossed the Greenwich Meridian.

Soon after that Dumas saw his first ship, a Brazilian steamer called the *Gyration*. The ship came close and Dumas asked for his position. He was told it was wartime and they were not allowed to give any information. One of the crew recognised Dumas and agreed to pass a message of the sighting onto the Argentine Ministry of Marine. As he approached the African coast Dumas saw more ships. When fifty miles from Cape Town, Dumas was stopped by a British warship who demanded to know who he was and what was his destination. They let him continue. As he entered harbour in the dark two searchlights were focused on him and a pilot cutter approached demanding they put a pilot on board. Dumas refused but they escorted him in anyway. He made fast alongside a large vessel undergoing repairs. It was ten o'clock in the evening of 25 August 1942. He had been at sea for fifty-five days.

Dumas was welcomed and lauded by all in Cape Town. He made a plan to stay there for twenty days and not to do anything about his boat until the last week, a somewhat unwise thing to do bearing in mind the leak and the state of the boat's planking. However, he enjoyed his interlude and received many letters of congratulations. He met a wealthy, cultured and well travelled Dutch lady who tried to persuade Dumas to abandon his voyage and settle down with her on an island in the Seychelles. Dumas was tempted but knew deep down that he had to complete his voyage, remembering the proverb *'Never let your friend's hand get hot in yours'*. With much regret Dumas declined the offer.

With all damage repaired, Dumas now set off on the second leg of his 'impossible voyage', a distance of 7,400 miles across the Indian Ocean to New Zealand. The pilot chart for the months of September and October predicted winds of over gale Force 8 for an average of twenty-seven days per month. There was the risk of cyclones in the Tasman Sea between Australia and New Zealand and the only possible shelter on the voyage were two small uninhabited islets, St. Paul's and Amsterdam Islands in the middle of the Indian Ocean. In those days there were stores of food and clothing there for shipwrecked sailors but landing on the islands was exceedingly difficult. Whilst making his preparations Dumas pondered on what he was about to undertake but he was doing what he wanted and he wrote: '*I had broken loose from habit and escaped the dreariness of everyday life.*'

On 14 September, Dumas slipped his lines and headed out to sea. As he passed the breakwater he met a British warship coming in. Dumas dipped his ensign in salute and the ship's captain saluted him from the bridge. *Lehg II* passed the famous sailing clipper the *Pamir,* still trading under sail, and he met a six-masted American ship, the *Tango*. He had light winds at first and it took him two days to reach the Cape of Good Hope, once upon a time, perhaps more appropriately, known as 'the Cape of Storms'. The second day out he once again found the bilges full – but this time it was fresh water. He discovered that one of his water tanks had leaked, losing its forty gallons. All he had left was another twenty gallon tank, together with some twelve gallons in cans. He decided to make do with this and carry on, collecting rain water if necessary.

He met gale after gale blowing against the Agulhas current which pushed him far to the south of his intended course. Rain squalls hit him in regular succession. He achieved daily runs of 120 to 150 miles but at the cost of Dumas spending hour after hour at the tiller. One day he remembered it was his forty-second birthday and he wrote in his log ' *I felt in the depths of my soul an insurmountable feeling of apprehension.*'

On 28 September he was 1,100 miles from Cape Town, still experiencing bad weather. He decided to head north to try to find better conditions. After a few days he was in calmer seas and lighter winds but these did not last. On 24 October, in the midst of another storm, he passed Amsterdam Island, hidden behind a bank of cloud. It was very rough and Dumas remarked on the huge number of albatrosses and stormy petrels he saw. He was still more than 1,800 miles from Australia. On 3 November he had sailed 3,800 miles and was approaching an area where cyclones were frequent. The barometer fell to 732, the lowest he had ever seen it, and dark clouds swept past him like black smoke. One enormous wave hit the boat hard and caused chaos below. On going into the cabin, Dumas found broken bottles and a foul mess of sodden food, bedding, clothes and tangled gear.

On 16 November he reached Australia and he passed the meridian of Cape Leeuwin, the country's south-westernmost point. He had crossed the

Indian Ocean, probably the hardest part of his entire voyage. His dwindling supply of fresh water was dark and muddy and Dumas began to feel the first effects of scurvy – painful gums.

Then, despite being in the Roaring Forties, he ran into a calm which lasted for over ten days. On 22 November Dumas drifted across the 120° meridian, the antipodes of his home port. He was halfway round the world. From now on every day would take him closer to home. To his surprise, the calm ended with a full gale from the east. He described it as a 'williwaw' which was accompanied by heavy rain, thick low cloud and lightning. To make up for lost time Dumas decided to sail through this gale with full sail set. As the gale passed the wind veered first to the south then west and Lehg II flew onwards, quickly crossing the Great Australian Bight.

On 10 December, after seventy-five days at sea, he sighted Tasmania's south-west Cape, which he passed in another gale. Dumas was briefly tempted to put into Hobart, which was only sixty miles away but he resisted. He wanted to get out of the cyclone area as quickly as he could.

Dumas struggled on, experiencing great pain from scurvy with his gums badly inflamed. When 160 miles from Cape Providence, the south-west tip of New Zealand's South Island, he was faced with another heavy storm which pounded Lehg II for several days. They headed north toward the entrance to the Cook Strait, which separated New Zealand's two islands. To prevent his boat from being overwhelmed by the following seas he kept speed up and tried to keep his stern to the largest waves. He appreciated Lehg II's pointed stern and felt safer running before these seas - as long as he could keep awake to steer. Dumas was at the point of exhaustion and was at the helm for hour after hour but was making 175 miles a day. On Christmas Eve he sighted Cape Farewell, the northernmost point of New Zealand's South Island. After 101 days without sight of land Dumas was only a quarter of a mile out in his dead reckoning – quite an achievement as he had found little chance of taking any sun sights during the recent gales. Despite being mid-summer, Dumas remarked how he suffered from the cold.

Dumas struggled on against head winds into Cook Strait and on into the channel to Wellington Harbour where he arrived on 27 December 1942, having sailed 7,400 miles in 104 days. Lehg II moored alongside some US warships, the crew of which gave him much help in repairing his yacht. Dumas made many friends in New Zealand and during his stay all signs of his scurvy disappeared.

He set sail for south America and Valparaiso on 30 January 1943. A forty knot northerly wind was blowing and Lehg II struggled with the heavy seas.

That afternoon Dumas passed Cape Palliser, the last bit of land he would see until he reached south America. He had over 5,000 miles to go to Chile with no port of call or refuge anywhere on the way.

For Dumas, it was more of the same - hour after hour sitting at the tiller. When approaching the 180° meridian, the barometer fell to 756 and Dumas found himself in the tail end of a cyclone. At the height of the storm, *Lehg II* escaped disaster by narrowly missing the floating trunk of an enormous tree, big enough to have sunk him. As he travelled east Dumas ran into more tranquil conditions and he was able to staunch a leak from yet another damaged plank just below the waterline. One day Dumas, whilst below, felt the boat strike something, give a lurch and stop. Thinking he had hit land or a rock he dashed on deck to find *Lehg II* trying to climb up the back of a whale. The boat was actually elbowing her way between two sleeping whales. Slowly, with no help from Dumas, *Lehg II* purposefully, and with exaggerated slowness, pushed her way through them and sailed on. Dumas sat quite still, terrified at what the whales reaction could have been.

As Dumas progressed across a now benign Pacific with light variable winds, Dumas wrote in his log about the places and islands he was passing, all lying far away to the north. Raratonga in the Cook Islands, 600 miles to the north, Maria Theresa Reef south of Tahiti, the island of Rapa 900 miles to the north-east and then Pitcairn Island also 900 miles north. He was maintaining a course along the 40° South line of latitude, making to the south when the wind allowed it. For many days he had light winds, even though he was in what was meant to be 'the Roaring Forties.' On days of calm, with little to occupy him, Dumas felt unsettled and overawed by the sense of being quite alone in the middle of the immense Pacific.

On 4 March he saw a ship, the first he had seen on this leg, and began to see many sea birds. On 9 March he calculated he had twenty-eight days to go to Valparaiso. The weather now changed with squalls and heavy gales from the north. Dumas began to head north to get to 31° South, the latitude of Valparaiso. For the rest of March Dumas experienced periods of calm between violent gales, often from the east. On 1 April, Dumas was 400 miles west of Mocha Island off the Chilean coast and he felt the favourable effect of the Humboldt current pushing him north. On 11 April at eight o'clock in the evening after seventy-seven days out of sight of land he saw the lights of Point Curaumillas flashing ahead. In front of him lay Valparaiso. His navigation had, once again, been faultless. The next day, in very light winds *Lehg II* crept toward the coast. It was was getting dark with the boat drifting toward some rocks when a naval launch, alerted by the lighthouse keeper, put out to tow her into harbour. On arrival at ten o'clock that night, Dumas moored up against a harbour tug and went ashore to celebrate.

Dumas was feted for his achievement by the Chilean navy, who gave him much assistance with preparing his boat for the voyage ahead. *Lehg II* was hauled up on a naval slipway and was given a thorough overhaul. Ropes and sails were replaced, his chronometer was repaired, he was given a full set of charts and a badly needed new wardrobe of foul weather gear. Throughout this interlude, although satisfied with his achievement to date, Dumas felt a dark cloud overshadowing everything - the knowledge of what was to come in his final passage - Cape Horn.

As we saw in the last chapter, the Argentine Nautical Instructions at that time said that the best time to navigate in Cape Horn waters was midwinter in the southern hemisphere. It was believed that one would then find winds on average less violent than during the rest of the year. When leaving Argentina, Dumas had already decided to follow this advice and he now decided to delay leaving Valparaiso until the end of May, even though many people gave him contrary advice. A Captain in the Chilean navy, however, believed that the season and route Dumas had chosen were the best, and persuaded Dumas he should be off the Horn at a full moon.

Dumas provisioned for six months with 3,000 miles to sail. It was the shortest leg of his voyage but the trickiest and he pondered on those who had gone before. He was aware that the body of his friend Alfon Hansen, the only man to have rounded the Horn alone, lay somewhere in the sea off the coast of Chile; only the wreckage of his wrecked boat had been found. He knew that both Slocum and Bernicot had avoided the Horn by passing through the Magellan Strait. Nevertheless, Dumas was determined to be the first to try to pass alone south of the Horn from west to east. In choosing his route Dumas decided to follow the path of the clippers and keep well to the west of the Chilean coast and not to stop anywhere. That way he should be able to avoid becoming embayed or being driven ashore by one of the many westerly gales he would surely meet.

On 25 May 1943, after attending Mass, Dumas was towed out of the harbour. The tow was cast off later in the afternoon and *Lehg II* sailed slowly south in a light westerly breeze. On 2 June Dumas passed Juan Fernandez, 'Robinson Crusoe's island', in very poor visibility. On 9 June Dumas ran into his first storm of this leg and, whilst running before it, *Lehg II* was badly pooped. Dumas clung to the mizzen mast to avoid being washed overboard. As they headed south it got colder and on 14 June they reached a latitude of 47° South. The temperature dropped to under five degrees

Centigrade during the daytime and Dumas' hands could not endure the open air for long. The wind backed to the south-west and *Lehg II* crashing, shuddering, shaking and creaking in the seas began to make water again. This time Dumas could not find the source of the leak.

In addition to the cold, days were short and the sun only just rose above the horizon. Waves crashed down on the cabin and Dumas could not stay dry, nor could he dry anything out below. He had no form of heating. He was being driven too close to the coast by an incessant south wind, so he took a tack out to the west. On 16 June he resumed his course to the south; he was now at 48º South. By 18 June he was 180 miles due east of the entrance to Cape Pilar, the western entrance to the Magellan Strait and the cold was so intense that Dumas could not leave the smallest part of his face exposed to the wind. Hail lashed down at him mercilessly. Despite all this Dumas was not at all tempted to turn to the east and make for the Magellan Strait. He had decided to round Cape Horn and nothing was going to dissuade him from this course.

When he was some 500 miles from the Horn he prepared himself for what was to come. He greased his gloves so that water would not make them useless. He did the same to his oilskins. He prepared some iron rations – chocolate, preserves, biscuits and fruit – in case he was kept at the helm for long periods and he put some Benzedrine sulphate tablets close by, ready to take to keep him awake. Dumas felt confident and believed nothing had been left to chance.

On 20 June Cape Horn was 400 miles away. Two days later a ferocious storm hit him with winds from the north-east. He took in the storm trysail and continued under mizzen, staysail and storm jib. He was now sailing due east in forty knots of wind. At five o'clock that evening he saw land to the north-east. The seas were not as bad as Dumas had been expecting and the next day the winds became lighter and the sky cleared. At noon Dumas saw 'ice blink', the reflection in the sky of the Antarctic ice pack, far to his south. Around midday on 24 June the wind veered to the north and rose to gale force. He now had only ninety miles to go to reach the Horn. In his book, Dumas reflects on the passage he was undertaking:

'How full of meaning and menace is the sound of those two words: Cape Horn! What a vast and terrible cemetery of seamen lies under this eternally boiling sea! Fear adds its chill to that of the atmosphere, the terror that lurks in a name and the sight of these seas. Here, everything seems to be attracted and drawn towards the depths, as by some monstrous, supernatural magnet. Had I had a larger surface of wood under my feet, I could have calmed my nerves by pacing the deck, but no; I could not walk my thoughts under control.'

Later he wrote: *'I remembered the enthusiasm I felt on hearing the news that Al Hansen had succeeded in rounding Cape Horn from east to west, a feat no wise diminished by his terrible end. Hansen had been powerless to escape the curse that broods between the 50° of the Atlantic and the 50° of the Pacific.'*

At midnight Dumas calculated that Cape Horn would be abeam. He was in heavy seas and *Lehg II* was being thrown about alarmingly. At one point Dumas, sitting below, was thrown forward and his face smashed into a brass deadlight on the the opposite side of the cabin. The pain was terrible and Dumas was stunned, with blood pouring from a broken nose. Gradually the bleeding stopped and the pain subsided. Dumas saw nothing of the Horn, merely a bank of clouds indicating where land was. His face was a horrid mess but Dumas thought nothing of this, merely relief at the fact he was nearly back in the Atlantic.

With the Horn now behind him Dumas reflected in his log on how he would feel being the first man to have rounded it alone and survive. He remembered his friend Al Hansen and wrote:

'It seemed unthinkable that he, with all his determination, should have finished as he did. What a loss that he should not have lived to tell, with more talent than I possess, what he felt on rounding the Horn. I realised that I was privileged and looking back, thinking of the sailors who got no further, I wept with joy.'

Dumas was now faced with a hard beat into a head wind to get clear. By nightfall on 26 June he was some ninety miles east of Staten Island, which lies close to the east of the mainland. He turned north and sailed close-hauled into a strong north-west head wind hoping to be able to weather the Falkland Islands. Snow lashed his face every time he went on deck and he spent much time below, not certain where he was heading. Gradually the wind backed to the west and on 29 June Dumas sighted the Beaver Islands, which meant he was past the Falklands. Now his way was clear to head straight for home. After a few more days, the look of the water, the number of porpoises and birds flying around him, all told him he was nearly there.

On 5 July he was 150 miles from Mar del Plata. The sun was higher in the sky and began to give him some warmth. At last he could dry out his clothes and sodden cabin. He saw a Chilean steamer with a four-master in tow, bound for the Strait of Magellan. The wind was fair and he knew that the worst was behind him.

On the morning of 7 July Dumas and *Lehg II* approached the harbour of Mar del Plata. A fishing boat towed them in to a mooring off the yacht club, Dumas 'as proud as a peacock'. A huge reception awaited him. Telegrams poured in, photographs, press interviews and autograph signing followed – Dumas felt he was the centre of the world and said to himself '*For this – I would go round the world a hundred times.*'

Dumas' voyage, however, was not finished as he wanted to sail the last 200 miles north to Montevideo in Uruguay, to see and thank all his friends who had supported him throughout his voyage. Only then would he head for Buenos Aires. After a few days Dumas tore himself away and set sail in the afternoon for this short run. The wind was from the north meaning Dumas had to beat along the coast. He decided to tack offshore for 2 hours and then tack back inshore. After thirty hours when he was level with Mar Chiquita. he tacked and headed inshore. Dumas slept for an hour and a half then went on deck. He was horrified to see waves breaking on the shore less than one hundred yards ahead. He leapt for the helm, which was lashed, but he had no knife to cut it free. He tried to undo the lashing so as to turn the boat but it was too late. *Lehg II* would not respond. A high sand dune appeared ahead and the breakers were very close. The boat lifted on a wave and dropped with a heavy crash. She was on the sands and the following wave broke over the deck, breaking the mizzen shrouds. Dumas decided the only way to save *Lehg II* was to get her as far up the beach as possible. Holding the tiller he took advantage of every breaker and she moved slowly inch by inch up the beach until she was well aground.

Dumas then started to lighten the boat by carrying whatever gear he could some fifteen yards up the beach. By the evening the boat was considerably lighter and was high and dry at low water. Dumas reflected that every ship he knew of which had gone ashore on these beaches had been destroyed.

The next day he went in search of help. He found a horseman riding by who took a message. The Ministry of Marine arranged a rescue attempt and a trawler and patrol boat arrived on the scene. A ship's boat came ashore through the breakers. They decided to pass a tow and try to drag Lehg II back into deep water. The tow would have to be at least 1,000 metres long! The next morning the trawler anchored a kilometre off the coast and it took the whole day to pass the tow ashore. Then the tow began and *Lehg II,* stern square on to the breakers started to move. Very gently, and without a scratch, she was hauled off and refloated. She was towed back to Mar Del Plata. *Lehg II* did not make a drop of water on the return trip.

Dumas and his gear were reunited and after a short interlude Dumas left again for Montevideo on 28 August 1943. This time he sailed the 200 miles without incident, arriving on 30 August. There he was greeted with a triumphal reception with cheers and shouts from the shore. Dinghies, boats and people crowded on and around the pier. He remained there for a week basking in the attention.

As Dumas was expected back at his starting point off the Argentine Yacht Club in Buenos Aries at eleven o'clock on 7 September, he took a tow from Montevideo for the 110 mile trip and arrived at the Yacht Club precisely on time to another tremendous welcome.

He had circumnavigated the globe by 'the impossible route' and was the first man ever to sail alone south of Cape Horn and survive. He was also the first man to sail past the Horn solo from west to east and in the depths of winter too. Dumas had achieved something quite remarkable and had proved that simplicity and determination, combined with the ability to accept almost total discomfort, can achieve real success at sea. Little went wrong on his voyage but then he had little to go wrong - a lesson that many of today's long distance sailors could learn.

Dumas, however, was not finished with the sea.

After his voyage he laid up *Lehg II*, went back to the land and his ranch and sat out the war until it was over. In 1945 he set off on in *Lehg II* once again, travelling 17,045 miles in 235 days in a somewhat meandering voyage that seemed to have little purpose or objective, apart from keeping Dumas alone at sea for as long a period as possible. He sailed from Buenos Aires north to Rio de Janeiro, then north to Havana (5,410 miles in sixty-one days) and finally on to New York. From there he sailed a large arc across the Atlantic passing, without stopping, the Azores, the Canary Islands, the Cape Verde Islands, arriving back at the port of Fortelaza in north-east Brazil after 106 days at sea having sailed 7,000 miles. He then sailed back home to Buenos Aires, calling in at Montevideo on the way.

After this voyage Dumas donated *Lehg II* to the Argentine Navy as a training ship. After a few years she became neglected, broke her mooring chain, and was wrecked on a rocky shore. A wealthy Argentine yachtsman paid to have her restored and then donated her to the Argentine Naval Museum in Tigre, a coastal town on a tributary of the River Plate, where *Lehg II* remains to this day.

In 1955 Dumas set off on what was to be his final long voyage, this time in a new boat - a tiny double-ended two and a half ton displacement sloop called the *Sirie II*, which Dumas had designed and which he built himself. He sailed alone from Buenos Aires to New York, with one stop in Bermuda, covering the 7,100 miles in 117 days.

In 1957 the Slocum Society inaugurated an annual prize to be awarded for the most remarkable trans-oceanic crossing achieved during the previous year. The Society awarded the first of these prizes to Dumas, not for a single voyage but 'to honour the extraordinary voyages made by the greatest solitary navigator in the world.' A fitting tribute to a great sailor and navigator.

Dumas died in Argentina on 28 March 1965, aged sixty-four, having spent the days before his death with Edward Allcard who was then setting off on his own voyage round Cape Horn (described in chapter 10 below). Dumas' book 'Alone Through the Roaring Forties' remains in print and continues to fascinate readers the world over.

Chapter 8
Marcel Bardiaux – The first Frenchman

M arcel Bardiaux was a strange character who achieved much but was little loved or liked by those who knew him. He was a driven man who, whilst being a loner all his life (he never married), liked partying and the company of women, at least when he was young. He claimed to have attended 5,000 parties during his eight year solo circumnavigation. Edward Allcard (see chapter 10 below) met Bardiaux in Casablanca in 1950. Before Edward died he told the author that he remembers not liking Bardiaux very much and thinking him somewhat conceited, self-centered and pleased with himself, even though at that stage he had barely started on the voyage which would make him famous. Later in his life Bardiaux became a Poujadist and a racist. He was probably antisemitic as well and espoused other right wing causes. This did not make him popular. None of this, however, should take away from his achievements as a great sailor and navigator.

The man

Bardiaux was born on 2 April 1910 in Clermont-Ferrand in the midst of the Auvergne mountains in southern France. His sister was born six years later. His father was killed by a bomb just a few days before the First World War ended in 1918.

His mother, unable to support the family on her war pension, moved the family to Paris to seek work. They set up home in Neuilly-sur-Marne, now but not then, a fashionable Parisian suburb. Bardiaux spent five years at a religious orphanage where he was one of the best pupils. However, when Bardiaux was thirteen his mother, no longer able to support the family on her own, removed him from the orphanage and sent him out to work. This was hard to obtain but Bardiaux found jobs variously as a plumber, a joiner and, surprisingly, as a seamstress.

During this time Marcel built his first boat, basically just a long wooden box, which he sailed on the River Marne. When Bardiaux was fourteen his mother married again. He did not like his new stepfather and ran away from home, making his way to Le Havre to try to find a berth on a ship. Unfortunately for him the police found him and returned him to his mother.

After this Bardiaux, a restless spirit, took up camping and canoeing. He designed and made a lightweight tent for hiking, using his sewing skills. He also designed a small kayak made of canvas stretched on a wooden frame which he built and marketed as a 'Bardiaux'. He was successful, selling all he could make. He was one of the founders of the Kayak Club de France, a group of youths who spent much time in their canoes on the Marne. When Bardiaux was nineteen he became French kayak and canoe champion.

In 1929 Bardiaux met the lone sailor Alain Gerbault who had just returned to France after his solo round the world voyage in the *Firecrest* (see chapter 3) which was moored at a quay on the River Seine. This meeting and the sight of Gerbault's yacht inspired Bardiaux to want to do something similar. When he eventually built a boat for his round the world voyage many people thought she had a strong resemblance to the *Firecrest*, although considerably smaller.

In 1930, aged twenty, Bardiaux set off on his first maritime venture. Alone in his canoe called *'Belle Etoile'* he paddled across the rivers and canals of western Europe to reach the River Danube. This he followed all the way to the Black Sea, then along the coast to Istanbul. From there he paddled across the Aegean Sea and the Mediterranean to Marseilles, returning up the River Rhone (for this he must have hitched a lift on a barge going upstream as in places the current against him could have reached ten or twelve knots and his trip was made before the river had been properly tamed for navigation.) Then he went along the French inland waterways to Paris. He paddled for 13,000 kilometres of which 8,000 were at sea. This was an extraordinary voyage by any measure.

Soon after his return he was conscripted and joined the French Navy. On completing his training he was posted to Paris as a naval telephone operator (hardly a suitable post for such an active and by then experienced seaman). At the end of his naval service, Bardiaux set up in business making and selling kayaks and canoes. He took up motorcycle and car racing and became European Kayak Champion. He had become a very self assured young man, robust and rugged, able to turn his hand to almost anything.

He remained a Naval reservist and was called up in 1939 at the start of the Second World War. When the Germans occupied France he was taken prisoner and shipped to a prisoner of war camp in Germany. He escaped twice. The first time he was captured but he succeeded on the second attempt. Pretending to drown in a river, he remained hidden underwater breathing through a metal tube until his pursuers gave up the hunt.

He returned to France and went back to live in Neuilly-sur-Marne for the remainder of the war. With little to look forward to Bardiaux decided to build a boat in which he could escape to sea when the war was over.

The boat

In a bookshop in Paris he came across the plans for a small yacht designed by the French naval architect Henri Dervin. This was for a 30 foot long sloop with a beam of 8 feet and 10 inches and a displacement of 4 tons. To Bardiaux's eyes her lines resembled Gerbault's *Firecrest* and looked seaworthy and fast, although not designed for ocean sailing. With the plans in front of him, Bardiaux modified the design to suit his purpose. He had read the accounts of Slocum, Harry Pidgeon, Gerbault and Conor O'Brien and knew exactly the sort of boat he wanted. He altered the lines and redesigned the deck to make it flush with only a small low streamlined cabin top aft of the mast and a very small foot well by the tiller. He added a bowsprit and altered the sail plan. The boat would now have the appearance of a submarine and would tend to sail like one, diving through the waves and throwing spray aft at the helmsman. Bardiaux designed the boat to be self-righting and unsinkable. She would have watertight compartments fore and aft and two buoyancy tanks each side in the forecabin. She was to be built as strong as Bardiaux could make her and her frames, reinforced by bronze straps, made a complete circle round the boat and across the cabintop. The small foot well by the tiller could be closed off in bad weather.

Bardiaux started to build his boat, which he had already decided to name *Les 4 Vents,* in a first floor workshop in Nogent-sur-Marne. He had the greatest difficulty in the midst of a war of getting the materials he needed. Everything in German occupied France was in very short supply but, bit by bit, Bardiaux assembled what he needed. For the lead keel Bardiaux got hold of 1,275 kilogrammes of scrap lead, most from old lead battery plates which he melted down bit by bit so as to cast the keel.

In 1944 the Germans began to retreat from Paris and as they did so they blew up a bridge over the River Marne some twenty yards away from Bardiaux's workshop, which was almost totally destroyed in the blast. However, Bardiaux was able to salvage most of his work and materials and he moved it all to a new workshop further away. When the war was over, he set up the frames, cast his lead keel and completed the boat. It was not until 19 July 1949, four years later, that the vessel was finished and was hauled through the streets of Perreux-sur-Marne, transported on two lorry axles, to be launched into the River Marne. Bardiaux spent the rest of that year preparing *Les 4 Vents* for his forthcoming voyage.

The voyage

This started somewhat ignominiously on Sunday 1 January 1950 near the Pont Alexandre III on the River Seine in Paris. *Les 4 Vents* was moored with her mast up, towering over the bridge with gear piled all over the decks. A typical Paris crowd gathered on the bridge and the quay making derogatory remarks about the boat. 'Must be mad to take off in a boat like that'; 'It's not a boat, it's a toy'; 'All right for a pond in the Tuileries, but for Cape Horn, well....', etc.

Bardiaux lowered the mast and prepared to leave, but the engine, meant to take him down the Seine to the sea, refused to start. So he threw down the starting handle, picked up his sculling oar, cast off the mooring and, amid cries of admiration from the crowd, pushed his boat out into the current. When out of sight of the bridge, Bardiaux accepted a tow, which took him to a quay some way downstream. There he tied up for the night. It took him two days to sort out the problems with the engine and, finally, he set off on Tuesday 3 January, with a friend on board. They reached Rouen on 7 January. The next day they entered the Tancarville canal, where Bardiaux spent a month preparing the boat and sorting out the rigging. It was one of the coldest winters France had seen for some time, with temperatures of minus eight degrees Centigrade in the day and minus fifteen at night. The canal froze over.

Early in February Bardiaux moved down the canal to Le Havre where he had to obtain his seaworthiness certificate from the Maritime Registration Authority. At last, on 14 February, Bardiaux was ready to leave and, in a lull between gales, locked out of the harbour and sailed westward to Ouistreham. From there Bardiaux made his way slowly to La Rochelle on France's west coast, stopping often on the way. On arrival at La Rochelle he learnt that Louis Bernicot (see chapter 4) was in harbour on board *Anahita*. Having been told it was unlikely he would get more than ten words out of the old Captain, Bardiaux found him friendly and talkative. They spoke, of course, of Cape Horn and the Magellan Strait. Bernicot commented that Bardiaux would be better off going through the Strait rather than try for Cape Horn. But if he did try for the Horn, Bernicot said be patient, wait for a rare lull and then make the most of it. Bernicot gave him a signed copy of his book and his charts of the Magellan Strait 'just in case'.

From La Rochelle, Bardiaux sailed south to the shallow inland sea of Arcachon, where Dumas had found his first boat *Lehg I.* There he put the boat ashore at the Couach marine engine factory to have his engine replaced. He also shortened the boom by two feet to make gybing easier and finished preparations for his voyage. He was better prepared than Dumas, but that does not say much by today's standards. At least he had an engine and some form of heating in his cabin but not much of anything else.

He left in the afternoon of 18 October 1950 but was back the next day as he found that his compass read 'west' in whatever direction he headed. He was told it could not be repaired so he exchanged it for a new one (and took a spare). Finally he left France and headed out to sea on 21 October, nine months since he had departed from Paris. Was he having difficulty in severing the knot or was he just enjoying the company, mostly female, he met along the way?

Bardiaux and *Les 4 Vents* had a rough crossing of the Bay of Biscay. He put into several small fishing harbours in northern Spain, often finding himself trapped behind shallow bars whilst heavy swells ran outside. Eventually, on 4 November, Bardiaux reached Vigo, where he was piloted into the yacht basin in front of the imposing Real Club Nautico.

His next call was to Oporto up the river Douro in Portugal, where he spent two days finishing jobs on board. He was advised not to leave the next day as a very rough sea was running outside. Bardiaux left notwithstanding and tried to reach Lisbon, the only harbour on this coast with an all weather entrance. He made only slow progress and, having been at the helm for some thirty-two hours, decided to put into Sao Martinho-do-Porto, a small lagoon reached via a very narrow (and shallow) entrance through a gap in the cliffs. Bardiaux had no large scale chart and his only pilot book rated the entrance as very dangerous. Ignoring all the rules about it being safer to stay out at sea in bad weather rather than try to enter an unknown and unsafe harbour (and it was dark by then), Bardiaux headed *Les 4 Vents* for the entrance. Huge seas were breaking against rocks which seemed to rear out of the sea all around him. Bardiaux could hardly keep his eyes open. Somehow he made it in but found little rest as there was a bad swell running in the harbour. He found the holding ground to be very poor and he dragged his anchor again and again, toward yet more rocks close astern of him. He ended up carrying his one-hundred pound anchor, walking on the bottom for over one-hundred yards, surfacing for air twice. This anchor held but back on board Bardiaux found he no longer had the strength to bring in the cable to haul the boat away from the rocks. The engine was useless against the wind. Luckily two fishermen saw his predicament and swam out to help him. They were amazed that he had got into the harbour at all with no proper chart.

He was lucky to have survived and then found himself stuck in harbour awaiting better weather. He left on 23 November 1950 and called in at Lisbon, where he had trouble with the Portuguese customs. He partied with the French Ambassador and others but remarked on the absence of any young ladies. 'Lisbon', he said 'is a womanless town.'

He left with some relief on 5 December, the Customs trying to fine him for not sailing at the hour he had said he would two days before hand. He had had enough of Portuguese officialdom. Once out of the river mouth, he met a strong northerly wind and heavy seas. He had an extremely cold crossing to Africa and Bardiaux was not able to leave the tiller for long. He slept for only four hours during the first seventy of the passage. On the night of 11 December he saw, with relief, lights on the African coast and the next day entered Casablanca under full sail; his engine being useless as he had run out of petrol.

Casablanca was then, as it is now, a crossroads and haven for numerous vagabond sailors of all nations enjoying the various and sometimes dubious delights of Morocco. Bardiaux had originally planned to stay for only a few days but enjoyed himself so much he was still there nearly six months later. One of the first of the vagabonds Bardiaux met was Edward Allcard (see chapter 10) who had recently arrived from the Azores in his yawl *Temptress,* along with his famous female stowaway, Otilia. Allcard had discovered her hiding on his yacht when one day out of the Azores, bound for England. He had diverted to Casablanca.

Allcard was an extremely experienced ocean wanderer who had just become the first man to sail alone both ways across the Atlantic. This was what he wrote about Bardiaux:

'....*The other boat was a little 25 foot Bermudan sloop called Les 4 Vents belonging to a Frenchman, Marcel Bardiaux, He was another of these round-the-world-singlehanded cranks; but he had made the mistake of publishing his route, with dates, prior to departure – 1950 said Cape Horn and the Pacific; anyway he had reached Casablanca. The boat was strongly built but it was obvious to me that he would have to endure much greater hardships as the design was not suitable for the job. She had a short rockered keel which made it impossible to beach with any safety for repairs and painting; and, like most racing boats, she could only be made to self steer with difficulty.*

'*The cockpit was self-draining but as there was no sliding hatch in the coachroof he had a door with a sill only four inches high. In a very rough sea he would be unable to open this door without letting volumes of water down*

below. There was not even a coaming round the cockpit and no life lines what-
soever. He will learn, I thought, hoping it would be before he got to the Cape
Horn area. He, too, had come in originally for only a few days but left after a
stay of five or six months.'

During his stay Bardiaux partied hard and enjoyed the company of other yachtsmen, various ladies, including Allcard's beautiful stowaway, and many ex-patriots living in the town. In February, he took a car trip inland with some friends, including a famous Parisian singer, to see something of the country. As they were entering Marrakesh, their car was hit by another and they somersaulted, dropped six feet off the road and landed upside down hitting some palm trees on the way. No one was seriously hurt, although they suffered several broken bones and ribs between them. Bardiaux was told to rest for a month and he worked out that this delay would mean he would be unable to get round Cape Horn before the coming winter. In March, Bardiaux witnessed the arrival of the Australian adventurer, Ben Carlin and his wife, who had just crossed the Atlantic in their amphibious jeep *Half-Safe*. In this strange vessel, only 14-feet-long, they went on to circumnavigate the world by sea and land.

Bardiaux was very attracted to Allcard's stowaway Otilia. Described by Allcard as his lovely mermaid, she had stowed away on Allcard's *Temptress* in the Azores, hiding in the forecabin and appearing on the second day out. Before leaving Casablanca she went on board *Les 4 Vents* to say goodbye. Bardiaux was tempted to ask her to accompany him on his voyage. He asked her, 'Are you looking for a place to stow away?' She replied, enigmatically : 'It would certainly be more fun than to be shut up in a London Office. What a pity you've only got one cabin.' Bardiaux had difficulty in suppressing his feelings but wrote that he saw a dangerous reef ahead and made haste to row the mermaid back to the club pontoon.

In March, Bardiaux had *Les 4 Vents* hauled out to find that her copper sheathing was badly corroded. He reinforced this with another layer around the waterline and, following advice received from Allcard, built a small doghouse at the aft end of the cabin top to give him some shelter from the wind and waves.

Bardiaux left Casablanca on 7 May 1951 and headed for Agadir, a little way south. He then finally left Morocco on 3 June bound for the Canary Isles, having been kept in harbour by an incessant strong west wind. He arrived in Las Palmas on Gran Canaria on 6 June. He stayed there for twelve days disliking the polluted harbour, whilst dodging the local thieves and socialising as usual. He left for an eight day passage to Dakar on 18 June. This was the longest leg of his voyage so far and he admitted in his book that, despite having been on board for eighteen months, he was still incapable of taking sun sights. He had with him everything needed for astro-navigation but had sailed so far by dead reckoning alone.

Bardiaux found the leg to Dakar frustrating with light following winds and he could not get *Les 4 Vents* to steer herself. He made a good landfall on 27 June and was forced to enter Dakar Harbour under sail as his batteries were flat. Here he lingered until 23 September 1951.

Bardiaux's voyage was turning out to be totally different from the voyage of his compatriot Captain Bernicot. Bardiaux had now been away for a year and nine months, had only just reached west Africa and had yet to cross the Atlantic. Bernicot completed his entire circumnavigation in the same period of time.

In Dakar, Bardiaux had fun ashore and carried out repairs and improvements to his boat. He also had the good luck to meet a retired French Naval Officer who had been round Cape Horn and who taught Bardiaux the essentials of astro-navigation in two afternoons.

Now he was ready to face the 3,000 mile Atlantic crossing to Rio de Janeiro. He left on 23 September 1951 and had a rough time for most of the way. For the first few days he made good progress with a fine north-westerly breeze but it soon went round to the south-west, headed him and freshened. Where he should have found the calms of the doldrums (which Bernicot had motored through a few years previously) he met Force 8 to 10 south-westerly winds. Bardiaux found taking sun sights extremely difficult in these conditions and the results were often quite useless. Bad weather followed him all the way until he was faced with a long beat into the prevailing trade winds to weather Cape Sao Roque, the extreme north-east point of Brazil. This rough weather continued and, unable to get any sun sights due to overcast skies, Bardiaux was approaching land very uncertain as to his position. On 20 October, believing he had rounded Cape Frio, he headed west to close the shore. Suddenly he saw waves were breaking on a dark mass a little way ahead of him. He turned round as quickly as he could only to find a rocky mass rising up in front of him. He managed to extricate himself and worked out from the charts that he had stumbled into the labyrinth of rocks surrounding the Comprida Islands, some thirty miles north-east of Cape Frio. He was way out with his navigation and was lucky to get out unscathed. He spent the rest of that night beating past Cape Frio against a strong north going current and just before dawn saw the flash of the lighthouse. He could now resume his course to the west. On 21 October Bardiaux entered Rio Bay and at one o'clock in the morning dropped anchor.

Here in Rio, Bardiaux expressed his considerable dislike of the formalities of the Brazilian way of life. As in Portugal, he was exasperated with the convoluted bureaucracy involved in gaining entry clearance, not helped by his refusal to adopt the normal and expected attire of Brazilian men - jacket, trousers, shirt and tie, felt hat and black shoes. Bardiaux, to much disapproval, continued to wear shorts with a nylon shirt and sandals when calling on officials. The French Consulate initially refused him entry when he turned up like this.

During Bardiaux's stay in Rio, the French naval training ship the *Jeanne d'Arc* visited the port. The French officers and officer cadets from the ship refused to talk to Bardiaux, who was just a mere able-bodied seaman. This despite *Les 4 Vents* being moored in a place of honour right in front of the terrace of the Yacht Club bar, where the visiting French officers gathered for aperitifs every evening. Bardiaux could hear every word they spoke but he was ignored.

Bardiaux left Rio after a month of partying and socialising and headed for what he referred to as the 'Polynesia of Brazil', the nearby island of Ilha Grande. It is a beautiful place despite it then being used as a leper colony and as a prison for some of Brazil's most dangerous prisoners. Otherwise the island was uninhabited and Bardiaux luxuriated in its peace and quiet, recovering no doubt from his over indulgences in Rio. It was now mid-summer and Bardiaux sailed slowly down the coast of Brazil and Uruguay, stopping often. He spent New Year's Eve digging a trench in the sand to refloat *Les 4 Vents* which had blown aground in an exposed anchorage whilst he was enjoying himself ashore He arrived at Punta del Este in Uruguay on 22 January 1952 and was immediately swept away to attend the World Film Festival taking place in the city. The party animal was in his element again. A few days later he set off for Montevideo where Bardiaux said of his stay in Uruguay 'it was one long round of dinners and parties.'

On 6 February he left for Buenos Aires and after a very rough crossing of the river Plate, tied up at the Argentine Yacht Club. Al Hansen and Vito Dumas had been there before him and it was from there they too had set out for their very different passages to Cape Horn, Hansen heading south and west, Dumas heading east.

Bardiaux left Buenos Aires bound for Cape Horn on 8 March 1952, somewhat late in the season as autumn was now approaching. Bardiaux stopped at Mar del Plata after a thirty hour battering against strong headwinds, to find not a single yacht afloat – they had all been laid up for the winter. Bardiaux pressed on to Bahia Blanca where, on entering the harbour in bad weather, the boat suddenly gybed and the boom flew across giving

Bardiaux a hefty blow on the head which knocked him overboard. By luck he managed to grab onto part of a sheet trailing in the water and he clambered back on board. Bleeding profusely from the blow and feeling dizzy with his jib blown into ribbons, Bardiaux somehow managed to pilot *Les 4 Vents* into the harbour. The Argentine naval base welcomed him, slipping the boat to antifoul the bottom and one of their sailmakers sewed him a new 'untearable' jib. He enjoyed his time there as an honorary officer of the Argentine Navy - a far cry from his treatment at the hands of the French Navy and something Bardiaux would never forget. His loathing of his home country probably began to develop here.

After two weeks he left the base at Puerto Belgrano and headed for Puerto Deseado 600 miles to the south. It was now getting very cold and the nights were getting longer as the southern winter was approaching. Bardiaux called in at San Julian where Magellan overwintered before discovering the Strait now named after him. Two days later he entered the estuary of Rio Gallegos. He was very tired and ran aground on a mud bank. He decided to stay put and get some sleep.

The next day, sailing on southward he passed the entrance to the Magellan Strait in good weather (he even anchored for the night in the entrance to the Strait, a place notorious for rough seas and strong winds). He was not so lucky after that and had a rough passage against headwinds and intense cold, so cold that Bardiaux claimed his sails froze stiff at night. Eventually he arrived at Rio Grande in Tierra del Fuego, the last inhabited place he would come to before the Horn. He entered the channel at night, lost his way and went aground on a gravel bank. In icy water he tried to dig the boat out but failed. Luckily the wind had died as otherwise his position would have been perilous. He floated off on the next tide and headed south-east to clear the eastern corner of the mainland, where he struggled against an adverse current, at times running at nine knots. Despite a huge swell Bardiaux entered and anchored in Bahia Thetis for some rest. Even with three anchors out and a line to the shore he was not safe. The next morning he navigated a narrow channel into a small cove where there was good shelter. As there was nowhere he could lie afloat at low water, he put *Les 4 Vents* aground on a bank of sand and mud. He got ten hours sleep. Bardiaux admitted that he could never have done all this in a larger heavier boat.

Cape Horn was now less than one-hundred miles away and Bardiaux set off to navigate the notorious Le Maire Strait, describing in his book how he had to dip his sails in sea water to unfreeze them. Here he had a favourable nine knot current which running against a west wind created enormous and dangerous breakers. *Les 4 Vents* charged through them like a submarine. The wind backed to the south-west and increased to Force 11 or 12. Bardiaux could do nothing but heave to. Whilst bringing up a sea anchor from the cabin, he faced near disaster. *Les 4 Vents* turned turtle, twice, the second time with Bardiaux on deck. Water poured below and the second time the boat was slow to right herself as she was now half full of water and floating with a pronounced list. The sails were in tatters as was the shelter he had built over the cockpit. The mess below was indescribable with broken glass everywhere. Bardiaux streamed a long warp to slow the boat whilst he pumped her dry. He then set some sail and headed for Aguirre Bay where he hoped he might find shelter and rest. He reached it in the dark and was at last able to put on some dry clothes and start to sort out his pitiable cabin. He lay awake that night on the bare boards of his bunk and considered the coming few days. Might he be near to achieving his ambition of rounding Cape Horn? He recalled his meeting with Louis Bernicot two years earlier at La Rochelle when Bernicot expressed his belief that when Bardiaux got near to the Cape he would stowaway his charts of the Horn and make for the Magellan Strait instead. Bardiaux had never had any such intention, the lure of the Horn being too strong. He remarked that he had only ever accepted Bernicot's charts of the Strait 'as a souvenir' with no intention of using them.

On Sunday 11 May 1952 in pitch darkness at three o'clock in the morning, Bardiaux set off into a strong south-west gale to sail to Isla Deceit, a small island a little to the east of the Horn itself. A study of the chart persuaded Bardiaux that he might find shelter to await daylight, in a crescent shaped bay on the east side of the island. Bardiaux held a secret ambition to land on Isla Hornos itself and leave a message in a sealed bottle confirming his passage past it. Unlike ships of old, who gave the Cape as wide a berth as possible and who often had to sail miles south into the ice in order to get past, Bardiaux decided to use the fact of his small light boat being handy and manoeuvrable enough to sail close in.

He sighted (or rather sensed) Isla Deceit at seven o'clock that evening having sailed eighty miles. It was by now quite dark as at this latitude there was only daylight between nine o'clock in the morning and three o'clock in the afternoon. He found no shelter. A huge swell was coming into the bay and anchoring was impossible. He hove to and tried to get some rest, but he got no sleep. He was suffering from the intense cold. His fingers were chapped and split, his face and ears were covered in chilblains and one ear was frostbitten.

At six o'clock in the morning of 12 May he set off again into a strong west-south-west wind with a huge swell running. He tacked south until he thought he was twelve miles south of the Horn itself. He tacked again and headed north. Just after midday he spotted Cape Horn a little abaft his beam. He put in another tack to get clear of Isla Hornos, on which the lighthouse stands. He went below to have a tot of rum and spotted the message bottle he had wanted to leave on the island. There was no way he could land in this weather.

He studied his chart and decided to shelter in an inlet on Isla Hermite, a large island twelve miles to the west of the Horn, but he realised he could never make it before nightfall. So he sailed on south until he was at Latitude 56º 20' S, where he met ice floes. The wind was even stronger now and he needed to roll in more mainsail. He found the sail frozen solid and Bardiaux had to boil water in his pressure cooker to thaw out the lower part before he could reef it. He tacked north and sailed on through the night, the wind and swell never relenting. At nine o'clock the next morning, Bardiaux sighted False Cape Horn, a cape about the same height as and thirty-two miles to the north-west of the true Cape Horn (in the past it had often been mistaken for the Horn itself with deadly consequences). Bardiaux hoped to find shelter in the lee of the land at the southernmost end of the Hardy Peninsular but it was not to be. A vicious williwaw flung *Les 4 Vents* onto her beam-ends. After that a seam in the mainsail had started and Bardiaux lashed himself to the boom for the two hours it took him to sew up the seam with hands so badly chapped he could hardly hold a needle. He was being driven by the wind to the north of Isla Hermite.

Bardiaux knew he had to find shelter. Somewhere where he could repair his battered and damaged boat. The only place for that was the Argentinian Naval Base at Ushuaia in the Beagle Channel. He thought he might be able to get there through the Murray Channel which ran to the west of Isla Navarino. With his newly repaired mainsail deep reefed, he headed north toward the Murray Channel. Suddenly there was a violent crash which shook the whole boat. Bardiaux thought he had hit a rock. Going up on deck he saw a white mass go by – he had hit an iceberg, fortunately a small one. He was then blown flat by another williwaw and all he could do was run off streaming a heavy warp to slow him. During the next eight hours he was blown thirty miles right across the bay.

Gradually the wind decreased and little by little Bardiaux worked into the channel between Isla Navarino and Isla Lennox, which led to the Beagle Channel. He was now less than twenty miles from his outward path, having sailed a circle of over 300 miles right round Cape Horn. Just before dawn he arrived at Puerto Harberton, when it began to snow heavily. The next day he sailed the seventy miles to Ushuaia. It took him ten hours and at last on 16 May he was safe and amongst friends. He was lucky to have survived. He stayed for nearly a month putting himself and his boat back together.

On 10 June, near mid-winter, he set off on the next leg of his voyage which would take him into the Pacific Ocean. He passed quickly through the Beagle Channel and on 15 June entered the Magellan Strait, stopping at the perfectly sheltered and isolated Playa Parda, which made such an impression on Bernicot when he stopped there. Bardiaux now wanted to hurry to get north and away from the southern winter. He had suffered badly during his exploits around Cape Horn and one of his legs was almost paralysed, with his right side causing him much pain. Reaching Cape Providence at the exit from the Strait, Bardiaux did not follow his prede-cessor Bernicot in *Anahita* who headed off out into the Pacific but set off to follow a different route through the 'Patagonian Channels'.

Through these, a series of fiords and inland channels, it is possible to navigate the coast of Chile from 56° South to 42° South, a distance of nearly1,000 miles in relative safety, making only a few short forays out to sea. Between 20 June and 7 August 1952 Bardiaux headed north, stopping often. He was always the centre of attention in the small harbours and fish-ing villages he stopped in. Few had seen a pleasure yacht before. Eventually he reached Ancud, close to where the wreckage of Alfon Hansen's boat was found. From there Bardiaux sailed longer legs out in the Pacific, stopping at Valdivia, Valparaiso and Coquimbo, from where he took his departure for crossing the Pacific.

He was now well and truly on his way home, having achieved the main objective of his voyage – to double Cape Horn alone, the first Frenchman and the third man ever to have done so.

Bardiaux left Chile on 4 April and arrived in Tahiti after forty-five days at sea and 4,885 miles. From there, the voyage back home took him via New Caledonia, Indonesia, Bali, the Cocos Islands, Mauritius, Durban. Cape Town, St Helena, the West Indies, New York, Bermuda, the Azores and then France. It was as if Bardiaux took the longest route possible so as to extend his voyage as much as he could.

It was by any measure a quite extraordinary venture, in what was a very small light-weight vessel, considered quite unsuitable at the time. Bardiaux claimed that he probably held the record for the number of landfalls made during a circumnavigation - 543.

Aftermath

In the light of all that he had achieved, it is interesting to note how Bardiaux was treated on his return to France, compared to the adulation meted out to those other two French sailing heroes, Alan Gerbault and, much later, Eric Tabarly. Bardiaux was the first Frenchman to sail alone round the world via Cape Horn, yet he received no awards for this at all. Gerbault who came before Bardiaux's voyage and Tabarly who came after were both awarded the Legion d'Honneur, France's highest award. Both these awards were given for merely sailing the Atlantic alone. In contrast, America honoured Bardiaux (although not until 1958) by awarding him the Blue Water Medal of the Cruising Club of America. France never recognised him.

Tabarly, hailing from Brittany, was rewarded for beating a Briton, Francis Chichester in the second *Observer* Singlehanded Transatlantic Race (the OSTAR) in 1960 - as one newspaper put it afterwards 'now a Breton rules the waves'. Gerbault did no race but was awarded merely for being the first Frenchman to sail the Atlantic alone. Not until thirteen years after Bardiaux's voyage did another man sail alone south of Cape Horn – this was the great Australian Bill Nance in an even smaller boat (see the next chapter).

So why was Bardiaux not rewarded in France? The answer most probably lies in that country's class system which was at that time, the 1950s, even more entrenched and more insidious than that prevalent in England. Tabarly was an Officer in the French navy; Gerbault was an aristocrat from the upper classes, was a French tennis champion and moved amongst the beautiful denizens of Monte Carlo and the French Riviera. Bardiaux was merely a seaman from the lower decks, an AB, who had built his own boat and who during his time in the French Navy never saw the inside of a warship but spent his time either sweeping floors or manning a military telephone exchange. The nearest he got to the sea was acting as a lookout for ships passing up and down *La Manche*, the English Channel.

Furthermore, as recounted earlier, Bardiaux was ignored and cold shouldered by French naval officers (and, more surprisingly, its officer cadets) when the French training ship, the *Jeanne d'Arc*, visited Uruguay. These officers and cadets turned their backs on Bardiaux. The final indignity came when Bardiaux, then in Argentina, received a letter from the French Navy Office telling him he had been transferred from the French navy reserve to the French army reserve. This seaman, who had just navigated himself half way round the world had suddenly, and at the whim of some French bureaucrat in Paris, been converted from a seaman into an infantry foot soldier. What sort of idiocy was that? Bardiaux passed this letter on to the Argentinian navy, who later circulated it round the world, making the French navy a laughing stock. Admittedly Bardiaux was not an easy man to get along with, described by Edward Allcard as someone a bit too self important, opinionated and pleased with himself.

Upon his return to France Bardiaux was not ready to settle down and he did not much like what he saw of his home country. He proceeded to build, with his own hands, what is believed to be the first ever yacht built entirely out of stainless steel. He named it *Inox* (being the French word for Stainless Steel, short for '*inoxydable*'). She was 15 metres long, weighed 30 tons and was rigged as a ketch. Bardiaux claimed she was unsinkable, having fifty-five watertight compartments. *Inox* was a strange shape, very narrow for her length and with a pronounced turtle deck. Bardiaux claimed that he undertook a solo non-stop circumnavigation in *Inox* taking 229 days (coincidentally three days longer than Francis Chichester's voyage in *Gipsy Moth IV*). Presumably this trip took place after Robin Knox-Johnston's non-stop circumnavigation in *Suhaili* in 1968/9 which is held to be the first such voyage. It is hard to find any independent authoritative confirmation for Bardiaux's claim.

Reports about his later life are all somewhat unreliable but he claimed to have completed voyages in *Inox* equivalent in distance to eighteen laps of the earth, to have fallen out with France and to have left the country between 1969 and 1995. During this time he roamed the oceans in his strange craft travelling to Canada, England, Ireland, Alaska, Japan and Australia. In 1981 he claimed he came across a castaway in a liferaft half way between south Africa and Australia. He rescued the man and took him on board. In November 1994, aged eighty-four, Bardiaux was caught out in hurricane force winds when crossing from Halifax in Nova Scotia to France, alone on board *Inox*. He claims he fell overboard but managed to climb back on board, arriving in France after thirty-three days at sea.

Two years later, he and *Inox* were back in Canada when he was caught out in a vicious storm close to Gaspé, a harbour at the entrance to the St Lawrence seaway. *Inox* was driven ashore onto rocks where she lay for twenty-four hours being pounded and battered by huge seas. With the help of a Canadian, called Robert Pagés, Bardiaux managed to free the boat and get her into harbour for repairs. Bardiaux believed that no other vessel would have survived and that this was proof of the indestructibility of his stainless steel creation.

After that Bardiaux returned to France (his fortieth Atlantic crossing) and took *Inox* up the Vilaine river to Redon in Brittany. There he spent the rest of his days, living a solitary life on *Inox*. He died in February 2000, aged eighty-nine, in complete anonymity and remembered by only a few.

During his life Bardiaux wrote six books, his later ones containing much of his peculiar philosophy of life as well as his sailing exploits ('*The 4 Winds of Adventure*' describing his world voyage round Cape Horn is the only one of his books to have been translated into English). He fell out with his publishers and tried to distribute his books on his own. He wrote much about Marshall Petain. the unpopular head of the Vichy Government during World War II, whom he admired.

He said he predicted the 1968 student revolution in Paris and was a supporter of the right wing populist anti-Government and anti-big business Poujadist movement, originally set up to protect the interests of small traders. He became bombastic and boastful and has been described variously as obstinate, stubborn, a braggart and even evil. He made many claims about his life, including having taught Bernard Moitessier (one of France's greatest sailors) how to sail. This seems unlikely as Moitessier was brought up in and learnt to sail in Vietnam, long before before he left for France (see chapter 14 below).

Controversy continued after his death. In his will, Bardiaux disinherited his nephews and a niece (he was never married) and left everything he had to Robert Pagés, the Canadian who had rescued him from the rocks in 1996. Pagés went to Redon after Bardiaux's death and removed everything from the boat, including all Bardiaux's trophies, books, log books, manuscripts and other valuables. He moved quickly as the nephews and niece were threatening to overturn the will in a French Court. At the same time the French government tried to recover the steel vessel as being of historic interest. Pagés put *Inox* up for sale and she is still sailing around the coasts of France today. As for *Les 4 Vents*, it is reported that she sank some years ago and now lies at the bottom of the Mediterranean, somewhere south of Sicily.

Today Bardiaux is hardly known outside France. Despite the vicissitudes of his later life, he will always be remembered for his outstanding and groundbreaking voyage in *Les 4 Vents*.

Chapter 9
Bill Nance – The smallest boat

The next man to round the Horn alone was the Australian Bill Nance, the youngest and least known of them all. He was only twenty-three when he set off from England in *Cardinal Vertue*, the smallest boat yet to attempt the feat, and he was a virtual novice sailor.

When I started to write this book it was impossible to find any reliable information about Nance and his voyage, or about his earlier or later life. At the end of his circumnavigation he sailed to Miami, sold *Cardinal Vertue* and disappeared into the hinterland of the USA. No books were written about his voyage; only a few, inaccurate, press and magazine articles were written and I found only a few references in the Australian press. That was all. No photographs of him could be found at the time. In Adrian Flanagan's recent book *The Cape Horners' Club* the only mention of Nance is a name in a list. Yet his voyage was one of the most extraordinary of them all. Whilst his name appears in the records of sailors who have rounded Cape Horn alone, beyond that almost nothing is known about his achievements or his life.

However, what I have now found out about him confirms this is exactly how he wanted it. The gentlest and kindest of men he is self-effacing and modest to a degree, believing he did not achieve anything remarkable. He wishes for no public approbation, acclaim or awards. He just wants to get on with his life, away from the limelight. In this, like everything else he has done, he has succeeded admirably.

When researching for this book I could only find two publications containing any information about him. First, a very brief description of Bill and his voyage appeared in a book written by Peter Woolass, the book being a paean to and history of the Vertue class of yacht. In only two short pages Woolass sets out a very brief sketch of Bill's voyage past Cape Horn in his yacht *Cardinal Vertue*. Woolass ended this account with the following words: '*This is but a brief record of a remarkable exploit by a remarkable man. An exploit which passed unhonoured and unsung. We who sail 'Vertues' on our humble voyages can appreciate better than most the enormity, the danger and the hardships which Bill Nance faced and overcame. And salute him.*' A few years after he wrote this, Peter Woolass did trace Bill's whereabouts through Bill's brother Bob who, whilst being protective of his brother, did let out that Bill had built a yacht on the lines of the famous Australian ocean racer *Freya* and had sailed this vessel across the Pacific to Honolulu. Beyond this I could find little.

Second, Don Holm, the American author of *'The Circumnavigators'* gives Nance a mere one page and ends his account by stating that in 1968 Nance was reported married and living on the Oregon coast, building a larger vessel for his next circumnavigation.

Then a year ago, during an internet search, I came across a reference on an American website (www.sailawaygirl.com) to an American yachtswoman called Pam Wall and the intriguing words: ' ...Our friend, Bill Nance who lives in Port Townsend, Washington, ...'.

Pam Wall has her own web site and I contacted her asking if her friend Bill Nance was the one I was seeking. 'Yes, he sure is' she replied and said not only that but that she was godmother to one of Bill's children, that she had introduced Bill to his second wife, Marie, and that Bill had bought from her and her late husband, Andy, the yacht *'Carronade'* in which Pam and Andy had sailed the world. She also told me that *Carronade* was the yacht on which her husband Andy, together with Bill Nance's brother Bob and one other, had undertaken a remarkable voyage from Australia around Cape Horn in 1965/6. This was just a year after Bills' epic solo voyage in *Cardinal Vertue*.

Serendipity, I had struck gold through one short email but the message came with a warning. I asked Pam if she would contact Bill and ask him if he would be prepared to talk to me. She said she was happy to do so but doubted whether Bill would respond as he rarely spoke to outsiders these days. Pam contacted Bill's wife, Marie (Bill never uses email or the internet) and for several anxious months we heard nothing. Then I sent Pam two copies of my last book, which had just been published, asking her to send one copy on to Marie and Bill, to give them an idea of the sort of book I wrote.

Neither Pam nor I heard anything further for two months until one day I received out of the blue an e-mail from Marie in which she said she had Bill's permission to speak to me on his behalf. She went on to say that he was, as ever, reluctant to speak about himself, but if I would let her know what information I sought, she would do her best to deliver it to me.

I replied to Marie explaining what I was looking for. No response came for several weeks until the telephone rang very early one morning at my house in France. It was Marie saying Bill had agreed to talk to me and we set up a time for a conference call later that day.

I spent the day very excited and wondering if she would actually call back. The telephone rang at the agreed hour and Bill came on the phone explaining that at nearly eighty and after years working underground in gold mines and in shipyards he was hard of hearing. He was quietly spoken and, at first, somewhat reticent. After a while he opened up and we then talked for over two hours, with Bill giving me his life story. At the end he said he would let me have some photographs of himself, of *Cardinal Vertue* and of his later yacht, 'if he could find any'.

What follows is an account of Bill's life and sailing career as told to me that evening in March 2017 and from subsequent discussions I have had with Bill and Marie.

Early life

Bill was born in 1938 in Wallaby Creek near Melbourne, Australia. He was the second of seven siblings. The family did not have much money and none of the family had any connection with or interest in the sea. The young Bill was a mad keen cricketer and as he grew up he hatched a plan so that, if he could get himself to England, he could play cricket there in our summer, returning to Australia to play more cricket in the southern hemisphere summer. Cricket twelve months of the year was his aim.

At the age of twenty Bill put this plan into action by leaving Australia for South Africa to earn sufficient money to get him to Europe. He got a job in the mines, working far underground drilling for diamonds. The work was physically arduous but the money was good. He stuck it for two years. Whilst working there he came across a book written by Edward Allcard about his singlehanded crossing of the Atlantic in his yacht *Temptress*. This book inspired Bill and it struck him that this was just the sort of thing he would like to do, despite knowing nothing about sailing or the sea. He became determined to sail around the world. To learn about all of this he started sailing and racing in a small 12-foot Firefly dinghy.

At around this time, Bill heard about an Englishman, D H 'Nobby' Clarke, who was beginning to write about and promote the idea of building and sailing multihulls, and trimarans in particular. Nobby had a long association with the pioneer American multihull designer, Arthur Piver and had been his agent in the United Kingdom for many years. His designs were simple and cheap to build and were fast and fun to sail. They appealed to Nance, who started a correspondence with Clarke about the possibility of his building one.

When he had sufficient funds, Nance travelled to England to talk to Nobby Clarke and to look for work. At first he got a job driving a motorised barge carrying cargo between the London Docks and Ipswich. But what Bill really wanted to do was learn to sail. One day someone told him about Bob Roberts, who was skipper of the Thames sailing barge *Cambria,* the last Thames barge still trading and carrying cargo under sail in and around the Thames estuary and England's east coast. Bill worked out that the best way to learn some seamanship in a short time would be to ship aboard such a vessel. He met up with Bob Roberts and the *Cambria* in Pill Mill on the River Orwell in Essex. Roberts happened to have a vacancy on the barge (it only had a crew of two) and Bill's sincerity and enthusiasm convinced Roberts to take him on as mate.

Bob Roberts was a fascinating character and, in addition to being skipper of the last cargo-carrying sailing barge, was a renowned folk singer, songwriter, storyteller, bargeman, broadcaster, author and journalist. The money from the barge was not sufficient for Bob to support his family, so he supplemented this by writing books, appearing on the BBC and appearing at folk clubs and festivals. He collected many songs which he heard from bargemen and fishermen he met along the East Anglian coast.

In addition to all this Bob Roberts was a highly experienced seaman with a reputation for hard sailing and fast passages. He had been at sea all his life and had made many long passages in sailing boats. He took over the *Cambria* in the 1950s and continued to trade in her in sail long after all the other sailing barges had gone. The *Cambria* carried its last cargo of one-hundred tons of cattle cake from Tilbury to Ipswich in 1970. (The *Cambria* has recently been rebuilt by the Cambria Trust at a cost of £1.4 million and can often be seen sailing today (still without an engine) in and around the waters of the Thames estuary.)

Roberts was just the perfect mentor for the young Nance. So throughout 1961 the crew, together with the ship's dog 'Dusty', sailed *Cambria* in all weathers through the shallows and narrows of the east coast creeks and estuaries, whilst Bill used his time ashore searching for a boat to buy. Having found his perfect mentor Nance now found, quite by chance, his perfect boat.

Nance found a boat called *Cardinal Vertue* for sale in Burnham-on-Crouch, fell in love with her on first sight and bought her. He spent the rest of 1961 getting her ready for a voyage home to his native Australia.

The boat

In 1936, soon after naval architect Jack Laurent Giles had set up in business in Lymington, Hampshire, he was asked by a yachtsman from Guernsey to design a five tonner suitable for serious offshore cruising. This was, at that time, a somewhat outrageous request in the light of what was then regarded as a proper yacht – in those days it was a maxim that you needed a foot of waterline length for every year of your life. Nobody then really thought a five tonner, only 21feet long on the waterline, was suitable to go offshore. Most offshore sailing and racing was carried out in yachts which today would be regarded as extremely large and heavy.

But Giles went ahead regardless and designed a yacht, named *Andrillot*, which was destined to become the forerunner of a class of small cruisers which, by their exploits, were to cause many a raised eyebrow amongst the diehards. She was only 25 feet and 3 inches long with a pronounced and graceful sheer. Being designed for cruising she was, of course, gaff rigged with a 5-foot bowsprit and she had no engine. *Andrillot* soon won her spurs when in 1937 she cruised the Bay of Biscay, covering 856 miles in twenty-three days.

Although *Andrillot's* gaff rig was rarely repeated, her underwater hull form has continued unchanged for decades. Giles described it as *'shaped to maintain the general outward character of the pilot-fishing boat, a straight forward little boat with a modest forward overhang, full displacement and moderate beam.'* He also remarked that he never changed the lines plan because he was never able to draw a better one. The second of the series was called *Sally II* (which the author owned and sailed for many years during the 1970s). More followed and in 1945 the name 'Vertue' was adopted for this class of little boats. The Vertues soon developed legendary status as more and more long and remarkable voyages were undertaken in them. The first of these voyages being undertaken by Humphrey Barton, then Jack Laurent Giles's partner, who in 1950 sailed *Vertue XXXV* with one crew from Falmouth to New York. This voyage was immortalised in Barton's famous book of the voyage titled simply *'Vertue XXXV'*

By 1948, eighteen of these hardy vessels had been built when Elkins Boatyard in Christchurch (who built many of the early examples, including *Sally II*) completed the construction of Vertue number nineteen, which was to be called *Cardinal Vertue*. She became one of the most famous of all.

In 1959 Dr David Lewis, a New Zealand doctor living and working in the east End of London took up sailing looking for a more adventurous life. He found *Cardinal Vertue* for sale on the east coast of England and thought her ideal for what he wanted. He bought her in 1959 and sailed her single-handed from Burnham-on-Crouch to Stavanger in Norway and back to England. He next heard about the very first *Observer* Single-Handed Transatlantic Race, which was due to start from Plymouth in 1960. He became fascinated with the idea of sailing the north Atlantic solo, the difficult way from east to west, against the prevailing winds. His interest was wider than just a single-handed sail across the Atlantic. He believed such an experience would enable him to study human behaviour and reactions (albeit his own) during total isolation and in the face of danger.

Lewis was a small man who showed exceptional courage and determination. There were five entrants in that first race and a few hours after the start the mast of *Cardinal Vertue* snapped about 12 feet above the deck and crashed down into the sea. He was disabled 3,000 miles from the finishing line. Undaunted, Lewis sailed back to Plymouth under jury rig and two days later set out with a repaired mast. This showed real determination, with the four other entrants way over the horizon by then and well on their way. Lewis completed the race coming in third, behind Francis Chichester and Blondie Hasler. He wrote a splendid book about his voyage titled 'The Ship Would Not Travel Due West'. After the race he sailed *Cardinal Vertue* home to England and put her ashore back in Burnham-on-Crouch, up for sale. In later life Dr Lewis went on to undertake many remarkable voyages, including a solo voyage to Antarctica. He studied ancient Polynesian methods of navigation without instruments and became a well known sailor and author. He died in 2002.

Without really knowing it, Nance had, with his Vertue, stumbled upon one of the best small boats ever designed for ocean cruising. Of heavy displacement, they are seakindly, seaworthy, fast for their size, will heave to in a gale like an old duck and will look after you when conditions get really bad. Perhaps more long distance voyages have been undertaken in Vertues than in any other class of boat of under 30-feet. They have achieved legendary status, helped of course by Nance's own voyage.

Vertues have sailed from England to New York (*Vertue XXXV*), from England to Newfoundland and back (*Icebird*), from Singapore to England (*Speedwell of Hong Kong*), from England to the Bahamas (*Easy Vertue*), from Gibraltar to South Africa (*Speedwell of Hong Kong* again), from Scotland to California (*Salmo*) and from Hong Kong to England via north Borneo, Ceylon and South Africa (*Mea*). None had yet circumnavigated the globe.

The voyage

Bill Nance left Burnham-on-Crouch in the autumn of 1961 planning to sail home to Australia. He set off with only a rough rudimentary knowledge of astro-navigation and the barest of navigation equipment – a few charts, a sextant, log tables, a kitchen alarm clock and a pocket transistor radio (for time signals) and, it must be admitted, with scarce or nil experience of how small yachts behave and how they should be handled in deep water and ocean gales. As we have seen, his only sailing experiences to date were sailing a 12-foot dinghy and sailing a 65-foot Thames Barge amongst the sandbanks and shallow waters of the Thames Estuary and the east coast rivers. However, Bill was strong, clever and resourceful and he soon learnt what to do. Bob Roberts had taught him well.

Nance met his first gale in the English Channel and ran aground off Chichester, suffering some minor damage which he had repaired in Cowes on the Isle of Wight. He headed west and spent a night in Brixham Harbour, sheltering from a strong westerly wind. He finally left the United Kingdom on 13 December 1961. His voyage eventually took him round the world.

Bill says little about the first leg of the voyage. He was learning as he went, particularly how to use the sun and stars to navigate. This was a relatively easy leg with following trade winds blowing him along for most of the way.

Nance arrived at San Fernando in Argentina, a harbour twenty kilometres north of Buenos Aires, after sixty-one days at sea. He spent only a short time there and having checked over his boat, departed bound for Cape Town. It is reported that he left amid considerable ridicule and harsh criticism about the size of his boat, his experience, his lack of equipment and, more probably, his age (he was still only twenty-three). Nance had another reasonably uneventful passage to Cape Town but he did meet one severe south-easterly gale, an introduction to what was waiting for him in the Southern Ocean,

He took thirty-nine days to sail the 3,995 miles to Cape Town, probably a record at that time. This is a remarkable time for a yacht only twenty-one feet on the waterline. Allowing for the inevitable periods of calm and light weather, Nance must have kept his boat sailing near her maximum speed for much of the way. Nance was a hard driver - sailing a yacht as small as a Vertue in gale or near gale conditions at high speed is not only uncomfortable but wet, both on deck and below, where everything becomes soaked and sodden from the never ending waves and spray which land on board, some of which always finds its way below.

It was after he left Cape Town for Australia on the next leg that his troubles really began. Soon after passing the Cape of Good Hope (the Cape of Storms), Nance ran into one of the frequent gales to be found in that area. *Cardinal Vertue* was knocked down by a huge sea which damaged the wind vane of his self-steering gear. When approaching Saint Paul Island, about mid-way between South Africa and Australia, he met another violent storm in which *Cardinal Vertue* was dismasted, once again. The mast broke at the lower crosstrees and was washed overboard, along with the rigging and the mainsail. Whilst trying to recover these Nance himself was washed overboard but he was wearing a safety harness and managed to cling on and haul himself back aboard. He set up a jury rig and continued toward Australia. He had some 2,000 miles to go to Fremantle.

Merely to say 'he set up a jury rig' totally diminishes the achievement of what he did next. When a mast breaks at sea in the midst of a storm, there is a total mess of broken spars, torn and shredded sails and entangled ropes and wire rigging, all half in and half out of the water. Without the steadying effect of the mast and sails, the boat would have been rolling fearfully from gunwale to gunwale making work on deck almost impossible. Add to this the fact that the broken upper part of the mast would be in the water, still attached to the boat by the tangled rigging, and would act as a battering ram trying to punch a hole in the hull every time the boat pitched and rolled in the oncoming seas. Many boats have been lost this way after a dismasting. The first thing Nance would have done would have been to cut free the mess of rigging and sails. There is no way he would have been able to bring it all on board. The wire shrouds would have had to be cut with bolt cutters or freed by unscrewing the bottle screws which attached them to the hull. This would have taken many hours whilst the boat lay broadside onto and at the mercy of the oncoming seas. Only then would he have been safe and able to think about setting a jury rig.

Thirty-six days later Nance sailed *Cardinal Vertue* into Fremantle. Nance had taken seventy-six days to sail 5,000 miles from Cape Town, the last 2,000 of which were under jury rig. On arrival Nance, having just limped into harbour in a severely damaged boat, was accosted by officials from the Australian Customs and Immigration Service (who have a reputation for rudeness and zero tolerance towards visiting yachtsmen). They gave him a churlish welcome by impounding his boat until he could raise a $1,600 fine they levied on him (that's about $20,000 or £12,500 in today's money). Bill did not have even fifty cents to his name and perhaps it was this, combined with his youth and the small size of his boat which led the Customs not to believe his story of having sailed from England. Nance's problems were solved after the Royal Freshwater Bay Yacht Club stepped in. They arranged for the fine to be settled but even then the Customs demanded that Nance and his boat be out of Australia within six months – all this despite Nance being an Australian national. Some welcome for a returning hero.

With the aid of many local yachtsmen, Nance stepped a new mast, effected minimal repairs and set off for Melbourne, pleased to be away from Fremantle. When rounding Cape Leeuwin a few days later, Nance met yet another storm and *Cardinal Vertue* was hit and pooped once again by a huge sea. This bent the self steering gear, putting it out of action, damaged the port bow, cracked seven ribs, split a plank just above the waterline and split a deck beam.

For two days Nance sat at the helm non-stop, steering the boat downwind but eventually had to get some sleep. He went below leaving *Cardinal Vertue* under bare poles. She was soon capsized by another rogue wave and she turned turtle through 360°. Nance lost the boom and the mainsail, which went over the side. Below there was utter confusion. Nance streamed heavy warps, to try to stop the boat lying broadside onto the waves, and once again left her lying a-hull. He tried to get some much needed sleep. Again *Cardinal Vertue* was knocked down and this time the main cabin hatch was smashed; water poured below. He headed for land under a trysail and small headsail and eventually made it to Albany, which lies some 350 miles to the east of Cape Leeuwin.

After the boat was repaired, once more with help from local yachtsmen, Nance sailed *Cardinal Vertue* across the Great Australian Bight to Melbourne, his birth place, in sixteen days, arriving on 27 October 1962, clocking up daily runs of 120, 130 and 155 miles – an exceptionally fast speed for such a small vessel.

Nance, who was now back with his family, could only stay a few days in Melbourne as his six month permit to remain in Australia was running out. He sailed on to Tasmania and then to New Zealand, where this nation of sailors welcomed him with open arms. He had none of the problems he experienced in Australia. He found Auckland hospitable and remained there until the end of 1964, working and earning enough money to pay for the next leg of his journey. During this time he crewed on a famous New Zealand ocean racing yacht, *Cotton Blossom* in a number of ocean races. He worked in shipyards and boatyards whilst getting *Cardinal Vertue* shipshape.

In November 1964, just as he was about to leave Auckland, he damaged both his hands in an accident with a wood turning machine. In order not to delay his departure he had protective steel caps made to fit over his

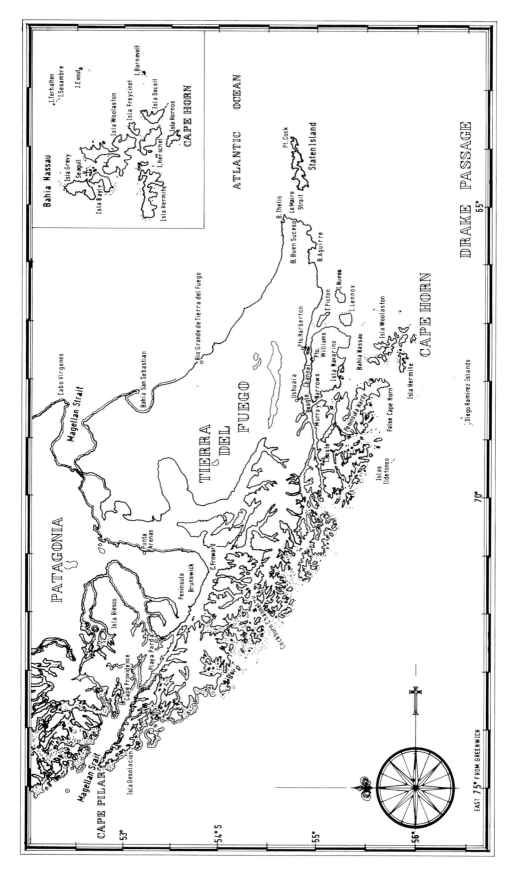

1. Previous page, map of Cape Horn

2. Joshua Slocum (1899)

3. Joshua Slocum's boat *Spray* (1898)

4. Yacht *Coronet* - First yacht to round Cape Horn in 1888

5. Alain Gerbault in the Pacific with Queen Marau of Tahiti
(between 1925 and 1929)

6. Alan Gerbault arriving at Le Havre at the end of his
circumnavigation in 1929

7. Photograph of Edward Miles on board *Sturdy II*. Photo dated 1931.

8. Louis Bernicot on board his yacht *Anahita* (1952)

9. Louis Bernicot's yacht *Anahita*

El Gráfico

Vito Dumas
El más grande
de los navegantes
solitarios

10. Vito Dumas on board *Lehg II*

11. Vito Dumas and Alfon Hansen with his cat and dog

12. Vito Dumas's first yacht *Lehg I*

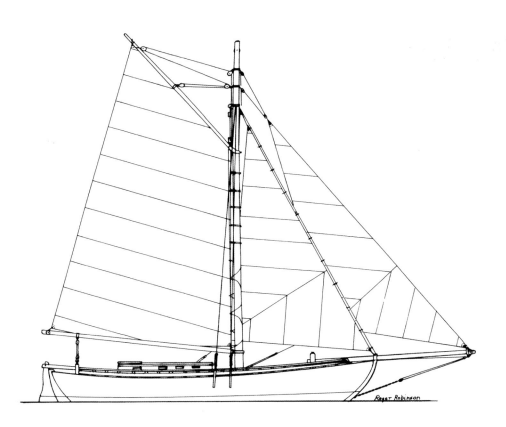

13. Drawing of Alfon Hansen's yacht *Mary Jane*

14. Bill Nance on *Cardinal Vertue*

15. *Cardinal Vertue* (opposite)
16. Bill Nance at *Cardinal Vertue's* chart table (opposite)

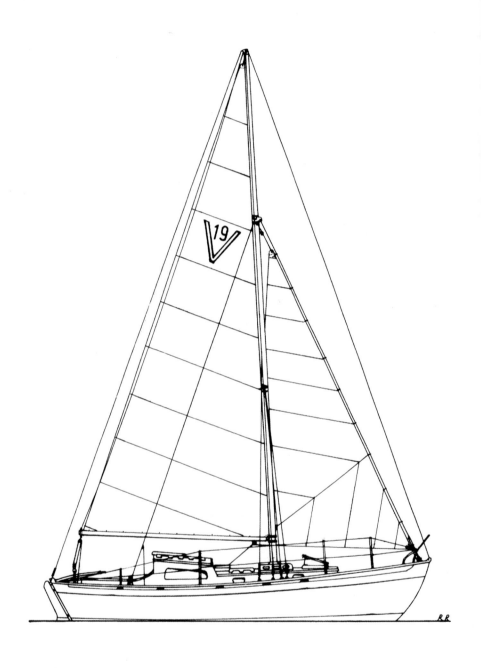

17. Drawing of Bill Nance's yacht *Cardinal Vertue*

18. Edward Allcard - a man who loved life

19. *Sea Wanderer* ashore on slip at Puerto Williams, Chile

20. Norman Fowler and Edward Allcard (with Ann Davison)

21. Edward Allcard's last boat *Johanne Regina* under sail

22. Cape Horn bearing N distance 1 mile

23. Portrait of Donald Crowhurst

damaged fingers. He set off on 1 December 1964 for the Southern Ocean and Cape Horn.

He made a very fast run across the Southern Ocean driving *Cardinal Vertue* hard day and night. During this leg he travelled 2,000 miles in thirteen days. He had no real problems until he approached Cape Horn. Nance sensibly, unlike Bardiaux and Dumas before him, decided to reach the Horn around mid-summer when there was almost perpetual daylight and relatively warm temperatures. On 30 December he was at 51° South running under bare poles streaming thirty-fathoms of warp in a full gale when the biggest sea he had ever seen crashed aboard and pooped *Cardinal Vertue*, breaking the tiller at the rudder head. He lay a-hull during the night, something Nance avoided after his experiences off Cape Leeuwin. He said later *'I have no great faith in lying a-hull and probably only survived because the weather eased and by the following day I was able to fit the spare tiller'*.

As he neared Cape Horn, the barometer dropped to a low of under twenty-nine inches, a pressure normally found in the centre of a hurricane. On 7 January he sighted the Diego Ramirez Islands which lie sixty-five miles south-west of Cape Horn. These islands extend for five miles north to south and are in the direct path of ships approaching Cape Horn from the west. Many ships have been wrecked there in the past. Now there is a lighthouse on the islands.

Later that day Nance and *Cardinal Vertue* passed close to Cape Horn in a driving rain squall. Nance said of the event: *'It was as usual a day of alternating squalls and sunshine, but a day to remember for me. I think most of all I was relieved to see it go astern.'*

Nance was the youngest man to have sailed alone past the Horn and he had done so in the smallest boat (a record which stood until 1973 when a seventeen-year-old Japanese boy completed a circumnavigation via Cape Horn in a 20-foot yawl named *Ahoudori II).*

After rounding the Horn, Nance carried on non-stop to Buenos Aires, where he arrived on 22 January. He had been at sea for fifty-three days and had averaged 122 miles per day. This was a record not beaten until Sir Francis Chichester, in his *Gipsy Moth IV,* double the size, achieved an average of 131 miles per day.

At Buenos Aires Nance had completed his circumnavigation and, much to the liking of this quiet self effacing man, there was no publicity and no fanfares. It should be remembered that Nance's voyage predated the voyages of Francis Chichester, Robin Knox-Johnston and Alec Rose, all of whom were subsequently knighted. Why was this remarkable exploit by this remarkable man not comparable with those of these now famous knights of the sea? Maybe he just wanted none of it.

In Buenos Aires Nance met the man who had inspired him all those years before, back in South Africa, to take up the sailing life - Edward Allcard. Allcard was on his way south in his yacht *Sea Wanderer*, having sailed from England and was, as we shall see in the next chapter, the next man to round the Horn.

From Buenos Aires Nance wrote to his old skipper Bob Roberts in Essex saying he was going to sail *Cardinal Vertue* to Nassau and then on to Florida. For many years nobody had any hard information on Bill's whereabouts after that. The following is what Bill told me about his life following his Cape Horn voyage.

On leaving Buenos Aires, Bill did indeed sail *Cardinal Vertue* to Miami, stopping in Antigua and the Bahamas, sailing alone as always. On the leg to Antigua he is reported to have averaged 123-miles a day. Between there and Nassau he logged 180 miles noon to noon on one occasion, - probably a record for a boat of this size. In Miami, Bill put *Cardinal Vertue* up for sale. She was bought by a man who lifted her ashore intending to refit her and install an engine. However, this never happened and, very sadly, *Cardinal Vertue* was left for many years to rot away on the banks of the Miami River. She is now no more.

Nance then moved to Portland in Oregon on the north-west coast of the USA, where he thought he could get work in one of the many shipyards there and where he could learn steel welding. This he did (and got married) and using his new found skills built himself a 39-foot steel sloop which he called *Phaedra*. She was a sister ship of the famous Australian ocean racer called *Freya*, which had been built and designed by the Norwegian Halvorsen brothers. In *Freya* the brothers won the prestigious Sydney to Hobart ocean race three times in succession - 1963, 1964 and 1965. She was a double ender in true Norwegian style, continuing the tradition of Colin Archer and the boats of both Alfon Hansen and Vito Dumas.

Bill and his first wife sailed *Phaedra* from Portland to Sidney on Vancouver Island in Canada and then onto Hawaii, where they spent time sailing amongst the islands, ending up in Honolulu. They then sailed back to San Diego in the USA. Bill's marriage broke up and he sold *Phaedra*.

Soon after that Bill met up with Andy and Pam Wall, who came to play a big part in his life. Some years before, Andy Wall, another Australian, had built a small 30-foot wooden yacht called *Carronade*. In this diminutive little ship Andy wandered the Pacific and Atlantic oceans for many years. Then at exactly the same time as the world was entranced by all the publicity and razzmatazz surrounding Sir Francis Chichester's epic passage round Cape Horn (see chapter 11 below), Andy along with Des Kearns and Bill's brother, Bob, were out there in the unfriendly Southern Ocean in *Carronade* just behind the great man also heading for the Horn. No one knew they were there and after a wild passage, in which they were knocked down and pitch-poled, they successfully rounded the Cape. *Carronade* ended the passage in Fort Lauderdale in Florida, where Andy met Pam and were soon married. The newly-weds set off on *Carronade* on their honeymoon, crossing the Atlantic to England. They spent three years sailing around Europe and the two then sailed back to the USA to build a bigger boat.

Back in Fort Lauderdale, Bill Nance, who was now divorced, bought *Carronade* from Andy, who proceeded to build a sister ship to *Phaedra*. Bill Nance set off alone on *Carronade* intending to sail across the Atlantic to Norway but off Cape Hatteras ran into an unexpected hurricane which had developed suddenly with little warning. It was not the hurricane season. The rigging on *Carronade* was old and worn and began to strand and break, unable to take the strains imposed on it by the bad weather and large seas. Before he lost his mast completely Nance diverted to Wilmington in North Carolina. He stopped there for six months working as a welder. Then he sailed south to the Caribbean, stopping in the Bahamas and Jamaica before sailing south to central America. He next headed for the Panama Canal. In the boistrous conditions he met, *Carronade,* which by now had sailed over 100,000 miles, began to suffer structural problems and Nance, becoming fearful that the old ship would break up under the strain, diverted back home to Fort Lauderdale.

He then had a respite from sailing and in 1978 and 1979 took a job on a USA research ship going to the waters of Antarctica. On his return Nance moved to San Diego and went back to school, enrolling in a California State College to learn furniture making. After completing his course he moved north to Port Townsend, in Washington State, which was a big centre of wooden boat building and where Nance's skills were put to good use. During 1981 he went to Florida to visit Andy and Pam where he met an English lady, Marie, who was visiting the Walls. Marie hailed from Lymington in England where she had originally met the Walls on *Carronade*. Bill and Marie fell in love and soon got married.

After several years the boatyard where Bill was working went bankrupt but he and four other employees got together and took over the business. They made a big success of it, changing with the times, becoming experts in the use of modern synthetic materials as well as traditional wood. They built a 161-foot yacht which was the largest Glass Reinforced Plastic boat to have been made in the USA at that time. The yard and Bill prospered.

Nance was eighty in 2018 and is now retired, living with Marie. He talks little of his exploits those many years ago but there is no doubt that his voyage around the world and round Cape Horn which ended when he was twenty-four remains one of the most outstanding voyages of all time. Nance has never wanted or sought recognition for his achievement. But those who appreciate what he did salute him.

As a postscript to this tale, Bill's brother, Bob Nance had an almost equally illustrious sailing career. After his trip on *Carronade* he joined Miles and Beryl Smeeton on their renowned yacht *Tzu Hang* for their third attempt to round Cape Horn, having been pitch-poled and damaged on their two previous attempts. Both times they had limped into Chilean waters lucky to survive. The third time, with Bob Nance on board, they sailed from England and then past Cape Horn from east to west and then on up to British Columbia where Miles and Beryl, who were getting old by then, swallowed the anchor. Bob bought *Tzu Hang* from the Smeetons, working in Canada for several years to raise the money to pay for her. Bob sailed *Tzu Hang* the length of the Pacific from Canada to Australia and then eastward round Cape Horn and north to Florida where the voyage ended in Fort Lauderdale. There he established, and still operates, a successful sailmaking and yacht rigging business under the name Nance & Underwood.

Eventually Bob sold his beloved *Tzu Hang*. The people who bought her were, unbeknownst to him, involved in drug running between south America and the USA. Eventually, the owners were caught and arrested in St Thomas, part of the US Virgin Islands. *Tzu Hang* was impounded by the USA Drug Enforcement Agency and left lying to her anchor in the harbour. With no one to look after or care for her, she remained afloat whilst a hurricane swept through the islands. *Tzu Hang* dragged her anchor, was thrown onto the beach and wrecked. Eventually the American authorities found someone prepared to buy the wreck and remove her from the shore. A crane loaded her onto a low loader truck to be transported inland. Unfortunately the driver of the truck miscalculated the height of his load and *Tzu Hang* was driven straight into the roof of an underpass on a busy highway, where she became stuck and unmoveable. In order to clear the road, *Tzu Hang* was there and then hastily cut up by power saws and ended up merely a heap of firewood. A devastatingly sad end to a wonderful, much loved and much written about yacht. She had given so much pleasure and adventure to the

Smeetons, to Bob Nance and to all those who had read Miles Smeeton's many books describing their adventures and travels together on *Tzu Hang*.

How sad it was for these two boats previously owned by the two Nance brothers to have had such ignominious endings. *Cardinal Vertue* rotting away to a pile of timber in Florida and *Tzu Hang* ending up as a pile of firewood underneath a flyover on a major highway in the US Virgin Islands.

Chapter 10
Edward Allcard – The oldest boat

Initially this chapter turned out almost as difficult to research and complete as the previous one. Whilst Edward Allcard's early life is well chronicled in his first three books, these only take him up to the time he reached Buenos Aires in his ketch *Sea Wanderer*. He stopped there having declared his intention to sail south to Cape Horn. There was then a long gap in his story until the time when, many years later, he turned up in the West Indies, married and with a young daughter. What had happened in between? This was almost a complete blank save I knew he had spent time in Patagonia, had sailed round Cape Horn in 1966 and had then passed through Singapore. I also knew that he had at some stage met and married his second wife Clare, who described their life together in her wonderful book *A Gipsy Life*.

As Allcard had been born in 1914, I rather assumed he was no longer alive and I was at a loss as to where to turn next. Then another piece of serendipity came along. One day I chanced upon an internet blog (what would we do without these) written by Charles Doane, a sailor, writer and journalist on the US magazine SAIL. In it he wrote about a recent visit he had made to the Allcards in Andorra, high in the Pyrenees between France and Spain, to talk to them about Thomas Tangvald, who the Allcards had taken in after the death of Thomas's father on a reef in the Caribbean, and about whom he was writing a book.

So I now knew that Edward was still alive aged 101, and, better still, Andorra was only three hours drive by car from our house in the south-west of France, where I was writing this book. I found Clare's email address in Doane's blog and sent her a message. A few weeks later I was sitting down with this amazing couple, listening to their story and yarning about the past. It was a joyous meeting and, as so often happens with sailing people, we found we had many mutual friends. But the best news for me was that Edward, with Clare's help, was putting the finishing touches to his latest book, which chronicled his voyage in *Sea Wanderer* south from Buenos Aires to Cape Horn, the time he spent there and his journey back to the West Indies to complete his circumnavigation. This was just what I needed and, not only that, but I had met the esteemed Edward Allcard, long a hero of mine as he was to so many other sailors of our generation.

Subsequently we became good friends and his wife Clare, a well regarded writer herself, became a much appreciated mentor and guide to me in my writing of this and my previous book. Edward's book was published in 2017 to much acclaim, but sadly he died a few months after publication. He was 102. The story of this amazing man follows.

The man

Edward Allcard was one of the most accomplished voyagers under sail of the twentieth and twenty-first centuries. He spent virtually the whole of his adult life wandering the world's oceans, usually alone. He was a well known author who, as mentioned above, wrote several memorable books describing his adventures. Today, whilst many people remember his name, few knew that he was still alive in 2017.

He was the sole surviving member of that band of sailors who opened up the world's oceans in the early days of small boat voyaging. Eric & Susan Hiscock, Miles and Beryl Smeeton, Alain Gerbault, Marcel Bardiaux, William A Robinson, Humphrey Barton, Peter Tangvald and the others are all long gone. They embraced the cause of long distance ocean sailing in small boats as an alternative simple way of life and Allcard was the last of these to have survived from that golden age.

Edward and Clare moved to Andorra when their sailing days were over. Asked by an immigration officer, concerned for his future happiness, if he wouldn't feel enclosed by the mountains after the ocean's wide horizons. '*No,*' he replied, '*It's all nature. Mountains are just waves standing still.*'

Edward was born in Walton-on-Thames, Surrey on 31 October 1914, three months after the start of the First World War. His grandfather had a house in Teddington on the banks of the Thames with its own creek and boathouse and Edward's first memories were of his grandmother storming across the lawn with a large parasol chasing off punts and rowing boats which tried to moor against their river bank.

Edward was educated at Eton in England and Chillon College in Switzerland following which he trained on the River Clyde in Glasgow to become a naval architect and marine surveyor. Until his death he was the longest serving member of the Royal Institution of Naval Architects. Sailing was in his family's blood and Edward started sailing at the age of six and was rarely out of a boat from that time onwards. Sailing became his passion and his life, almost a religion.

During World War II he worked with the RAF and the Air Ministry helping design, build and test air-sea rescue craft. After the war had ended, he took to the sea and only stopped sailing in 2006 at the age of ninety-two, when he sold his last boat. He owned sixteen boats during his lifetime, many of which he bought in a derelict state. He made his first single-handed voyage in 1939, just before the start of the Second World War, sailing from Scotland to Norway and back.

Allcard's early voyages

In the winter of 1947 Allcard set off alone in an attempt to reach Gibraltar in a twenty ton cutter called *Content* but he experienced many problems in a succession of winter gales and returned to England after eight days at sea, making it to Newlyn in Cornwall. He repaired the boat and set off again in January 1948, this time with a friend as crew. They stopped in Dartmouth, where Allcard spied a 34-foot yacht named *Temptress*. She was smaller than *Content* and far better suited for a single-hander. *Temptress* was rigged as a gaff yawl, had a small petrol/paraffin engine and was comfortable below. She had been built in 1910 at Calenick on the River Fal and had previously been owned by Humphrey Barton, who in 1929 had sailed her to Spain and back. Allcard described her as '*a little ship who for her size was remarkably stiff, able and dry*'. Allcard bought *Temptress* there and then and, after selling *Content*, left England on 27 August 1948, this time alone. He was aiming for a direct passage to Gibraltar. He had a rough time crossing the Bay of Biscay and put into La Coruna and then Lisbon before reaching Gibraltar on 8 October. Allcard spent the winter there. He made a new main mast and gave the boat a thorough re-fit. He left on 21 May the next year bound for New York.

Allcard and *Temptress* followed the classic Trade Wind route. Humphrey Barton, who sailed the Atlantic eighteen times, said of this route 'Sail down the Channel. Turn left. Then sail south until the butter melts. Then turn right.'

Despite the normally benign nature of the 'trades' Allcard experienced heavy weather at first with many headwinds. On 10 July, after fifty days at sea, Allcard reached the 'Horse Latitudes', an area of variable winds and calms. He crossed the Gulf Stream in August, the middle of the hurricane season, somewhat fearful of meeting one coming up from the Caribbean. Allcard arrived in New York on 9 August 1949 after 4,800 miles and eighty days at sea.

Soon after his arrival in America, Edward noticed a neglected and derelict yacht called *Wanderer* moored in a mud berth nearby. Edward, who had a predilection for saving abandoned vessels and an eye for a good boat, immediately bought her for a song. Clare wrote later that *Wanderer* had grass growing on her decks, hornets nesting in her masts and rats everywhere. To Edward's eye she seemed an ideal vessel for a future project – a trip to the south Atlantic, the waters of Cape Horn and, perhaps, a circumnavigation. Edward spent the next few months sorting out *Wanderer* and making her seaworthy. He re-rigged her, moved the mizzen mast forward and altered her into a ketch, with a rig suitable for the waters of the Southern Ocean and Cape Horn.

But first Edward had to sail *Temptress* back home to England. Allcard moored *Wanderer* in a mud berth under a tree at Port Washington on the north shore of Long Island, then a small hamlet, now a fashionable resort studded with yacht marinas and golf courses. He set off in *Temptress* on 15 August 1950, despite a warning that a hurricane was coming his way. Allcard rode this out in Gravesend Bay on Long Island.

On 24 August he set off properly, bound non-stop for Plymouth. As was to be expected, the passage started off with calms and much fog, followed by favourable westerly winds which blew him on his way. Often he found a strong gulf stream under him helping him on his way at the rate of twenty miles per day. In the latter part of the passage he had a very hard time, experiencing a number of gales, in one of which *Temptress* was knocked down and damaged. Allcard decided to divert to the Azores.

As he approached the islands, Allcard experienced more hurricane force winds. A huge sea picked *Temptress* up, rolled her right over, breaking the mizzen mast (along with some of Edward's toes) and clearing the whole back end of the boat. Allcard wrote:

'it was as if a giant with a massive sword had razed everything down to deck level. The boom gallows had gone, the compass had gone, the mizzen mast had gone, the bumpkin had gone and the main boom sagged on deck like a broken wing. The mizzen mast was in the water, still attached, acting like a large battering ram against the hull.'

Temptress was in grave peril and Allcard got her running down wind with the mizzen mast acting as a sea anchor. Suddenly the wind disappeared as they passed into the eye of the storm. Allcard used this respite to cut the mizzen free. Soon the wind returned from the opposite direction, as ferocious as ever, and Allcard ran before it streaming heavy warps over the stern whilst steering the boat to keep her heading dead down wind. He was at the helm non-stop for fifteen hours. Two days later he was able to start sailing again and he managed to get a sun sight. He had been blown to within fifty-six miles of the island of Fayal.

On 28 October, he and *Temptress* limped into the small harbour of Horta and anchored. Edward had been at sea for seventy-four days. *Temptress* was leaking badly, even at anchor, and Allcard had to pump her out regularly. The harbour was then unprotected (today a large breakwater has been built) and hardly safe but Allcard rode out a gale attached to a large mooring buoy. *Temptress* was then lifted ashore by a quayside crane in order for the leak and rudder to be repaired and for a new mizzen mast to be stepped. In late December the repairs were completed and the boat relaunched. Allcard took her on a trial sail with several islanders on board, including an attractive young woman. The evening before he left, in early January, the locals threw a farewell party where the same woman came up to Edward and asked him when he was leaving. Edward shrugged and said merely '*Oh, sometime tomorrow*'. He never liked being tied down.

Allcard, alone, slipped his mooring and stole out of the harbour later that night in the pitch dark, aiming to sail the 150 miles to the island of San Miguel, before heading for Madeira and then Gibraltar. *Temptress* met a good breeze from the north-west and soon left the island behind. Just as day dawned Allcard started with momentary fear as he saw movement at the main hatch. He saw, rising out of it, a hand followed by a frightened white face, half hidden by unkempt black hair. It was a girl. Allcard realised immediately who she was. She was called Otilia and it was she who had spoken to him at the party. Alarm turned to anger and then to laughter, as Allcard realised he had shipped a stowaway. With no common language between them, Allcard eventually understood that she had come on board as she wanted to get to England. At first he said he could take her only to San Miguel or Madeira where she would, no doubt, be returned to the Azores. Otilia burst into tears. Edward then thought further about the beautiful girl he had on board; slim with long black hair, large dark eyes and olive skin, he realised that her life would be made unbearable if she was returned home. Edward, always the gentleman, believed that one should never take advantage of a girl, nor refuse any request from a lady. Therefore, strictly speaking he could not refuse to take her to Europe. He tried to talk her out of continuing. He tried to tell her they were at sea at the worst time of the year, had very little food for two people and would have to drive the boat hard day and night. Otilia merely shrugged her shoulders. Edward then decided to take Otilia as far as Gibraltar.

As they neared land Edward decided to head for Casablanca instead and they arrived there on 1 February 1951. Once the story of the beautiful stowaway got out they were bombarded by reporters and cameramen. Stories abounded about their married state or, more importantly, their lack of it – this was the 1950s after all.

Crews on boats in the harbour were all agog at Edward, the long term loner, striding around the harbour with his lovely mermaid alongside him. As we saw earlier, one of these was Marcel Bardiaux, the young Frenchman sailing alone around the world in his tiny yacht *Les 4 Vents*. He even tried to persuade Otilia to join him. She responded by saying what a shame it was that he had only the one cabin.

Her story went around the world and letters to Otilia flooded in, some containing proposals of marriage from total strangers. One letter came from a kindly lady in London who offered to pay Otilia's fare to England and give her accommodation for a year. Otilia accepted this offer and one day, Edward said a sad goodbye to his lovely stowaway. In London, Otilia sold her story to a Sunday newspaper, immediately making Edward newsworthy.

They went their separate ways and did not see each other for fifty-eight years until 2009, when Edward and his wife Clare caught up with Otilia through the Internet. They spent Edward's ninety-fifth birthday together. Amazingly, Otilia and her husband were now living a mere four hours drive away from Edward's home in Andorra.

Left on his own, and at first entirely miserable, Edward prepared *Temptress* for the voyage home to England. He dallied in Casablanca until 5 June when he set off. He stopped only once, to anchor for a night in Vigo Bay in Spain. He arrived in Plymouth late in the evening on 13 July and tied up in Millbay Dock, hoping for a quiet arrival. This was not to be. He was greeted by a battery of cameras and newsmen. He was now famous, not only as the first man to sail the Atlantic alone in both directions but as the man with the beautiful stowaway.

The next year, 1953, saw Edward return to New York to collect *Wanderer* from her mud berth under her tree on Long Island and to sail her back to England. Edward wrote the following account of how he got to New York:

The story went like this. I'd sailed Temptress back to England and was searching for the cheapest way to be reunited with Wanderer, still laid up near New York, when I heard of a sailing yacht called Catania, in Cornwall. Apparently she had a new American owner who wanted to sail her to the States, but had no experience of the sea. He was looking for a skipper. However, I was warned, there were certain snags…

I promptly headed to Mashfords Boatyard at Cremyll in Cornwall to find out what the snags were. After careful inspection I saw that there were none with the boat, which was in tip-top condition. Then I met the owner, a young man called Norman Fowler, and there, I soon realized, lay the problem.

The local tittle-tattle was that Norman had murdered the boat's previous owner – who was also his wealthy lover – in his bath. He had not been arrested because, when the police broke in, the key of the locked bathroom door was found by the dead body. The boat Catania was a small part of Norman's inheritance.

Despite an instinctive antipathy, I decided to risk it. I had to get back to Wanderer. A couple of weeks later, the two of us set sail for the West Indies, with me simply hoping to finish the voyage alive and on the other side of the Atlantic. I could then hitch-hike up to New York and start rebuilding the boat.

We made it down to the Canary Islands, where we called in to fill up with fresh water and food. By this time, I had had enough of Norman's snide remarks and his constant rebuttals of all and everything I said. I would call down excitedly from on deck, 'There's a ship on the horizon!' He'd come up, take a cursory look and say, 'No there isn't.' His eyesight must have been poor. Then, when the ship passed quite close, he would refuse to come up on deck to see it.

Reluctant to become surplus to requirements, I was careful not to teach him too much about sailing or navigation. Hoping to cut the journey short, I suggested heading to Bermuda, from where I could fly to New York. He would have no difficulty in picking up crew there to sail on to the West Indies.

When we finally sailed into Hamilton Harbour, Bermuda, I moved ashore and took the first plane possible to New York. There, after an absence of three years, I moved on board Wanderer. Meanwhile I wrote to a friend in the West Indies to seek out news of Norman. I soon received a reply: 'Norman had no trouble in getting two crew for the trip from Bermuda to the West Indies. But he was subsequently murdered in a public bath.' I was not altogether surprised. There had been times when I would gladly have wrung his neck myself.'

Before Edward left New York he changed his boat's name to Sea Wanderer. The reason was that her original name was also the name of a little 21-foot yacht in which Eric Hiscock, later to become a famous voyager and author, had started his and his wife's world girdling career. The Hiscocks were building a new boat and wished to call her Wanderer III. Eric, fearing confusion with two yachts sailing the oceans and being written about under the same name, contacted Allcard virtually demanding that he change the name of his much travelled forty-year-old vessel. Allcard, being the gentleman he was, readily agreed but, as changing the name of a boat is considered bad luck, offered only a compromise. He said he would change the name from Wanderer to Sea Wanderer.

He stayed in New York only long enough to get her ready for a passage via the Intra-coastal Waterway to Miami and thence to the Bahamas, where *Sea Wanderer* was refitted for an Atlantic crossing. The Atlantic crossing took Allcard seventy-six days which Allcard described as 'a voyage of some austerity'. He sailed her to Chichester Harbour for a thorough re-fit.

The boat *Sea Wanderer*

Sea Wanderer was built in Lubeck in Germany on the shores of the Baltic Sea in 1911 for a Mr Bone, an Englishman who planned a circumnavigation. Mr Bone was interned by the Germans during the First World War but his German paid hand continued to live aboard. His yacht had the unique distinction of being the only vessel in Germany during the war to have the Red Ensign flying all day, having been hoisted regularly each morning. After the war, Mr Bone gave up the idea of sailing around the world and had the yacht shipped to New York, where he lived on board for a number of years, moored in the Hudson River. He died in 1946, aged eighty-three. The boat then sat on her mooring unloved and uncared for until Edward came along four years later in 1950.

Sea Wanderer was originally a Bermudan yawl, 36 feet long and 11 feet wide with a draft of 5 feet and 4 inches. She had no engine. She was a big, heavy and seaworthy vessel. In the Bahamas, Allcard built a strong doghouse over the fore end of her cockpit, in which he could shelter in bad weather. Upon his arrival in England he spent the next three years preparing his boat for his planned trip to southern latitudes. He tore out the interior and rebuilt it to his liking. He installed an eighteen HP Lister diesel engine. A coal burning stove was installed for cooking and heating in cold weather. He beefed up the hatches and skylights and made the cockpit self-draining making the boat, in theory, capable of being temporarily submerged or turned upside down without letting too much water below.

During this interlude from seagoing Allcard was now, much to his dislike, a famous personality. He appeared on the BBC radio programme 'Desert Island Discs' on 26 July 1955. That programme was very different from what it is now, was much more superficial with Roy Plomley, the presenter, seemingly little interested in his guests' characters or motivations. Surprisingly, no mention was made of Allcard's stowaway incident, the one thing which had made Edward famous. Perhaps the idea of Mr Allcard being alone on a boat with a pretty young girl to whom he was not married was too much for the stuffy BBC or the straight laced Mr Plomley. Also the BBC did not broadcast a section where Edward criticised the accuracy of British Admiralty marine charts – Edward said they were his biggest hazard to navigation, being dangerously inaccurate, adding that he went aground less when he stopped using them. Presumably the BBC did not want to upset their Lordships of the Admiralty. Allcard chose an eclectic selection of eight records, professing at the outset he would really like to take only an eight record set of a Linguaphone Spanish Language Course. Mr Plomley graciously said he would treat these eight as one and as his first choice. For his last choice he chose a recording of a conversation between himself and his cousin Barbara, who was married to the author John Masters, discussing, amid much laughter, boat's rigs at a lively party in New York.

Famously, when asked by Mr Plomley what luxury he would like to take with him to the island, Allcard replied, *a five ton block of lead*, which he said would be useful as a keel for the new schooner he would build upon being rescued. Surely the most preposterous, original and unlikely luxury ever chosen on the programme.

The voyage south

Allcard and *Sea Wanderer* left England in the autumn of 1956 on his longest voyage yet. Edward planned to sail to the higher latitudes of south America via Gibraltar and the West Indies and then, hopefully, on around the world. He called in at Vigo in Spain, Lisbon, Gibraltar (where he left *Sea Wanderer* for a short trip back to England) and Tangier. On the last leg to Tangier he had a companion called Ashley, who he had met on the aeroplane flying him back to Gibraltar. On arrival in Tangier, Edward moored *Sea Wanderer* between two large fishing boats (or more likely smuggling or gun running boats) which promptly exploded, blown up by mines killing one man. That very same day two French destroyers hurriedly left the harbour. Somehow *Sea Wanderer* received no damage.

As Allcard was experiencing problems at home in England (probably in connection with his impending divorce) and needed to earn some money he, along with Ashley, started offering day charters and fishing trips to visitors to the port. Soon they had a thriving business but it could not support the two of them. It was agreed that Ashley would go back to England to put Edward's old *Temptress* back into commission and offer her for charter in England. However, this venture all went wrong.

Some time later Edward was told that *Temptress* had caught fire and was very badly damaged. It later transpired that Ashley had deliberately set fire to the boat, intending to destroy her and disappear with the insurance money. (*Temptress* survived and was in due course sold to the well known sailor and author, Mark Fishwick, who still sails her in the waters of the west Country).

After five and a half months, having filled his coffers, Allcard set off on his next leg to the West Indies. After a slow eleven day passage of 700 miles, Allcard reached the Canary Islands and moored *Sea Wanderer* in Las Palmas, on the island of Gran Canaria. There his first visitor was a fair haired lanky Norwegian who, with an infectious grin, introduced himself as Peter Tangvald. Peter was also sailing singlehanded to the Caribbean, bound eventually for San Francisco, on his yacht *Windflower*. She was a yawl some nine feet longer than *Sea Wanderer*. The two became firm friends and Edward would later play a big part in the life of Peter's son, Thomas.

As Peter and Edward wanted to get to the West Indies by Christmas they decided to make a race of it and thus was born the first east to west singlehanded transatlantic race. There were virtually no rules save the first to get to English Harbour in Antigua would win the prize of one US dollar and they were allowed to use their engines. The start was fixed for half past two in the afternoon on Wednesday 20 November 1957. Only thirty-four days remained until Christmas.

The trade winds behaved themselves and both boats achieved good daily runs. Allcard had the slower boat but the advantage of a self steering arrangement using twin staysails. Tangvald had to spend many hours at the helm whilst Allcard slept. Tangvald arrived on 21 December after thirty-one days and Allcard came in two days later. Both had made it by Christmas. A dollar bill was signed and framed and mounted in *Windflower's* cabin.

Soon after their arrival, Tangvald sailed off west to the Panama Canal and California, whilst Allcard remained in English Harbour taking out charter parties on *Sea Wanderer*. Over the next four years Allcard cruised the Windward and Leeward islands with one, two or three people on board. Allcard slept in a small bunk in the fo'c'sle. *Sea Wanderer,* with Allcard's gentlemanly manner and ready wit, would have been a happy ship during this time, with many contented charterers. Edward generally liked his guests, most of whom he said were American doctors.

In July 1961, at the end of that year's season, Allcard finished with chartering and concentrated on getting the boat ready for the high latitudes to come and the long voyage to south America. He designed, built and installed a new wind vane self steering gear and sewed by hand a new working jib. Finally on 29 November 1961 Allcard left English Harbour with official clearance for passage to Valparaiso.

The trip from the Caribbean to the River Plate is difficult at the best of times. Cape San Roque, the easternmost point of south America, is 2,000 miles east of the direct route, and the ubiquitous south-east trade winds, combined with a north going equatorial current, make it hard for any sailing vessel to weather the Cape from the north. The old pilot books used to recommend that in order to achieve this sailing ships should pass at least 500 miles to the east of the Cape. If they then failed to make it, they had to sail a huge circle back into the north Atlantic and try again. Edward decided to sail north and east from the Caribbean until he picked up the north-east trade winds on the east side of the Atlantic and then follow the recommended sailing route to Cape Horn.

He made the passage non-stop arriving at La Paloma, 110 miles east of Montevideo, on 9 March 1962. It had taken Edward one-hundred days but he had chosen his route well. Inevitably he experienced some periods of bad weather together with a vicious *pampero* when approaching land. There were periods when Edward felt his mental and physical powers weaken and his legs became weak through lack of use.

Edward came close to losing *Sea Wanderer* on his first night at anchor in La Paloma. The harbour was open to the south-west and he was warned that he should move to a nearby more sheltered anchorage but he stayed put. That night a fierce south-westerly gale did blow up (he had been warned) and the boat dragged until almost in the breakers close to some rocks to leeward. Edward managed to lay out a second anchor.

But then the main anchor chain, attached to a thirty-five pound CQR anchor, broke and he could feel the boat grounding. He laid out a further sixty-six pound 'hurricane' anchor but in doing so the handle on his windlass broke free and whipped round giving his left hand a mighty blow just clear of the wrist. The wrist and his left arm became useless. Luckily a boat appeared from the shore and with help he was able to get the anchors up and move ship across the harbour into some shelter. It was not until five days later that the wind died sufficiently for Allcard to be able to motor (he could not hoist sail with his damaged wrist) to the sheltered anchorage close by and at last he was safe. Once ashore a doctor told him he would have to rest his wrist for three months. After two weeks he could row his dinghy and after another two months he was able to hoist sail. He left on 9 May and, using his motor for much of the time, reached Montevideo, arriving the next day.

Allcard spent the next four years in and around Buenos Aires and the River Plate, sailing frequently between Argentina and Uruguay. One time he ventured into Argentina's interior and moored up at an American rancher's private jetty. He was introduced to two elderly unmarried sisters who owned the adjoining estancia. On leaving after a happy week, the American rancher suggested to Edward that if he stayed he could become a million-aire. Edward was told that the two sisters were the last of their family and when they died the huge and very valuable estancia would be seized by the State unless one of them had married. *'Edward, this could be yours, this is your chance - think seriously about it'* he was told. Edward did just that and after two days cast off and fled downstream, 'to freedom' as he put it.

During his time in Buenos Aires Edward met the renowned Vito Dumas, the first man to sail south of Cape Horn and survive (see chapter 7). Allcard, who thought Dumas looked unusually frail for a man of only sixty-four, was delighted to meet him. Dumas came back the next day but on the following day, 28 March 1965, a friend told Edward that Dumas had died during the night. Edward also met Bill Nance in *Cardinal Vertue,* who called in at Buenos Aires after his dash across the Southern Ocean and around Cape Horn. Nance was overjoyed to meet Edward as he had been Nance's inspiration to take up ocean sailing all those years ago in South Africa.

In December 1965 Allcard eventually left Buenos Aires for his voyage south to Cape Horn and beyond. This was not to be a-dash-around-the-Horn-and-onwards voyage. Edward's dream was to explore this uttermost part of the earth, to experience its southern winter and to immerse himself in its simple life style. It was rare in the 1960s for yachts to venture there, let alone linger and, as we shall see, he nearly didn't make it.

On the way south he stopped in Mar del Plato and Puerto Madryn before arriving in the paradise harbour of Caleta Horno. With a very narrow twisting entrance the harbour itself offers perfect safety sheltered from all winds and sea and with no sign of human habitation. Allcard's perfect sort of place. He stayed for ten days getting the boat ready for what lay ahead. Going south from there he spent a short time in Puerto Deseado and then sailed the long haul to Rio Grande de Tierra del Fuego, which Allcard described as *'the best port on this part of the coast - it has to be as it is the only one'.* He had a very uncomfortable time there, with the continual fight of wind against tide and a very strong current at that. He left after a week and on 22 March headed for Bahia Thetis at the entrance to the Le Maire Strait, which separates Staten Island from Tierra del Fuego. Sheltered from all but winds from the north and east, the bay is an ideal place to wait before tackling the Strait. The next day he moved on to the Bahia Buen Succeso (Bay of Good Success) only thirty-two miles away and half way through the Strait.

The next morning, almost exactly 350 years after the Dutch Captain Willem Schouten and his partner Jacob Le Maire had discovered Cape Horn, Allcard set sail. This is how Allcard described what happened next:

After sailing at a good clip for more than two and a half hours and with the coast to windward falling away to nothing, I suddenly saw a mass of white breakers approaching from the north-west. Wind! - and increasing faster than I could claw down the sails. I grabbed down the mizzen and hardly had it lashed when the wind struck like a ton of bricks, pinning the side deck under, as I scrabbled to lower the staysail and then furl the jib. Still not enough! With the ketch on her beam ends and bursts of spray like grapeshot raking over her full length, I struggled to lower the flogging mainsail.

Hour after hour of unrelenting wild water continued to bombard us. A Cape Horner! and the murderous coast of Staten Island was only thirty miles to the north-east.... The wind had already begun to veer more westerly and as it went south-west, as it was bound to do, we would be drifting towards a lee shore. To continue lying ahull was now bad seamanship. I decided to hammer back and return to the Bahia Buen Succeso.'

Allcard was unable to make it even with his faithful Lister engine going full blast. The wind was just too strong and the engine not powerful enough. He could now just see the coast (and a ship's anchor light) ahead. All he could do was to try to maintain his position during that long cold ferocious night. He was at the helm for twelve frigid hours. When dawn came no land was in sight!

Allcard takes up the story: *'Then a white peak appeared...over the southern horizon. I stared stupidly at it, and automatically at the compass. south? How could land be to the south? Could it be Staten Island? Surely not! I blinked my salt-encrusted eyes. It was unbelievable. We must have been swept, stern first, downwind some fifty miles during the night.... I wrote in the log 'very bad news'. Shaking my head, I groped my way below to escape the searching wind and to stop the engine. Wedging myself in the galley I lit the primus stove and was soon enjoying a fortifying cup of hot coffee. Whenever the engine runs it automatically pumps the bilge, so I was a bit surprised to hear water sloshing about inside.*

With the coming of daylight the wind had abated sightly and I set the mizzen. On going below I received a second shock. The boat was awash! Water was cascading over the cabin sole. A leak! and a bad one at that! We were in real trouble now. Highly alarmed, I promptly started the engine with its powerful pump.'

Allcard searched for the source of the trouble and found a steady stream of water running down from the rudder trunk. This was not something he could cure at sea. He pumped the boat out but two hours later water was again over the floorboards. He pumped regularly every two hours.

The wind never relented for three more days whilst *Sea Wanderer* lay hove to drifting away to the north-east with Allcard pumping. When the gale relented he found himself away to the east of Staten Island and that fifth night he just managed to make shelter in Port Cook on the island. The next day he was back in the 'Bay of Good Success', from where he had started - sixteen miles out and over one-hundred to get back - some progress.

Allcard then headed for the haven of Harberton, well into the Beagle Channel and the home of the Bridges family, made famous by Lucas Bridges in his book *The Uttermost Part of the Earth*. He was welcomed there and able to dry out *Sea Wanderer* against a stone quay wall. He managed to reduce but not stop the leak. He was lucky to have made it and could so easily have been lost, without any trace, somewhere out to the north of Staten Island. Nobody ashore had any idea at all as to where he was.

On 10 April, with the southern winter approaching, Allcard, still pumping hard, headed east back down the Beagle Channel trying for the Horn for the second time. He made it to an anchorage on Isla Lennox planning to cross the open waters to the Horn the next day. This dawned bright and sunny with a light west-north-west wind. Ideal. He sailed across Bahia Nassau and anchored in a small bay on Isla Herschel. Cape Horn was now only eight miles away. The next day, with the barometer beginning to fall, Allcard sailed through a narrow pass between Isla Herschel and Isla Deceit and headed for the Horn. To the south, far beyond the horizon, was Antarctica and to the west lay Horn Island. This is what Edward wrote about his passage past the Horn:

All went well as I cleared the pass and Sea Wanderer started to lift to an enormous swell setting in from the west; another sign of imminent bad weather. We ploughed on always pumping. I'd have to be quick.

Since I was a small boy, my imagination had been fired by tales of rounding the Horn. Compared to today's yachts, the great windjammers of yore faced a far bigger challenge. They couldn't take shelter in the little anchorages behind Horn Island and wait for a good moment. They had to face whatever the sea gods threw at them. Luckily for today's yachtsmen, the situation is different.

That morning however the god's at last were with me. Suddenly there it lay, my quarry. Cape Horn. I couldn't take my eyes off it, bathed in sunlight and getting closer and closer. Too close in fact, for a rock spouted ahead forcing me further out. With a moderate wind, coming unusually from the north-west, I doubled the Cape under full sail! What a fantastic stroke of luck! I quickly grabbed my camera. Then, as giant swells thundered and clawed, albatrosses wheeled and watched, I pulled the logbook toward me and wrote a treasured entry: '12th April 1966. 09:45 Cape Horn bearing N. 1 ½ miles.' Sea Wanderer's forefoot then trod the Pacific'.

Allcard headed north looking for an anchorage sheltered enough to ride out the threatening gale. He found this in a bay on the north-eastern corner of Isla Bayly, which bay went under the improbable name of Seagull Anchorage. This gave good protection with winds from north-west to south.

The next day, the 14th, the storm hit, accompanied by snow blizzards and a white out. Allcard snuggled down in his cabin with the wood burning stove keeping him warm. He spent five days in Isla Bayly safely anchored from the storm. He had been mighty lucky to get round the Horn before it struck.

Two days later, in light winds, he motored back through the Beagle Channel to Harberton. He then undertook an expedition to nearby Isla Gable to investigate a renowned Yaghan Indian site, dotted with the famous *conchales* or circular mounds of shells. The Yaghans, now extinct, built the circular wooden frames for their wigwams within these banks of shells. In summer this framework was covered in bark, kelp or grass and in winter with animal skins, sewn together. The Yaghans subsisted mainly on giant mussels. Allcard then moved on westward down the Beagle Channel to Puerto Williams, a Chilean naval base. There he hoped to use the slipway to haul out *Sea Wanderer* and fix the leak in the rudder trunk.

After a somewhat chilly reception, Edward was welcomed with the happy news that the slipway and its cradles had rotted away through the action of Teredo shipworms and had collapsed, that nothing could be slipped and anyway the navy had an 18-metre patrol boat in need of urgent repair, which would have to be done first.

'Well,' Edward said to the Commandante of the base, 'I'm a naval architect and I've owned sixteen wooden boats. Maybe I can help?' After a long discussion it was agreed that Edward would design a new cradle and slipway suitable for his boat and the patrol boat, that the Navy would build them and in return they would haul out *Sea Wanderer* and do any repairs free of charge.

Five weeks later work on the new slipway was complete, *Sea Wanderer* was slipped and the rudder repaired. A new bronze flange was brazed to the rudder tube and new graving pieces fitted when the tube was reinserted. Edward gave the bottom a fresh coat of antifouling paint and the old girl was relaunched during darkness with a blizzard blowing in a temperature of minus eleven degrees Centigrade.

It was now July, just past mid winter, and Edward's plan from then on was to sail westward along the Beagle Channel to enter the Magellan Strait and then head for Punta Arenas. From there he would pass through the western end of the Strait and then up the Patagonian Channels to Valparaiso.

However, he was advised that the ice was very bad that winter. The Patagonian Channels are much more ice bound than the waters of Tierra del Fuego, which rarely freeze. In Patagonia the sea ice can be two feet thick and floating bits of this or chunks broken away from glaciers could easily sink *Sea Wanderer*. Edward decided to wait for warmer weather. He remained in the area for the rest of the winter making frequent trips to Ushuaia in Argentina, on the north side of the Beagle Channel, for supplies and mail. There were no shops in Puerto Williams.

It was not until the end of September that the cold let up and after one final visit to Harberton, Edward set out on 1 October 1966 on the next leg of his extraordinary voyage. He made his way slowly to Punta Arenas in the Magellan Strait, which he found exceedingly inhospitable, with no real shelter, and where the wind blew a gale on nearly every day. This was where both Slocum and Bernicot had stopped. Edward was hoping to meet up with the famous mountaineer and explorer Bill Tilman in *Mischief*, who was following in his wake. Not being able to endure the sufferings in the Harbour any more he left a note for Tilman and departed.

By mid November Allcard was nearing the end of the Magellan Strait and called into the renowned harbour of Playa Parda (which Bernicot before him had entered) and Edward remarked that it was even more beautiful than he had expected. On 20 November he cleared the Strait and entered the Patagonian channels or canals. These he found magical, with good weather most of the time, plenty of sheltered anchorages together with an abundance of giant mussels, on which he mainly subsisted, and a surfeit of wild geese for shooting for the pot. Edward heads one chapter in his book '*Of geese, rain and perfect anchorages*'.

On 12 December he arrived in Puerto Eden, an isolated hamlet accessible only by sea with its nearest neighbour over 200 miles away. It was just the sort of place Edward liked, apart from the rain! (Its chief claim to fame is that it has the highest minimum rainfall of anywhere on the planet). He left on 20 December, mid summer, and continued onwards, stopping each night, foraging for mussels and meeting the local Indians. He was still less than halfway between the Beagle Channel and Valparaiso. He spent Christmas day in a sheltered anchorage eating a Christmas goose, which he had shot a day or two before.

Once past the island of Chiloe, he was faced with an open sea voyage. Chiloe is the second largest island in Chile and lies near where Alfon Hansen was lost in his yacht *Mary Jane*. Having stopped awhile on Chiloe,

Edward made a seven day passage to arrive in Valparaiso on 30 January 1967, to be welcomed by some cousins who lived in Santiago.

The latitude of Valparaiso is almost identical to that of the River Plate which he had left twelve months and twenty-six days earlier. He had now doubled the world's most notorious cape, having sailed 4,000 miles. This leg of his long voyage was now over and Allcard had carried it out in exemplary fashion.

After a lengthy stay in Valparaiso, Edward, still alone, crossed the Pacific to New Zealand, where he learnt that his father had been killed in a car accident and that his mother was dying. Mooring *Sea Wanderer* in Auckland Harbour, he flew back to Britain.

Later life

Enter Clare Thompson, then aged twenty-two. She was said to be suffering from depression and was incarcerated in an 800 bed nineteenth-century psychiatric hospital (dismal enough to make anyone depressed). One morning she picked up a discarded copy of The *Sunday Express,* which was lying on the floor of her ward. In it she saw an article about Edward (he was by then very well known) in which he said, on being asked if he ever got lonely, '*no, but it would be nice to find a woman with the same interests to come along too'*. A glimmer of hope stirred in Clare and she wrote to this man of fifty-four. She was frank, saying she couldn't sail or cook, was nothing much to look at but she could swim and speak French. And she would love to sail with him into the blue yonder. But there was one hitch – she was locked up in a mental asylum. Could he possibly wait until she was released?

Being a kind man Edward replied. They met for a picnic and one thing led to another. Then Edward, having found the long flight from New Zealand exceedingly tedious, bought a Land Rover in which to drive back to Singapore. Clare offered to go as co-driver. They left England on 27 July 1968. This was the first of their unlikely adventures together.

Edward then sailed *Sea Wanderer* alone to the Seychelles, where he and Clare bought a house, their love nest, which Clare soon called the 'Ants Nest' on account of the termite mounds inside the hut. It was no more than a native shack. There Edward bought a 54-foot local trading schooner, the *Black Parrot,* and a stash of timber to build a 70-foot replica of Columbus's *Nina* (surely Edward's craziest scheme of all). Edward had Colin Mudie produce some lines plans, he cleared a site and cut a stock of timber. But Edward decided to complete his circumnavigation before entangling himself with this project. Slipping quietly away he sailed *Sea*

Wanderer alone, past the Cape of Good Hope to Antigua in the West Indies, arriving 12 years after he had departed. Clare and their four-year-old daughter joined him there.

Then one day in 1974 Edward called to Clare *'Quick. Come and see. There's the most fantastic boat on the slipway. It's our dream ship, it really is!'* She was a 69-foot (with an 18-foot bowsprit) ex-Baltic trading ketch called *Johanne Regina,* distressed and near derelict and in urgent need of repair. Of course, they bought her (for a song). They spent two years sailing the Caribbean restoring her as they went (Clare told me they were still restoring her when they sold her thirty-two years later). They sailed her to her birthplace in Denmark where she had been built in 1929. Picking up assorted crew as they went along, they travelled down the west coast of Europe, through the Mediterranean and the Red Sea (where they were attacked, captured and jailed for spying by the communist South Yemen Navy) before finally arriving back at their home in the Seychelles.

A communist coup on the Islands some years later led to their having to leave their beloved home. To save *Johanne Regina* from being impounded and requisitioned (and probably destroyed), they sailed off in her and spent the next five years sailing the waters of Singapore, Malaysia and Thailand. They had many adventures, including outwitting pirates three times and rescuing Tim Severin and the *Sohar,* a replica ninth-century lateen-rigged Arab dhow, when they got into trouble on the much publicised Sinbad voyage.

By 1984 Edward was seventy and exposure to the tropical sun was doing him no good. They decided it was time to return to Europe. Clare found some land in Andorra (- *'no other houses in sight and no barking dogs'* Edward insisted) and they had a house built on it. They set sail via the Red Sea (terrible – Edward had remarked on the way down *'remind me never to go north up here'*), Cyprus (where the engine broke down irreparably) and Turkey (where they stayed a year). Eventually in 1986 they sailed for Spain and moored *Johanne Regina* in a marina in Catalonia, three hours drive from their house. Edward used to spend nine months each year on board and skied in Andorra in the winter. Aged eighty-seven he fell off *Johanne* and broke his leg. His doctor tried to stop him skiing but he carried on regardless until he was ninety-two. During this time Edward and Clare took in Peter Tangvald's orphaned son, Thomas, following the shipwreck that killed Peter and Thomas's seven-and-a-half-year-old half-sister on a Caribbean reef. Thomas had already lost his mother, shot by pirates in front of him, and his step-mother, who fell overboard and was drowned in mid Atlantic.

In 2005, with many regrets, they put *Johanne* up for sale. Miraculously, the city of Badalona agreed to buy her to convert into a sail training ship. The Allcards had long dreamed of her being used to bring adventure to young people. Now the old girl has never been so well cared for and she has a volunteer crew of eighty to scrape, sand and paint her. She is now called *Cuitat Badalona*, simply known as *El Quetx* ('The Ketch') and there is even a local choir called *Canta Quetx* to sing sea shanties. What more could she ask for?

Edward remained in amazing health until the middle of 2017 but with sadly diminished memory. Despite lots of new building in their valley, if he looked from his chair in the right direction, he could still see nothing but those waves standing still. He died in July 2017.

Chapter 11
Francis Chichester – The largest boat

The days of the lonely romantic voyager, sailing the seas simply for his or her own satisfaction, alone, self sufficient, asking nothing of anyone else, quietly departing and quietly arriving, were nearly over. Allcard and the others before him asked nothing more than to be left alone to plough their lonely furrows across the world's oceans, disturbing no-one and leaving no trace once they had moved on.

By 1966, with only a few exceptions, the age of what I might term 'the commercial voyager' had arrived where ocean voyages were primarily made for gain, for publicity and for the record books. To achieve this, money was needed, lots of it and sponsors were avidly sought. Special purpose boats were built, book and film contracts were drawn up, publicity merchants were engaged and newspapers were signed up to report on the participants' derring-does. Navies were asked to look out for and shepherd these intrepid voyagers round dangerous headlands. Boats were laden with liferafts, safety equipment and ship-to-shore radios or satellite phones, to ensure that these brave yachtsmen could call on aircraft, lifeboats and other rescue services around the world to rescue them when they got into difficulty.

The days when a lone sailor crossing an ocean would be totally self reliant, never expecting to be rescued and to 'die like a gentleman' were now over. Such a philosophy was well expounded by Blondie Hasler (of Cockleshell Heroes fame) to whom this expression is attributed and who founded the series of *Observer* Single-Handed Transatlantic Races. He said a competitor in such a race should sail it at his own risk and nobody else's, adding *'I would be happy to accept the fact that I should drown if I couldn't solve my own problems. I dread the idea of ships having to conduct rescue operations.'* This was very much the sentiment Allcard and his like propounded. Not however this new breed of voyagers.

Whilst the advent of money and commercialisation had begun to creep into some sailing in the early 1960s, it was Francis Chichester, the next Cape Horn astronaut to go, who first commercialised long distance solo sailing. His boat was paid for by a third party and was emblazoned with a sponsors logo (the Woolmark sign). He signed a book deal, engaged a publicist and sent regular radio reports to a weekly newspaper. He was escorted round Cape Horn by a Royal Navy vessel whilst being photographed from above by an aeroplane chartered by the *Sunday Times*. On arrival back in Plymouth he was greeted by a huge flotilla of little ships and by a vast crowd on Plymouth Hoe. He was knighted by the Queen.

Sir Francis Chichester's round the world voyage, taking in Cape Horn as he went, in the much maligned yacht *Gipsy Moth IV* is probably the best known, most read and written about and best documented of any voyage under sail since sailors took to the sea. It therefore serves little purpose merely to repeat the facts of the voyage, which will be known to most readers of this book. What is instructive, however, is to visit again not only the boat itself and what, if anything, was wrong with it (in view of all the criticism it got, most from Sir Francis himself) but to look anew at the sailor's character and personality, which led to the voyage becoming what one Scottish newspaper described as 'splendid but without charm.'

First, the facts – Chichester left Plymouth on 27 August 1966 and arrived in Sydney in Australia 107 days later on 12 December. He left Sydney, after carrying out alterations to the boat, on 21 January 1967, passed Cape Horn on 21 March and arrived home on 28 May 1967.

He was not, as he often claimed, the first person to achieve a circumnavigation of the world solo from west to east via the three great Capes. As we saw earlier in this book, Vito Dumas, the Argentinian, had done it first in 1942 in the middle of World War II and the young Bill Nance had done it in 1964, in the diminutive 25-foot *Cardinal Vertue*, two years before Chichester.

The boat

Gipsy Moth IV had confused beginnings. After Chichester had come in second behind Eric Tabarly in the 1964 *Observer* Single-Handed Transatlantic Race (always known as the OSTAR), his cousin, the wealthy Lord Dulverton, agreed to pay for Chichester to have a new boat built to beat the French in the next one, due to be held in 1968. Chichester had other ideas and told his cousin of his round-the-world-and-Cape Horn ambitions. Dulverton agreed to provide Chichester with whatever boat he wanted – announcing that the boat must be built in the best possible way by the best builders regardless of cost. Tony Dulverton assured Chichester that he was to have no worries whatsoever about finance.

Chichester appointed the firm of Illingworth and Primrose to design his new wonder boat. Illingworth was a retired naval officer with no real technical knowledge of yacht design but who was regarded as the father of ocean racing. His protégé, Angus Primrose, was a highly qualified naval architect at the very forefront of innovative yacht design. Chichester had already used Illingworth to design a new rig for his old *Gipsy Moth III*.

Some of what I say next comes from discussions I had with Angus Primrose in the late 1970s before his untimely death at sea in 1980. The story differs markedly from what Chichester wrote in his book about the voyage.

From the start it all got off on the wrong foot. Illingworth, without telling Chichester, decided to reserve him a space with the well regarded firm of Cowes boat builders, called Souters, who produced revolutionary and lightweight boats built to their own cold-moulded process. Illingworth told Chichester that he could almost half the cost of the boat, if he agreed to share a mould with an identical hull. This had already been designed by Angus Primrose for Welsh sailor Valentine Howells (Chichester's rival in the 1964 OSTAR), the boat to be paid for by a wealthy Pembrokeshire landowning squire, Lieutenant-Colonel Patrick Lort Phillips. When told this, Chichester was irate and was having nothing to do with a shared boat, despite the large cost saving. This project was abandoned (with the dire results we shall see later) and Val Howells failed to get his boat, as the Lieutenant-Colonel could not come up with the money without a shared mould.

Dulverton then demanded that Chichester's boat should be built, regardless of expense, at Camper & Nicholsons, a very well regarded traditional boatyard in Gosport on the banks of Portsmouth Harbour. Chichester and his wife Sheila agreed with this. Campers, as they are always known, had built Dulverton's grandfather a yacht in the past.

Now the problems started. Illingworth pleaded with Chichester to give him and Angus Primrose a free hand in the design but Chichester gave them some very particular, and conflicting, parameters. First, he said, the boat must not displace more than eight tons, second no sail should be bigger than any sail on his previous boat *Gipsy Moth III* and, third, the boat must be fast enough to sail to Australia in under one-hundred days.

Angus Primrose reasoned that to do the trip in such a time, the boat had to have a waterline length of at least 38 feet, with long overhangs to give added speed when under way. But the displacement limit, together with the need to provide large fuel and water tanks and lots of heavy radio equipment and batteries, meant the boat would have to have less ballast than Angus believed desirable. Other problems were that Camper & Nicholsons did not have Souters skills in building light-weight hulls and further the boat had to have, at the insistence of Lady Chichester, a fully fitted out interior identical to that on *Gipsy Moth III*. This all meant that the hull was much heavier than necessary. These factors all affected the boat's ballast ratio, which was lower than the designers would have liked. Nowadays this can be compensated for by an increase in a boat's beam but beam was not considered desirable in 1965 - an increase in beam was then believed to lead to a slower boat.

During the design process Chichester reluctantly allowed the designers to increase the displacement to nine tons but there was still not enough ballast. After sailing trials he agreed to the addition of another ton of ballast. Chichester says the boat ended up with a total displacement of eleven and a half tons but Angus believed it was less and said the problem was that most of the added weight was high up in the hull (radios and batteries) and not ballast. Chichester then makes in his book a very confusing remark when he says the boat with all this extra weight ended up with a Thames Measurement of no less than eighteen tons. This is nonsense. Weight does not affect Thames Measurement which started and ended the same.

Sir Francis grumbled and complained that the boat was bigger than he had wanted, was too tender and heeled alarmingly, even in a light breeze. These attributes were a direct and unavoidable result of the restrictions he had given the designers. Chichester should have known better and not blamed the designers.

Soon Sir Francis had another concern. Despite his cousin's assurances that Chichester was not to worry about money and that all costs would be covered, Dulverton telephoned Chichester a few weeks before the boat was launched to say the cost had far exceeded all estimates and please would Chichester find the difference. Chichester claimed that this last minute request, meaning he had to search for funds and money from sponsors, distracted him badly from his preparations.

At the launch of the boat, Sir Francis and Dulverton, had a bad tempered argument with the designers and the builders about the cost of the boat. Later Primrose felt very sorry for the yard workmen at Campers who had put everything they could into the building but got nothing but kicks from a cantankerous Sir Francis during his wireless reports and in his book about the voyage. He pinpointed every minor difficulty as we shall see later.

One thing which is forgotten today is that *Gipsy Moth IV* was a new sort of boat. In 1965 people were not used to light displacement yachts. At that time, boats considered seaworthy enough to cross oceans were in the main small heavy displacement, lumbering things with short overhangs and small low aspect rigs. *Gipsy Moth IV* was a new type of experience for most people, but she was exactly what Chichester needed to achieve his objective, even if he did not appreciate that himself. He continually complained at the angle of heel at which she sailed. Others who sailed on her, including the very experienced Blondie Hasler, did not think her heeling was in any way excessive.

Several commentators shared Chichester's criticisms of the boat calling her jinxed, cranky and one of the worst racing yachts ever to have been built. It was reported that, at her launch, Lady Chichester on seeing the hull react to the wash of a passing ship said 'My God, she's a rocker!' Others commented that it would be suicide to take a boat like that out of the harbour.

These are all quite unfair descriptions of a yacht which achieved everything it was designed for. A few years ago, one of Angus's former colleagues, himself now a distinguished naval architect, Angelo Lavranos, who worked with Angus on the design of the boat, said it was now time to give the designers credit for Sir Francis's achievements. Angus had to give Chichester the biggest, lightest, fastest boat he could and he did this remarkably well. She had to be light enough to keep moving in light airs and strong enough to cope with the Southern Ocean.

It was all very well for Chichester to moan continually throughout his voyage that his boat was too big but as he himself wrote, he had to have one fast enough to achieve his self imposed target of one-hundred days for reaching Australia. To succeed he needed to average 141-miles a day, or nearly six knots. His book clearly shows that Chichester was aware that a boat's speed is a function of its waterline length (somewhere around one and a half times the square root of the waterline length). He wrote that *Gipsy Moth IV's* theoretical maximum speed with a waterline length of 38 and ½ feet was eight knots. Any boat smaller, and therefore slower, would never have been able to keep up an average of six knots for one-hundred days. Chichester needed all that waterline length plus those long overhangs.

Primrose never saw eye to eye with the grand old man and their biggest falling out was when Sir Francis reached Australia and sent Angus a bad tempered telegram stating how he now had 'proper designers design a new keel profile.' Angus's reply was simple: 'Just get on with it. If you've only reached Australia, she's not even run in yet.' According to Angus's son, Dan, what really made his father's blood boil was seeing *Gipsy Moth IV* encased in concrete next to the *Cutty Sark* in Greenwich.

What else was wrong with the boat? Lots according to Sir Francis, who detailed them all, with much relish, in his book. These included:

Leaks – the deck leaked, the coachroof leaked, the hatches leaked.

The cabin lockers were continually wet, the doors would not stay shut and the backs of them could not be reached. They were too deep. When the doors got wet they jammed.

She sailed at an alarming angle of heel.

The lower mainmast aft shrouds fouled the mainsail and had to be put on levers to be let go on the lee side.

The toilet could not be used at sea.

The self steering gear kept breaking and eventually packed up completely.

Lady Chichester could not get out of her bunk when the boat was heeled.

He could not use the basin in the heads (toilet compartment) when heeled.

On 27 August 1966 a very unhappy Chichester, suffering from back pain caused by a recent fall on the deck of his boat, set out on the first leg of his voyage.

The man

Francis Chichester had been born in 1901 into an aristocratic north Devon family of squires and landowners. This family, and the manner of his child-hood, had a large influence on his character and later life. Anita Leslie in her biography of Francis Chichester describes the Chichesters as proud, brave and rigidly faithful to their own code, seeming more laudable than human. Francis's father was the Reverend Charles Chichester and his grandfather was Sir Arthur Chichester, the Ninth Baronet. One of my aunts married the Eleventh Baronet, Sir John Chichester, a second cousin of Francis, and from what I learnt about the Chichester family, I share Anita Leslie's views. Francis's father was an extremely dour and severe figure who made Francis's childhood a misery and the atmosphere at home was akin to a refrigerator. His mother, Emily, came from a cultivated artistic middle-class musical family of modest means. She was brought up in London and how she coped with the loneliness of a rambling old Devon rectory and with the hearty, arrogant, self opinionated and conceited Chichesters is hard to imagine.

Francis was his father's least favourite child (Francis had an elder brother, the favourite, and two younger sisters) and did not behave as a Chichester should, i.e. stolid and submissive. Instead he was highly strung and prone to tantrums. As was normal amongst such upper-class families, Francis was soon sent away to a private boarding school at the tender age of seven. There, a sadistic headmaster disliked Francis from the outset, noticed his independent spirit and tried to beat it out of him. Francis was beaten (having first been made to strip naked) seven times in his first term alone.

142

After a couple of years he was moved to another school near Bournemouth. There he hardened into a tough and somewhat priggish child. He became head boy, threatening and bullying younger boys with 'you've got to win or else!'

In 1914, aged thirteen, Francis was sent to one of England's most famous public schools, Marlborough College. At that time it was a pretty hateful place, mean and niggardly with a prison-like iron discipline. The food was terrible and the whole place freezing cold in the winter. Discipline was solely in the hands of the senior boys who ritually thrashed any boy who infringed the complicated social code of the school.

Francis became a lonely boy who headed off into the countryside whenever he could. He suffered from terrible eyesight but refused to allow it to let him down. The place hardened him, instilled in him a desire to succeed and to cope with discomfort, cold and damp. He hated the school and at age seventeen announced to his parents that he was not going back. His father was furious as he had planned for him to go to University and then join the Indian Civil Service. Francis stood his ground and, eventually, his father relented and agreed that he should be allowed to travel to New Zealand as a farm apprentice.

This was the making of Francis and in New Zealand and later Australia, Francis flourished and became determined to make his fortune. He vowed not to return to England until he had made £20,000 (equivalent to over £800,000 today). He dug for coal, prospected for gold, sold books door to door, grew trees, acted as a land and property agent, started an aviation company, married, had a son and then divorced his wife. He returned home to England having made his £20,000 (although most of it was tied up in trees and property and substantial loans were outstanding).

Life back at home was a disaster where his success was pretty much ignored. He was not certain what he wanted to do next. He took up flying and bought a Gipsy Moth aeroplane. In 1929 he became the second man to fly solo from England to Australia. He then shipped the plane to New Zealand and became the first man to fly solo across the Tasman Sea. To do this he converted the plane into a seaplane so he could land in the sea at Norfolk Island to refuel. In order to find this tiny island he adapted the seaman's trick of 'aiming off', i.e. to deliberately aim for a point to one side of your actual destination so that when the correct distance had been covered the navigator knew which way to turn to find it. Chichester then set off to complete a circumnavigation of the globe. He flew north to Japan where he flew into some overhead cables, crashed and barely survived. He returned to New Zealand to recover, where he found his finances in disarray as a result of the 1930s slump. He salvaged what he could and decided to fly back to England, this time with a partner who had bought a two seater Puss Moth. They flew via Peking and Siberia.

He arrived back in England in 1936 where he met a tall languid brunette called Sheila Craven, who had just returned from a solo journey through India and Abyssinia. Francis was attracted to her and liked her independent spirit. He asked her to marry him with the bold but scarcely enticing words 'I've got £100 in the bank, an overdraft of £14,000 and some trees. Will you marry me?' She accepted and they went back to New Zealand but came home to England when war was imminent. Chichester was taken on by the RAF as a navigation instructor, a position he held throughout the war.

When the war was over, Chichester bought a house in St James's Place in London and set up a small business making jigsaw puzzles using obsolete wartime Air Ministry maps. Later he started designing new maps for his jigsaws until he found he could sell them as actual maps. The business thrived sufficiently for Chichester to afford to buy a yacht (he had already started sailing by crewing as navigator on several ocean racers). He bought an eight ton yacht called *Florence Edith*. He immediately changed her name to *Gipsy Moth II*. With Sheila amongst the crew, Chichester raced and sailed her for four years, learning as he went along.

Then he was diagnosed with advanced lung cancer. The doctors wanted to operate to remove one of his lungs. Sheila, a believer in natural cures and the power of prayer, refused to allow this. She prayed and harangued the doctors and oncologists who eventually agreed not to operate. Chichester remained in hospital for several months, very weak and unable to speak. Gradually he began to recover whilst Sheila asked everyone to pray for him. Sheila then removed Chichester to a nature cure clinic, where he stayed until she took him to the south of France. There they met an unorthodox doctor who treated Francis with vitamin injections and persuaded Francis to have confidence in his body. He recovered rapidly and in April 1959 the doctor pronounced *'Monsieur, ce n'est rien.'* Four months later, Chichester was navigating a yacht (*Pym*) in the Fastnet Race.

Chichester then commissioned Robert Clark, who had designed *Pym*, to design him a new ocean racing yacht. She was to be 40 feet long and was built in Arklow in Ireland. She was called *Gipsy Moth III*. One day back in London, Chichester walked into the Royal Ocean Racing Club, whose clubhouse was just up the road from his own house, and saw pinned on the notice board Blondie Hasler's proposal for a solo Atlantic race. He made up his mind there and then to enter and contacted Halser, who was having trouble finding anyone interested in organising the race. The pair decided to race each other across the 'pond' for half-a-crown come what may. In the event and after much effort from the pair of them, the Royal Western Yacht Club of Plymouth agreed to start the race and the *Observer* Sunday newspaper agreed to sponsor it.

The story of that race and the amazing success of the subsequent OSTAR races, as they came to be called, is well known. Francis won the first race in a time of just over forty days, sailed the same course on his own in 1962 in a time of thirty-four days and then came in second in the second OSTAR, in a time of just under thirty days. After the first OSTAR, Chichester's fraught relationship with John Illingworth began. Illingworth was commissioned to design a new rig for *Gipsy Moth III*. Chichester had no cause for complaint about the improvement Illingworth made to the boat's performance. It was after the second OSTAR that Lord Dulverton, a wealthy cousin of Chichester, announced that he would pay for Francis to have his new boat capable of beating the French and, as we saw, Chichester engaged Illingworth to design it.

Dulverton, whose mother was one of Francis Chichester's aunts, was the scion of the immensely rich Wills tobacco family from Bristol and saw himself as a bit of a sportsman himself. '*If British industry, unlike the Frenchies, won't do anything for Francis, then I jolly well will*' he thundered to all and sundry.

Thus it came about that Chichester was able to build a spanking new yacht, *Gipsy Moth IV*, in which to undertake his planned solo-with-one-stop circumnavigation.

As we saw earlier, Chichester set off on this voyage in an unhappy frame of mind but nothing would have stopped him going. He was always a driven man, impatient of others and impatient for success. He had overcome many problems in his life, financial, medical and personal. He had nearly been killed by an aeroplane crash, had nearly died of lung cancer and yet had recovered sufficiently to sail the Atlantic alone three times. He always relished a challenge and believed that a man's body was made to endure wet, cold and sweat but was not designed to withstand city centre petrol fumes, financial worries and lack of exercise.

Despite being only sixty-four when he left on his voyage to Sydney, he was not in good health and looked old for his age. He was having mobility problems, some as a result of a heavy fall during sailing trials which left him with chronic pain and cramping in his right leg. But nothing would prevent this man from proceeding in spite of whatever doubts he had about his boat, his body or his state of mind.

Despite all his problems and frustrations, Chichester made it to Sydney in 107 days. His account of the voyage in the book he wrote afterwards is exceedingly detailed and is not an easy read. It is full of repetitive detail about his routine, life on board, tales of grief and mishap and tales of the boat failing him and of gear breaking. He often recounts feelings of despair, weakness, anxiety, spiritual loneliness and self doubt, all curious attributes for such a seasoned and well travelled adventurer to admit to. Admittedly he set out with severe pain in one of his legs, suffering from lack of proper preparation brought about by last minute money troubles and lack of sailing time (Chichester complained that the boat spent too much time on the slipway when the additional ballast was being added).

One factor which has often been missed in accounts of his voyage, and which may account for much of his oft expressed melancholia, was just how much alcohol the grand old man drank. He took with him copious amounts of wine, brandy, gin, whisky, Bacardi, Drambuie, Benedictine, Grand Marnier and champagne together with a keg of beer. All are itemised in the 'Stores and Stowage' section at the end of his book and all these for one man to consume in 100 days. While loading some gin onto Gipsy Moth IV, Chichester is reputed to have said; 'Any damn fool can navigate the world sober. It takes a really good sailor to do it drunk.'

Chichester recounts in his book how he was constantly rewarding himself with bottles of champagne or strong cocktails after sail changes, sudden weather changes or whatever other excuse he could find. At one point in his voyage he recounts how he had only four bottles of gin left. 'My favourite drink and I was pretty stupid not to have brought more' he wrote. He lamented that he would have to ration it and not have any hard drinks at lunchtime. The beer keg he had on board fed the brew to a tap fixed onto his gimballed chair installed next to the galley.

17 September, twenty-one days into the voyage, was Chichester's sixty-fifth birthday. He records in his book that he drank a bottle of wine at lunchtime and in the evening was quaffing champagne cocktails. On the basis that, like most men, he underestimated his consumption of alcohol and in the light of the amount of drink he carried, it is likely he was in fact half drunk during much of the voyage. In some ways this makes the voyage even more impressive.

The account of the first half of the voyage is full of frustrations and complaints about the boat and its vices. He complained about the steep angle of heel she sailed at and the fact that as the heel increased the boat's lee helm became so excessive that the self steering gear could not cope. He soon learnt that there was an optimal angle of heel and he reduced sail so as not to exceed that. He complained about the boat slamming when pounding to windward at a steep angle of heel. This was really a function of the speed at which she sailed. All boats slam when sailing fast in those conditions. Then he complained that *Gipsy Moth IV* continually broached when running fast downwind. This could have been caused by Chichester carrying too much sail and being over reliant on his self steering gear. Wind vanes of the type carried by Chichester are at their weakest with the wind dead aft and often cannot react fast enough to prevent a broach.

On entering the Roaring Forties, Chichester records the bad deck leaks he found everywhere and how he broke a tooth in half whilst eating some mint-cake. The next day he cemented it back together using a dentist's repair kit but it did not hold. So he merely got out a file and filed down the jagged edges. Soon after that the stainless steel frame of the self steering gear which held the servo blade broke in two beyond repair. Chichester spent the next few days working out how to set the sails to get the boat to steer herself. He rigged a small storm staysail with the clew attached to the tiller. This worked after a fashion and over the next few days Chichester was able to get sailing again. He reached Sydney on 12 December 1966, after 107 days at sea.

In Sydney

On arrival *Gipsy Moth IV* was hauled out on the Royal Sydney Yacht Squadron's slipway and Chichester enlisted the help of two of Australian's best known yacht designers, Warwick Hood and Alan Payne. The first thing they did was to try to dissuade Chichester from continuing his voyage as they considered the yacht to be unsuitable for the job. When Chichester said he was continuing regardless they set to and tried to improve the boat's handling as best they could, not that in some people's view it needed much improving. They decided to construct a steel extension to fill in the gap between the lowest part of the keel and the rudder and they altered the rig. They also rearranged the storage of all gear and stores below, concentrating the weight in the centre of the hull. They also worked hard to stop the deck leaks - they were quite successful in this. The self steering gear was repaired.

It was at this time that Chichester sent his bad tempered telegram to Angus Primrose. Another unfortunate incident was the result of two photographs taken upon his arrival. One, taken of Chichester's son Giles giving his father a hug on arrival, made it look like an ancient man weeping on his son's shoulder. The other, taken from above, showed Chichester with a policeman holding one arm and Giles the other looking like they were supporting an old and disabled man unable to stand on his own. These photographs, together with some of Sir Francis's criticisms of the boat, were circulated in Britain and Tony Dulverton, the owner of *Gipsy Moth IV*, cabled Australia to say on no account was Chichester to continue with the voyage. Chichester ignored this.   Another of his sponsors wanted to publish a statement disclaiming any responsibility in the event that he came to grief on the second half of the voyage. Captain Alan Villiers, who knew the waters of Cape Horn better than almost anyone from the days of square riggers, wrote in several newspapers pleading for Chichester not to attempt Cape Horn alone but, at the very least, to take a crew with him. The *Sunday Express* wrote an article stating that a clairvoyant believed that Chichester was doomed to failure in his attempt to sail round the world and that he would give up due to lack of physical strength. Another retired sea captain, the Australian John Jargoe, stated that Chichester had only a fifty-fifty chance of survival and must be 'a glorious bloody fool' to attempt it.

Then Chichester jumped off the stem of *Gipsy Moth IV* onto the jetty, missed his footing and crashed heavily onto the planking. This was all seen by a journalist and more articles appeared saying he was unfit and should be stopped from carrying on.

Chichester probably rather relished all this publicity which only increased his 'mystique' amongst the burgeoning band of admirers and swelled the number of his supporters back home in Britain. Sheila Chichester did not like it at all and hated all the questions she kept being asked, such as 'Aren't you frightened that he will be drowned?' and 'why don't you stop him?' To cap it all, the Sunday before Chichester left, Sheila stood up suddenly whereupon her ankle doubled up underneath her weight and she tore three ligaments. Some people took this as a bad omen but Sir Francis set out on the voyage home nevertheless.

The voyage home

Probably thankful for a bit of peace and quiet Chichester left Sydney on 29 January 1967, despite being warned to delay his departure because of a tropical cyclone close by to the north-east. He could have, and probably should have, gone south but Chichester made a big mistake by sailing to the north round the top of New Zealand. This added considerably to the distance but more importantly took him straight toward the edges of the cyclone. On the first day out he experienced storm force winds. A huge sea picked up *Gipsy Moth IV,* flung her onto her beam ends and capsized her, with her masts 140º from the vertical. The boat suffered structural damage and the mess below was indescribable. Chichester was very sea sick for the first week whilst he cleared up the mess and repaired the damage.

After this the passage to the Horn was reasonably uneventful and Chichester probably kept too far north as he experienced light winds until he had to duck to the south to pass Cape Horn. As he neared the Horn he met a fierce storm and was unable to take a sun sight for three days but he was on course and, early on the morning of 21 March 1967, sighted the Horn whilst being driven forward by huge waves. He reduced sail until just a small spitfire jib was set. HMS *Protector,* a Royal Navy ice patrol vessel, loomed out of the murk and kept station with *Gipsy Moth IV* as she rounded the Horn. Suddenly, to Chichester's amazement, a tiny yellow aeroplane, a Piper Apache, appeared overhead. It circled round *Gipsy Moth IV* six times, buffeted by the wind and spray, taking some of the iconic photographs shown in the numerous books which have been written about the voyage. On board the aeroplane was *Sunday Times* reporter Murray Sayle, who later said the flight was a magnificent and terrifying experience.

Chichester sailed east of Staten Island and then east of the Falklands and on the seventy-third day out from Sydney crossed his path of the voyage out. He had circumnavigated the globe in 173 days of sailing.

When he was nearly home and approaching England, a BBC chartered minesweeper took up station alongside him, followed by a Royal Navy escort ship. Chichester related how he actively disliked and resented this intrusion into his voyage and the thought of meeting people again made him tremble. On the afternoon of Saturday 27 May 1967 a small convoy had collected behind him whilst planes and helicopters scuttled overhead. That night beacons were lit on the hilltops of Devon and Cornwall to guide him home. The next day, Sunday, saw huge crowds flocking to Plymouth and at nine o'clock that evening in light winds, having kept everyone waiting all day, Chichester passed the breakwater into Plymouth. The Royal Western Yacht Club fired a finishing gun.

In July, Chichester, with a crew, sailed *Gipsy Moth IV* to Greenwich where on 7 July the Queen knighted him.

How special was his voyage? Whilst Chichester made all sorts of claims regarding it (and it was undoubtedly outstanding) when considered in comparison to other circumnavigations, was it really so magnificent? Despite his claims, his voyage was not the first 'true' circumnavigation via Cape Horn but the third (the first was Conor O'Brien in Saoirse - see chapter 3), the second was Marcel Bardiaux in *Les 4 Vents* (see chapter 8). Edward Allcard in *Sea Wanderer* passed Cape Horn a year before Chichester, although his twelve-year circumnavigation ended many years later. (Vito Dumas and Bill Nance were not regarded by Chichester as having made 'true' circumnavigations as they both began and ended their voyages in the southern hemisphere).

As for speed, his voyage was clearly the fastest but he had by far the largest boat and his speeds were not much better than those achieved by Bill Nance in his diminutive *Cardinal Vertue*, only 21-feet on the waterline compared to 39-feet for *Gipsy Moth IV*. Bill Nance achieved an average of just over 122 miles a day for much of his crossing of the Southern Ocean, whilst Chichester achieved 131 miles per day. Nance's achievement was quite extraordinary.

Was the boat as bad as Chichester made out? Definitely not and the designer Angus Primrose was right when he reminded Chichester in his famous telegram that having only just reached Australia the boat was hardly run in. Chichester complained little on the way home, achieved all his fastest speeds then and not all this can be attributed to the alteration made to the keel in Sydney. It is all very well for Chichester to continually complain that the boat was too big but he would never have got to Sydney in 100 days in a smaller boat. Technology was not as far advanced as it is now and he needed this size of boat to carry all the supplies, heavy radio equipment and batteries which he demanded. No other singlehander of his day felt the need for such equipment and preferred to do without the complications and frustrations of the primitive communication equipment available then. Most of them wanted to get away from the intrusion which such stuff brought into their lives.

Gipsy Moth IV after the voyage

Chichester commented: *'Now that I have finished, I don't know what will become of Gipsy Moth IV. I only own the stern while my cousin owns two thirds. My part, I would sell any day. It would be better if about a third were sawn off. The boat was too big for me. Gipsy Moth IV has no sentimental value for me at all. She is cantankerous and difficult and needs a crew of three - a man to navigate, an elephant to move the tiller and a 3-foot 6-inch chimpanzee with arms 8-foot-long to get about below and work some of the gear.'*

Chichester wanted no more of her and nor did Lord Dulverton. She was exhibited at the London Boat Show in January 1968 after which Dulverton donated her to the City of London, who entrusted her to the Cutty Sark

Society. They decided, amid much opprobrium from the British yachting establishment, to encase her in concrete in a specially built dry dock next to the *Cutty Sark*. There she sat for many years, rotting and corroding away and was eventually closed to visitors as it was deemed unsafe to have the public walking on her decks.

So she remained, forlorn and forgotten, until 2003 when Paul Gelder, the then editor of the UK sailing magazine *Yachting Monthly*, launched a campaign to restore the yacht and sail her around the world in 2006 which was to be the fortieth anniversary of Chichester's voyage, and also the one-hundredth birthday of his magazine. In 2004 the yacht was purchased by the United Kingdom Sailing Academy for the grand total of £1 and a gin and tonic (Chichester's favourite tipple). She was dug out of her concrete coffin and taken by road to her original builders in Gosport for a total restoration, which cost more than £300,000.

She set sail on a second circumnavigation in September 2005 with an experienced professional crew plus changing teams of disadvantaged youths. This time she went westabout through the Panama Canal and nowhere near Cape Horn. Unfortunately in April 2006, when crossing the Pacific, a navigational error led to *Gipsy Moth IV* running hard aground on a coral reef at Rangiroa, an atoll in the Tuamotus, known, very appropriately, as the Dangerous Archipelago. After several days she was refloated and then transported to New Zealand to be repaired. She sailed back to the UK arriving in May 2007. The crew experienced none of the behavioural problems expounded so forcibly by Chichester and they found her a safe, fast and easily handled ship. Perhaps she was not jinxed after all and maybe Don Holm should retract the statement he made in his authoritative book *The Circumnavigators* that '*Gipsy Moth IV was perhaps one of the worst racing yachts ever built.*'

Chichester's life after the voyage

As soon as he could Francis and Sheila escaped to the south of France to recuperate. He wrote his book of the voyage, gave many lectures and talks, attended many grand dinner parties and in 1968 became Chairman of a Committee overseeing the *Sunday Times* Golden Globe solo-non-stop round the world race. He was not well during this period and the outcome of the race left him extremely depressed. He blamed himself for the ensuing tragedies through his not having insisted on proper rules and better supervision of the entrants.

However, you can't keep a man like Chichester down and he soon dreamed up a new project – to build a new boat to achieve a sustained run of 1000 miles at 200 miles per day, sailing solo, something which no single-hander had achieved before. (By comparison, nowadays the latest generation of fast multihulls being sailed solo achieve over 800 miles in a single day!). He went to Robert Clark, the creator of *Gipsy Moth III*, to design him a suitable boat. Clark had just designed the fast, narrow and elegant *Sir Thomas Lipton* which Chichester admired and which had just won the 1968 OSTAR. Clark came up with a boat 57 feet overall and 42 feet on the waterline. She was rigged as a staysail ketch which with no large mainsail made for easier sail handling. The boat was built at Crosshaven in Ireland and was launched in June 1970, named *Gipsy Moth V.* She had a Thames Measurement of twenty-nine tons and the whole thing was far larger all round than her disliked predecessor, which Chichester used to berate for being too big.

The Chichester family took *Gipsy Moth V* on a shakedown cruise to the Mediterranean. Then Chichester's literary agent, the legendary George Greenfield, persuaded Chichester to up his 1,000-mile-voyage to try to sail fast for 4,000 miles at 200 miles a day from one fixed point to a predetermined destination. They decided on a course from Portuguese Guinea then straight across the Atlantic to a port in Nicaragua, a straight line distance of 4,000 miles. After fraught preparations, Chichester set off in December 1970 to sail to Guinea Bissau. He had a rough trip and the boat suffered some minor damage.

Eventually he left on his Atlantic dash on 12 January 1971 but had a slow start meeting headwinds. After he had covered 2,000 miles he needed to up his average to 216 miles per day for the rest of the trip. Then his problems started. He broke his spinnaker poles, ran into a huge floating fishing net and met contrary winds. Eventually he covered the 4,000 miles in twenty-two days sailing, an average of 181 miles per day. He meandered home slowly across the Atlantic seeming not to want his voyage to end. Then, having reached a latitude of 40° North he turned south and tried to sail 1000 miles in five days. Again he was out of luck as the trade winds deserted him. He stopped in the Azores and then headed back to England. On the way he ran into a bad storm in which *Gipsy Moth V* was knocked down and capsized. He arrived home on 11 May having sailed over 18,000 miles in five months but had achieved little.

He wrote a further book (*The Romantic Challenge*) and became very ill. He was in and out of hospital and health farms for a year until he was diagnosed with an inoperable malignant tumour near the base of his spine, which the doctors said was poisoning his blood. He was given blood transfusions but they did not help. Then, despite dire warnings from his doctors, he entered *Gipsy Moth V* for the 1972 OSTAR. He was by then Commodore of the Royal Western Yacht Club, who organised these races, and there was really no one who could stop him from going. At the pre-race dinner where he took the chair, he could hardly stand up. Sheila in her determined way thought that the race would do him good.

The race was a very different affair from the first one twelve years before. There were fifty-five starters, comprising everything from a 128-foot three masted schooner (*Vendredi Treize*), many multihulls and the smallest entry, the 19-foot *Willing Griffin*. Chichester had agreed to make regular radio calls to the *Sunday Times,* which arrangement contributed to the tragedies that followed.

The fleet met a westerly gale on the second day out which began to sort out the competitors and many retired. Chichester found the wild motion agonising, could not get his radio to transmit and had to spend much time lying down to alleviate the pain. He headed south planning to take the southerly (and longest) route where he hoped he would find better weather. His pains grew worse and, after taking strong pain killers, he fell into a heavy sleep. He awoke hallucinating, not knowing how long he had been asleep or where he was. The expert navigator was beaten and unable to work out his position. He turned for where he thought home was.

Back in England, Chichester began to make headlines once more. Where was the ancient mariner, the press asked. Why the radio silence? (The press had precious little else to write about as the rest of the OSTAR fleet sped westwards). Giles, Chichester's son, tried to calm everyone down and said the radio silence should not mean 'missing' (this being one of the things which Blondie Hasler had warned about many years before when refusing to carry a radio transmitter). Giles reminded the press that his Marconi transmitter had failed before.

As so often happens in these cases, officialdom took over with unintended consequences. Portishead Radio sent out messages asking Chichester to report in. RAF aeroplanes on routine missions were asked to look out for the old man's boat. A merchant ship, SS *Barrister,* sighted *Gipsy Moth V* half way between the Azores and Land's End. The ship reported that Chichester was heading for America and that he did not seem to require assistance. Once his position was reported it was easy for the RAF to find him but they noticed he was now sailing on a direct course to England. Then everything became more confused. A RAF Nimrod plane was despatched and flying low using lamp signals asked 'are you O.K?' Chichester signalled back 'I am O.K. No rescue'. The next evening another Nimrod found him. Francis's log on board *Gipsy Moth V* states that he signalled 'Wish son and Anderson could meet me in Channel'. This message was never seen by the Nimrod. It is exceedingly difficult even for an experienced signaller to use an Aldis lamp on the swaying deck of a small ship and the masts and sails often get in the way. Chichester closed down with the words 'Weak and cold. Want rest.' This part of the message was received by the Nimrod.

The next day newspapers thundered 'Francis Chichester weak and cold.' Later the same day a French weather-ship the *France II* which happened to be stationed nearby heard a radio request from a passing Nimrod asking any ships in the vicinity to investigate. The *France II* promptly steamed to the given position and arrived around noon on 30 June. Chichester, who like all yachtsmen feared big ships approaching at sea, signalled 'Go away. No aid needed.' However France II stood on and when a few yards away a man on her deck shouted 'I must know where you are going?' *France II* then overtook *Gipsy Moth V* and crossed her bows. She was too close and parts of the big ship caught in the yachts rigging bringing the top of the mizzen mast down with a crash. The weather ship lowered a launch which came over and a man in it asked Sir Francis if he wanted a doctor. No, he is reputed to have said, but *Gipsy Moth* does. The weather ship then steamed away leaving Chichester surveying the damage.

Back home events took on a world of their own, unbeknownst to Chichester. The *Sunday Times,* believing Sir Francis needed rescuing, persuaded the Royal Navy to send a warship to the stricken mariner's aid. The Navy diverted a frigate, HMS *Salisbury*, which was on its way home to Plymouth, to go and find the yacht and offer assistance. The *Sunday Times* then persuaded Francis's son, Giles, and John Anderson to agree to be helicoptered onto the frigate to join in the rescue. By that evening the two were flown 200 miles offshore and winched down onto the deck of HMS *Salisbury,* where a volunteer crew of three experienced yachtsmen from the aircraft-carrier HMS *Ark Royal* were also waiting. The next morning HMS *Salisbury* approached *Gipsy Moth V* and asked if they could send a launch across. Chichester agreed and accepted the offer of help whilst stating he was quite capable of getting home on his own. The new crew quickly cleared up the damage and were soon underway with a jury rig. They arrived back in Plymouth three days later. Chichester was admitted to the Naval Hospital where he remained until early August.

During this period a furore erupted over the cost of the rescue. Questions were asked in the House of Commons and angry letters were written to the press about the waste of taxpayers money. All Chichester could do was reiterate that he never needed help and did not ask to be rescued; it had all been a big misunderstanding. When all this was dying down a worse blow fell, as reports came in about the *Lefteria* affair.

Twelve hours after leaving *Gipsy Moth V*, the weather ship *France II*, at around midnight, ran down and sank an American yacht, the *Lefteria*, which had eleven people on board. Four of her crew were rescued and one body was recovered. The other six crew members went missing. In all seven lives were lost. The four who survived were taken to La Rochelle by the *France II*. A press communique stated that both the yacht and the weather ship had gone to the aid of the stricken mariner. The United Kingdom press picked up on this and a number of vitriolic articles were published accusing Chichester of going to sea in an unfit state, endangering peoples lives, refusing assistance, being responsible for the drowning of seven people and generally being a menace at sea. Chichester responded by stating in an article in the *Sunday Times* that he lamented the loss of life and that it had been a terrible shock when he learnt that the *Lefteria* was on its way to help him.

The *Lefteria* was an eighty-year-old Baltic trading schooner which the two American owners and their wives were sailing to the Caribbean, with an assorted crew of Americans, two Swedes and one Canadian. They were planning to operate the ship as a charter business. One of the survivors was Philip Bates. He was one of the owners (his wife was drowned). Once he had recovered he made a statement that those on board the *Lefteria* knew nothing of *Gipsy Moth V* or her whereabouts and they never deviated from their course to the Caribbean. He said that during the night a large ship came up to them and they exchanged signals by Aldis lamp. The ship was the *France II* which Bates said then steamed ahead and when the ship was clear he went below. Two minutes later the *Lefteria* heeled violently having been struck amidships. Bates climbed into the cockpit and was washed overboard. The yacht sank almost immediately and only four survivors were pulled out of the water by a launch from the *France II*. This story does not really make sense and Bates must have misjudged the ship's bearing or position. Whatever happened it was a major tragedy which has never been properly explained and was an exceedingly sad ending to Chichester's last ever voyage.

The ancient mariner never recovered and he died quietly in bed in a hospital in Plymouth on 26 August 1972. He was seventy-one years old.

Chapter 12
Alec Rose – In Chichester's wake

After the razzmatazz of Chichester, the voyage of Alec Rose, which came next, was a bit of a throwback to earlier days and also a bit of a sideshow. Whilst Rose wanted to sail in Chichester's footsteps (and even thought he might be able to race him) in actuality Rose was more akin to some of the earlier solo sailors. He did not seek publicity or acclaim, although for some strange reason he got both in big measure, nor did he rely on other people's money but undertook the whole venture using his own financial resources and purely for the satisfaction of it. For that he deserves our admiration and respect.

However his fame and fortune came very much from his finding himself, wittingly or not, in Sir Francis Chichester's shadow and wake. The first time mention is made of Chichester in Alec Rose's book about his Cape Horn voyage, comes after Rose had completed the 1964 OSTAR. Rose came in fourth to Chichester's second and Rose mused that, having heard Chichester was planning to sail to Australia along the clipper route, why could he not follow him round the world making a match of it. This is an idea the mercurial Chichester would probably have hated, not wanting anyone else to share the limelight or take away the glory of being the first to complete a solo one-pit-stop circumnavigation. However, as we shall see, the 'race' was not to be and Alec Rose left England for his circumnavigation and passage round Cape Horn a year after Chichester.

Early years

Unlike Sir Francis Chichester, Alec Rose was a simple character who came from an uncomplicated lowly background and led a quiet, fulfilled, life. He was born in Kent in July 1908, seven years after Chichester. His father was a haulage contractor in Canterbury and Rose had a happy rural childhood. He had an elder brother and sister and two younger sisters. He was educated at Simon Langton Grammar School in Canterbury where, having recovered from various childhood illnesses, he grew up with a wish for adventure and the sea. He was always happy spending time on his own and he recalled how he went to Gravesend one day to try to get a job on a merchant ship but was told to go home and grow up. Instead he got a job in an insurance office. He could not settle there and after trying other jobs took a one way ticket to Canada. He found work on a farm in Alberta. After a year away he returned home.

Rose married when he was twenty-three. He bought a smallholding and ran it as a market garden until he was called up by the Royal Navy in 1939. He joined the crew of a sloop, HMS *Leith*, engaged in convoy duties in the North Atlantic. In 1944 he was commissioned and promoted to sub-Lieutenant but his nerves were shot after a long period on convoy duties. He was invalided out of the navy in 1945 with the rank of Lieutenant.

Rose went back to his market garden and nursery and prospered for a while until a bad season and over expansion left him unable to reduce his overdraft. He was forced to sell up. At the same time his marriage of twenty-eight years broke up. He took to living in Ramsgate on board a converted lifeboat which he had bought a few years earlier. He acquired a taste for singlehanded sailing and decided he rather liked being alone at sea.

Rose had bought the boat as a bare hull and named her *Neptune's Daughter*. In her he learnt to sail and navigate. He met his second wife, Dorothy at this time. They had a sailing honeymoon on the boat. Intending to sail to Spain they only made it to Brest. On their return Rose looked for a new business to buy and found a greengrocer and fruiterer business in Southsea. It was 1961 and the Roses remained in Southsea for the remainder of their lives.

In 1963 Rose became fascinated with the idea of the second OSTAR which was to take place the next year and he became determined to enter. *Neptune's Daughter* was not up to such an undertaking and Rose cast around looking for a more suitable steed. In Yarmouth on the Isle of Wight Rose found a 36-foot cutter called *Lively Lady*.

The boat

Lively Lady had been built in Calcutta in 1948 by a Mr Cambridge (who still owned her in 1963). She was built to a pre-Second World War design by Fredrick Shepherd, a much respected English naval architect. During the war, Mr Cambridge made a study of yacht design and construction and started building the yacht in 1947, with the assistance of two Indian cabinet-makers.

He modified Shepherd's design in many respects. The keel profile was altered, a long coachroof was eliminated and replaced by a flush deck with a skylight. The topsides were raised to compensate for this. Instead of the designed steam bent timbers, she was built with grown timbers, all doubled, throughout making her immensely strong (but also heavy). Planking was 1 3/8-inch teak where 1-inch was specified in the design. The result was a very heavy displacement yacht with too little sail area. She was very typical of what was then thought correct for a proper cruising yacht, i.e. short ends, narrow beam, deep draft and heavy displacement. Her displacement is around fourteen tons, which is over two tons more than the far larger *Gipsy Moth IV*, who is half as long again as *Lively Lady*.

Lively Lady was very under canvassed when Rose bought her, carrying a traditional cutter rig set on a heavy wooden mast. Following in the footsteps of Chichester, Rose engaged the firm of Illingworth and Primrose to design a new enlarged rig for the 1964 OSTAR with a new aluminium mast. She proved to be still under canvassed. Before Rose's circumnavigation, the same firm produced a second rig with a taller main mast and a mizzen mast stepped abaft the cockpit. The purpose of this mast was, strangely, not to set a traditional mizzen sail but to allow the setting of a large mizzen staysail, with its tack near the foot of the main mast. The area of this sail was not very different from the mainsail and could be used to replace the mainsail in light airs. It was an odd arrangement and one wonders whether the weight of and complications of the rigging for such a mast outweighed the benefits.

One oddity of the Illingworth rigging plan was its simplicity. Each side there was a single topmast shroud and a single lower shroud, being balanced by a lower inner forestay. This arrangement is pretty normal for a weekend or coastal cruiser but is hardly sensible for a yacht undertaking a passage across the Southern Ocean. The only real problems Rose experienced during his circumnavigation related to her rig, of which more later. (For the technically minded, another reason for these problems may have been due to Rose's somewhat conservative choice of 7 X 7 galvanised wire for the standing rigging, rather than using better quality stronger 1 X 19 construction or by using stainless steel wire with swaged ends. The benefit to Rose was that his 7 X 7 wire could be hand spliced and was much cheaper, without the need for expensive terminal fittings). It is the authors' view that Alec Rose was exceedingly lucky not to have lost his mast during the outward part of his trip. In Australia a second set of lower shrouds was fitted.

Below decks the layout of the boat was simple if somewhat severe, with much heavy teak joinery, but perfect for a single-hander. The galley was on the starboard side just beside the main companion way. Opposite was a quarter berth with a chart table above. The saloon had two narrow settees with pilot berths outboard of them and there were a further two berths in the foc'sle.

All in all *Lively Lady* was an ideal boat for Rose's purposes provided you were not in a hurry or out to beat any records. She had a safe, very strong and seaworthy hull which would see out any weather thrown at her. On her return from the circumnavigation, commentators remarked on the perfect state of the boat's planking with no seams showing; a testament to the strength of her build. However, the idea of a race against *Gipsy Moth IV* was a bit fanciful.

At sea

On 23 May 1964, Alec Rose set sail with thirteen other contestants from Plymouth racing singlehanded to Newport on Rhode Island in the USA in the second OSTAR. All those who sailed in the first OSTAR were back and the favourite to win was a then unknown French naval officer called Eric Tabarly, in a specially built lightweight 44-foot yacht called *Pen Duick II*.

For most competitors the weather that year in the north Atlantic was fairly benign with following winds for much of the time. As is well known, Tabarly came in first after twenty-seven days and became the toast of France, being feted at home and awarded the Legion d'Honneur, France's highest award. Chichester came in second, two days later and Alec Rose arrived after thirty-six days in fourth place. He beat *Jester* and Blondie Hasler, the founder of the race, by only one day. It was a good effort by the relatively inexperienced Rose in a heavy and slow boat.

After the race he sailed *Lively Lady* home expecting a downhill run but met several easterly gales and experienced rough and unsettled weather the whole way. He made it without too much incident but arrived back in Plymouth very battered and bruised, much more so than on the outward journey.

Rose then began to think about what to do next and as soon as he heard of Francis Chichester's plans Rose decided to follow him in a solo one-stop circumnavigation, planning to stop not in Sydney but in Melbourne, where one of his sons now lived. Rose decided, out of courtesy, to tell Chichester of his plans and wanted to be the first to do so. Rose telephoned Chichester who said he had already heard about it. Rose wrote in his book that Chichester told him he was planning to leave Plymouth on 27 August 1966 and suggested that Rose be there to leave with him. The author doubts whether this is true as Chichester was not the sort of person to want to share the limelight. Chichester makes no mention in his writings of his ever having suggested or agreed to share his 'race against himself' with anyone else.

Whatever occurred, news of Rose's plans got out and the press announced that he was to race Francis Chichester around the world. The grand old man ignored these reports and you can be certain that he looked at them with disdain and disbelief as to how a slow heavy pre-war cruising boat sailed by a relatively unknown greengrocer could possibly compete with a super fast expensive purpose built racing yacht sailed by the world's best known single-hander.

However, the 'race' never happened. In the first place, Rose decided that 27 August was far too late for him to leave if he was to get round Cape Horn before the onset of winter in the southern hemisphere and secondly, as we shall see, Rose had to delay his departure by a year.

Relying on his own resources and money raised from local business-men, Rose prepared *Lively Lady* for the voyage, intending to leave from Portsmouth at the beginning of August, three weeks before Chichester. Not giving up the idea of a race, Rose had calculated that it would take him that extra time to reach Australia at the same time as Chichester.

Sunday 7 August dawned raining hard and Rose had an inauspicious departure. He ran the boat aground in Langstone Harbour and his engine would not start, flattening his batteries. Eventually at three o'clock in the afternoon a starting gun was fired and Rose departed, passed through the Forts, which guard the entrance to Spithead, and was on his way. He was very unhappy at the state of his ship with no working engine and nothing stowed properly below. Then the BBC broadcast a gale warning and Rose had a miserable beat into a rising wind down Channel. He decided to put into Plymouth to have his engine looked at. He stopped at Mashfords boatyard for three days. On setting sail outside the breakwater he lost his jib halyard up the mast and being unable to climb it, put back to Mashfords.

He set off again in much better condition. By midnight the next day he was ghosting along in a light wind approaching Ushant, when a large vessel came straight at him. Rose could not get out of her way or start the engine in time. The vessel struck *Lively Lady* on the starboard bow, breaking her bowsprit and the yacht proceeded to bump and scrape along the ship's side. The ship then disappeared in the darkness, probably quite unaware of the collision. Rose, shaken, found the bowsprit splintered and useless, several guard rail stanchions broken off, the mast damaged and the spreaders bent backwards. With a heavy heart, Rose once more turned back to Plymouth. Back at Mashfords the yard quickly began to put things right and the mast was lifted out for repairs.

On the eve of his delayed departure *Lively Lady* was moored alongside the wall, under a crane, ready for the mast to be lifted in the next morning. It was now 21 August, a mere six days before Chichester's planned departure and *Gipsy Moth IV* was about to arrive in Plymouth, planning also to berth at Mashfords yard for last minute preparations. So it looked as if Rose was going to have his 'race' after all.

The next morning Rose, who was sleeping ashore, was woken with the dreadful news that during the night *Lively Lady* had fallen away from the wall at low tide and had crashed heavily onto her starboard side. Damage was extensive but would have been a lot worse had the boat not been so heavily constructed. Several frames were cracked and the caulking disturbed showing up some seams. There was major work needed on the boat which would take many weeks to complete. This would mean Rose could not leave until well into October and would not then reach Cape Horn until mid winter. Rose had no alternative but to call off the trip until the next year.

Rose stayed on for a few days to clear the boat of stores and gear, and was there when Chichester arrived on *Gipsy Moth IV* on 26 August. Rose went on board and commented that he was very impressed by her but thought she had too much beam for bad weather. The next day Rose went out in a passenger launch to see Chichester off, feeling very miserable with his crippled *Lively Lady* ashore in a shed.

She was repaired over the winter and in May 1967 Rose sailed her back to Portsmouth. On 16 July, Rose made a second start and was soon heading down Channel, this time with no problems and with a much better prepared boat. He had a slow and uneventful voyage south to the Equator, not crossing until 26 August (a slow time of forty days). When off Madeira, the radio station misheard a message purported to have come from *Lively Lady* and Rose learnt that a search was on for him as he was missing. (In fact another yachtsman also called Rose had put out a distress call from west of the Azores and this may have caused the confusion – Alec Rose was furious.)

After the Equator, Rose met some rough weather beating into the southeast Trades and problems with the rig and gear began to emerge. The mainsail stripped off all the luff slides which needed re-seizing, the servo blade on the self steering gear broke and Rose himself became very battered and bruised. By the middle of October he had passed the Cape of Good Hope and was in the Indian Ocean.

On 7 November *Lively Lady* was nearly dismasted. The starboard lower shroud parted and only the topmast shroud was preventing the mast, which was stepped on deck, from coming down. The mast was banging in its socket and whipping in the middle. Rose let the jib halyards go and set up a staysail halyard as a temporary stay. This broke after a while and Rose set up one of the forestays as a temporary shroud. The broken one had parted at the splice at the top end. This incident showed up the weakness in the rig in only having one lower shroud on each side (and on relying on spliced ends). Rose had to wait two days until it was calm enough to hoist himself up the mast to the crosstrees to refit the repaired stay. He was lucky it was not the topmast shroud that had parted – if it had he would have lost his mast. He was half way across the Indian Ocean with 3,000 miles to go to Australia. A few days later the bobstay, holding down the end of the bowsprit, came adrift from the lower fitting on the bow just below the waterline. He was unable to reattach it but rigged a strut under the pulpit to help strengthen it. He was lucky his bowsprit was short and strong.

Two weeks later, Rose was woken by a banging on deck and found the port lower shroud had parted in exactly the same place as the repaired starboard one. It was two weeks before Rose was able to repair and reset it. During this time he could not set his mainsail and made very slow progress. On 27 November he passed south of Cape Leeuwin. Then a rough crossing of the Great Australian bight brought Rose to Melbourne on 17 December. It had taken him 212 days to reach Australia, as against Chichester's 107. As he passed through the Heads one of the watchers on the shore was the Australian Prime Minister, Harold Holt, who disappeared a few minutes later whilst swimming in the sea. His body was never found.

In Melbourne repairs were carried out to the rig, an additional pair of lower shrouds was fitted and the bobstay chain replaced. The boat was hauled out and painted and the sails repaired.

On 14 January 1968 Rose departed Melbourne and headed south to pass to the west and south of Tasmania. He ran into strong headwinds and only covered 330 miles in the first five days. During the night of 24 January Rose went forward to lower the genoa and on letting the halyard go the whole lot, genoa and the twin forestays, fell with a rush and ended up in the sea. The stainless steel tang at the masthead to which the forestays were attached had broken. He set up a jib halyard as a temporary stay.

Rose decided to make for Bluff at the southern tip of New Zealand to effect repairs. As he approached he was advised not to try to enter Bluff on his own but to wait for a pilot boat. A full gale was blowing and there is a vivid photograph in Rose's book showing *Lively Lady* rolling giddily in a huge swell amid spindrift and breaking seas as she motors toward the harbour. Another photograph shows an exhausted and haggard looking Rose looking anxiously ahead out from under an oilskin hood with a breaking sea in the background. Rose was very glad of the pilot as he would never have found the way in on his own. On arrival he was told that David Mackworth of Illingworth and Primrose was flying out with a new masthead fitting. This was fitted without the mast having to be taken out and four days after arrival Rose departed. Straight away he ran into a strong westerly gale and large seas as he passed through the sixteen mile-wide Foveaux Strait.

Four days later Rose was down to 48° South and was getting near to the northern limit of icebergs. It was very cold. Soon Rose was facing a Force 12 storm with only a baby storm-jib hoisted. He remarked that he had never before faced such a fierce wind. The night of 18 February nearly put paid to the whole trip and to Rose. He ran his small generator without connecting up the exhaust pipe and on going below was overcome by exhaust fumes and carbon monoxide. He collapsed and came too some time later slumped over the galley. He had been 'out' for about three hours. Luckily he had left the main hatch open and this had cleared the air below.

It took Rose the rest of February and the whole of March to cross the Southern Ocean to reach south America. He had bad weather most of the way, often having to face south-easterly gales. It was very slow progress. On 28 March, when Rose was 150 miles south-west of Noir Island off the coast of Tierra del Fuego, he was overcome once again by exhaust fumes. This time he collapsed at the bottom of the companion steps. One would have thought he would have learnt his lesson after the first time.

On 30 March Rose made radio contact with the Royal Navy Fleet Auxiliary tanker *Wave Crest* which, unbeknownst to him, was keeping a lookout for him. He passed north of the Diego Ramirez Islands and headed for the Horn in a strong north-westerly gale. On 31 March *Wave Crest* took up station astern of *Lively Lady*.

At dawn on 1 April Rose woke to find Cape Horn standing out majestically some twenty miles away. He was running under trysail, staysail and working jib. At noon he rounded Cape Horn eleven miles off in a light north-westerly wind. An aeroplane appeared and circled him. It had been chartered by ITN news and the *Sunday Mirror*. Whether Rose sought it or not he had equalled Chichester in the amount of publicity he was getting. In his quest to emulate Chichester this must have pleased him.

By the next morning he had passed the Le Maire Strait and was off Staten Island heading for the Falkland Islands. Now his self steering gear started playing up and he spent much of the next few days screwing and bolting the whole thing together. Although Rose was climbing north, it was not until the middle of April that things began to warm up and the weather settled down. On 7 May Rose tied the knot and completed his circumnavigation by passing his outward track. He passed some 650 miles east of Cape San Roque, the easternmost point of South America and crossed the equator on 19 May. He was making slow going of it but gradually getting home.

On 29 June he was 160 miles from Lands End. The Royal Navy kindly sent a minesweeper, HMS *Letterston*, to accompany him into harbour. She met up with *Lively Lady* the next day. Then a second minesweeper, HMS *Laleston,* arrived and took up station ahead of *Lively Lady* to keep off oncoming shipping. They were joined by three press boats and the convoy made slow and erratic progress up Channel in light and variable winds. On 3 July the launch *Southerner* joined in and put a TV crew on board *Lively Lady* and Rose gave a live TV interview.

The next morning, 4 July, three Royal Navy fast patrol boats joined the escort fleet which made its way past the Nab Tower and then the Bembridge Ledge Buoy and into Spithead and the Solent. They were joined by many pleasure yachts and motor boats and as the flotilla neared Portsmouth, Rose's wife Dorothy was brought out to *Lively Lady* on board the Commander-in Chief's Admiral's barge. There was a crowd on the shore estimated at 250,000 to view the proceedings. So ended the 'Great Adventure' in Alec Rose's life.

Aftermath

Alec Rose attended a civic reception at the Portsmouth Guildhall where he was made a Freeman of the city and later appeared, waving like royalty, on the tiny balcony of his greengrocer's shop in Southsea. He was knighted by the Queen at Buckingham Palace and was received by the Speaker of the House of Commons at the Palace of Westminster. Later, he and Dorothy were entertained by the Elder Brethren of Trinity House at Greenwich, very near to where *Gipsy Moth IV* was to be encased in concrete. They also attended a *Lively Lady* exhibition at the headquarters of the *Daily Mirror.*

At the end of Rose's book, there is a chapter written by Dorothy headed 'When Alec's Away' in which she detailed her daily life in running their greengrocer's shop, how once Alec had rounded the Horn she began to be asked to open bazaars and functions and how a variety of rose was named after him. She also described in gushing terms the events following Alec's return and their trip to the Palace to meet the Queen. She finished *'so you see the whole thing has been a fairy story with a happy ending. I cannot say more.'*

Was all this adulation, and the knighting of Rose, really justified? I fear not and in hindsight the whole thing appears a little ridiculous. Rose did not do anything new but merely followed in Chichester's wake. He broke no records, save possibly achieving some of the slowest ocean passages ever made and, unlike most of the people in this book, carried out no further voyages of any note after his return.

As this book makes clear many others had already sailed around Cape Horn as part of a solo circumnavigation and why were they not knighted? Edward Allcard, a fellow Britain, passed Cape Horn alone two years before Rose in his boat *Sea Wanderer* (still today the oldest boat to have done so) and went on to complete the longest circumnavigation ever - twelve years. Why was he not knighted? Similarly Bill Nance in *Cardinal Vertue* rounded the Horn three years before Rose in what was an extraordinary voyage. Nance was an Australian but why was he not honoured for his circumnavigation or one of his later voyages? Subsequent to Rose many other yachtsmen have made voyages around Cape Horn but none were knighted for this feat alone. Robin Knox-Johnston and Chay Blyth (see later) were both knighted subsequently but not for their Cape Horn exploits alone. They were knighted for 'services to yachting' and both made successful careers enabling hundreds of people to sail around the world, many round Cape Horn, on specially prepared yachts. Naomi James was made a Dame for her solo circumnavigation via Cape Horn but this was well deserved as the first lady to achieve this feat.

Sir Alec Rose kept *Lively Lady* for the rest of his life but used her little and virtually disappeared from public life. On his death in January 1991 he bequeathed *Lively Lady* to the City of Portsmouth.

There is today a pub in Bracklesham (a village lying, very appropriately, near Chichester in West Sussex) called 'The Lively Lady', a street in Portsmouth named 'Alec Rose Lane', an old peoples home in Gosport called 'Alec Rose House', a Wethersoon pub in the Port Solent marina named 'The Sir Alec Rose' and of course there is that variety of rose named after him.

After Sir Alec Rose's death, Portsmouth City Council handed *Lively Lady* over to a local charity but nothing much happened to her and she deteriorated badly. In 2004 Alan Priddy and a team of supporters began an extensive refit following which, in 2006, she set sail on another circumnavigation with an ever changing crew of disadvantaged youngsters from the Portsmouth (once again *Lively Lady* seemed unable to avoid following in the footsteps of *Gipsy Moth IV* which had set sail a year before on a circumnavigation also crewed by disadvantaged youngsters). *Lively Lady*, in a new paint livery with, somewhat incongruously, the name 'RAYMARINE' painted in large letters on her topsides (the power of sponsorship), sailed westabout round the world the 'easy way' via the Panama Canal and she returned in 2008.

There was then a long drawn out and acrimonious legal case with the former charity who had care of the boat and eventually she was handed over to a new charity, called Around and Around also, strangely, led by Alan Priddy, charged with looking after the boat for the years to come. Currently she is being totally rebuilt in Portsmouth by shipwright apprentices and it is planned for her to set sail in 2018 to circumnavigate the world again, to celebrate the fiftieth anniversary of Sir Alec Rose's original voyage. She is also due to take part in the forthcoming celebrations to remember the fiftieth anniversary of Sir Robin Knox-Johnston's first non-stop circumnavigation.

Lets hope she will be ready in time.

Chapter 13
Robin Knox-Johnston – The first non-stop

After Chichester's one-pit-stop voyage (and Rose's failed attempt at the same thing) the floodgates didn't exactly open but a trickle began, which soon turned to a torrent. It became obvious that the next 'best thing' had to be a non-stop circumnavigation and it was only a matter of time before someone tried it. In fact a handful of people thought they would try, each trying to keep their plans to themselves.

And thus the matter rested, while people scurried around in secret, seeking money or suitable boats, lining up book and newspaper sponsorship deals but not announcing anything. Amongst these was a Frenchman, Bernard Moitessier (who already had an ocean-ready vessel and who had recently completed the longest non-stop passage yet attempted) and Robin Knox-Johnston, a young tough merchant navy officer, who had recently sailed his tough little yacht home from India.

Then the whole thing was turned totally upside down by a piece of journalistic bravura emanating from the desk of the pugilistic editor of the *Sunday Times*, one Harold Evans (now Sir Harold). Upon learning that a number of potential solo non-stop sailors were signing up newspaper sponsorship deals (*The Mirror, Sunday Mirror, Express and Sunday Express* in particular) and not wanting the *Sunday Times* to be left out, Evans came up with a mouth-watering suggestion - why not institute a race for these guys in such a way that no-one has actually to enter but in which no-one can avoid taking part. It was pure journalistic genius (albeit with tragic consequences) on the part of Harold Evans. So the '*Sunday Times* Golden Globe Non-Stop Around the World Race' was inaugurated - a golden globe to go to the first man home and £5,000 (equivalent to about £80,000 today) to the fastest 'competitor'. The only rules were (1) anyone leaving any port in the United Kingdom before 31 October 1968 was automatically entered (whether they wanted to or not!) and (2) 'competitors' had to sail alone non-stop south of all southern Capes (other than any in Antarctica) and return to the United Kingdom having had no outside assistance. It was glorious in its simplicity and it guaranteed that the *Sunday Times* would receive the bulk of all publicity, leaving all other newspapers scrabbling in its wake. What a scoop.

The next three chapters tell the story of the only three race participants (one hesitates to use the term competitors or entrants) who actually sailed round Cape Horn during the currency of the 'race'. Others tried and failed, one faked his voyage and pretended he had done it and one succeeded three years later. The first to leave on a non-stop attempt, and the first to pass Cape Horn, was Robin Knox-Johnston. He was the first 'entrant'.

Today Robin, or Sir Robin as he is now, is undoubtedly the grand old man of British yachting (the author, who knows Robin, is sure he would not mind being described as old – he is now eighty). He has led an extraordinary life, is one of the most likeable, generous and approachable people you could meet and just seems to keep going on and on. Only recently has he re-launched his famous and beloved *Suhaili* after a complete rebuild, much of it carried out by Robin himself.

Early life

Born in London in 1939 and christened William Robert Patrick Knox-Johnston, he has always been known as Robin. At age four he built his first boat – made out of orange boxes; it sank on being launched. His next boat was a 10-foot canoe made in his grandparent's attic. This too sank on trials in the Grand Union Canal. He attended Berkhamsted School as a day boy, the same school which the explorer and sailor Bill Tilman went to. At school Robin hated team sports and was no good at them. At seventeen he decided to join the Royal Navy but failed to pass the entry examination. He chose the Merchant Navy instead and in 1957 joined the British East India Company's cadet ship SS *Chindwara* on which he spent three years steaming between London and various African ports. Then he passed the Ministry of Transport exam and got his Second Mate's Certificate. In 1960 he joined the SS *Dwarka* running between India and the Persian Gulf. By now he was engaged to be married and a year later took his first Mate's Certificate. After his marriage, he and his bride set up home in Bombay, where Robin joined the SS *Dumra* as Third Officer.

Robin, along with two fellow officers, came up with the idea of buying a dhow and sailing it back to England but soon realised they would never sell such a boat back home. They decided instead to build a yacht, sail her back to England and then sell her, hopefully, at a profit. They sent for a set of plans from a company in England who offered 'full plans and a free advisory service'. The plans arrived and were for a very old fashioned looking ketch. They were for a boat called *Eric* designed by William Atkins in 1923 which was based on the Colin Archer Norwegian type of double ended hull. The vessel was 32 ½ feet long (extended to 44 feet with a bowsprit and bumpkin) with an 11 foot beam and a draft of 5 ½ feet. She was a sturdy and seaworthy design but no racer. What was missing was a proper rigging plan. They asked for one but were told this would cost extra. As time (and money) were short Robin and his fellow officers bought copies of Douglas Phillips-Birt's book on rigging and Eric Hiscock's *Cruising Under Sail* and designed their own rig for the boat.

None of the three merchant navy officers really realised what they had got in this boat and I am sure none of them suspected she was to become possibly the most famous small yacht of all time.

The boat *Suhaili*

She was built in the Colaba workshops in Bombay in 1964 of Indian teak throughout. Indian shipwrights still used the traditional tools and methods which they used in the nineteenth century to build wooden warships. She was heavy and immensely strong, an attribute she shared with Alec Rose's *Lively Lady*, also built in India. She floated some two inches below her designed waterline as a result. A diesel engine and sails were shipped over from England.

The boat, named *Suhaili* (the name given by Arab seamen in the Persian Gulf to the south-west wind), was eventually launched, very late, in December 1964. A coconut was cracked on her bows whilst the men who had built her chanted traditional blessings. She was still not ready by February, which meant they missed the north-east monsoon to blow them across the Indian Ocean.

Robin's two fellow officers, who shared the boat with him, were by then short of money and time and withdrew from the project, going their separate ways. Knox-Johnston managed to scrape sufficient money together to buy them out. He laid up *Suhaili* and returned to England to take his Masters' Certificate. He wrote '*I had an unfinished, half-paid-for boat 10,000 miles from where I wanted her and no crew to bring her home.*' Robin persuaded his brother, Chris, and a friend to join him as crew for the trip home and they met up in Bombay in November 1965. After completing fitting out they left in December heading across the Arabian Sea to Muscat. They then sailed to Durban arriving in April 1966. As they were too broke even to buy stores for the next leg to Cape Town, they all found local jobs. By November they were ready to leave and set sail for Cape Town. They left there on 24 December and arrived at Gravesend seventy-four days later after a non-stop passage.

Of *Suhaili* Robin wrote: *'she proved herself to be a seaworthy boat able, when close hauled, to sail herself for long periods without attention because of her remarkable balance. There was too much weight aloft which caused her to heel over alarmingly at times but she was tough, safe and at 112 miles a day faster then we had expected.'*

The Golden Globe challenge

Robin had a month's leave in England before he joined a new ship. Something which probably changed his life for ever. One day during this period, whilst staying at his parents home, his father told Robin he had read that Eric Tabarly, the famous French yachtsman, was building a new trimaran. The two mused as to whether it would be suitable for the Transatlantic race or possibly to beat Chichester's time or even to go round non-stop. His father then said *'that's about all there's left to do now, isn't it?'* This got Robin thinking. Chichester and Rose had stopped on the way and it was inevitable that someone would try for a non-stop trip.

Robin thought that Tabarly was quite capable of doing it but a strong patriotism in him came to the fore. Surely a Frenchman could not be allowed to be the first, he said to himself. Imagine the headlines – they were bad enough when Tabarly won the OSTAR. *'Frenchman supreme on the Anglo-Saxon ocean'* thundered the French Press. This made Robin's blood boil and he really believed that by rights an Englishman should do it.

In many ways Robin was a man out of his time. Whilst it was the 'swinging sixties' and Robin was the same age as the Beatles, he was extremely 'square' and old fashioned, with a strong belief in the God given superiority of the English. So, he thought, who could this Englishman be? Could he go? Could he in *Suhaili* really race Tabarly in a 65-foot trimaran? Could he stand being alone for all that length of time? Then he realised he was hooked. He had no idea if anyone else was of the same mind but he became determined to do it. He put *Suhaili* on the market and went to see the yacht designer Colin Mudie.

Mudie was then 'the' yacht designer you would go to if you wanted something out of the ordinary or wanted some original thinking (or had little or no money). David Lewis of *Cardinal Vertue* fame had Colin Mudie design him an innovative catamaran (*Rehu Moana*) to take him and his family to Australia (one of the first multihulls to make this trip), Tim Severin had Mudie design his Arab Dhow, *Dohar*, for his Sinbad Voyage.

Mudie designed the square-rigged sail training ship, *T S Royalist* and the replica of the *Matthew* originally built in 1497 for John Cabot's voyage to Newfoundland. He had even drawn up the plans for Edward Allcard's proposed replica of Columbus's *Nina* (referred to in chapter 10).

Mudie, who relished a challenge, was not put out when Robin told him how little money he had to spend but merely started to draw something out. He came up with a 53-foot steel schooner constructed in a novel (and hopefully cheap) way with two identical masts to be bought off the shelf. With no interior fittings and keeping things as simple as possible Mudie thought Robin could put it all together for £5,000. But Robin did not have £5,000. All he had was *Suhaili*, worth no more than that, and he owed £2,000 which he had borrowed to pay for her. So he looked for a sponsor. Nobody came forward and even his employers, the British India Steam Navigation Company, turned him down.

When told this he decided on the spur of the moment that, damn it all, he would go in *Suhaili*. But she needed a complete overhaul, a new set of sails and some form of self steering. All this, plus the stores he would need, would come to over £1,500 and he still owed the £2,000.

Then luck arrived in the person of George Greenfield. He was a successful literary agent who had built up a business specialising in adventure. Amongst others he represented Sir Francis Chichester, the mountaineer Chris Bonington and the Arctic explorer Wally Herbert. He agreed to take Robin on and told him not to worry but get on with his preparations. Greenfield soon signed up London publishers Cassell and an American publisher for a book. He also signed up the *Sunday Mirror* (who had helped sponsor Alec Rose's voyage). Robin recalls how during a lunch with some top brass from the *Sunday Mirror* to discuss the project, held in a restaurant on a boat on the Thames, a tug went by throwing up a considerable wake. It rocked the boat and Robin lost his balance and fell off his chair. In an embarrassed silence the *Sunday Mirror* people looked anywhere but at Robin and not a word was said. Greenfield still pulled off the deal.

So Robin, in early 1968, had the funds to go ahead and prepare, which he did. By this time he had learned of two others who were planning a similar voyage – army Captain John Ridgway (who had recently rowed across the Atlantic with Chay Blyth) was preparing to go in a very small and unsuitable yacht, not much more than a weekend cruiser, and Commander Bill King, a wartime submariner, was building a radical Angus Primrose design called *Galway Blazer II*. Robin worked out that these two would leave around the beginning of June and, if he was to stand any chance of beating Bill King, he would have to leave much earlier than that. He started his preparations putting it about that he was planning to sail to Australia.

Then the *Sunday Times* announced the Golden Globe Challenge (the origins of which are described at the start of this chapter). This announcement brought people's plans into the open and horrified others. First to react against it, most violently, was Frenchman Bernard Moitessier, whose reaction is set out in the next chapter. Next, Donald Crowhurst publicly declared his intentions. Not to be outdone by his former rowing companion, army Sergeant Chay Blyth did likewise and announced his 'entry'. Then naval officer Nigel Tetley declared he would go in his trimaran *Victress*, a near sister ship to Crowhurst's proposed mount. Finally, two virtual unknowns declared. Frenchman Louis Fougeron who proposed to go in a tough little 30-foot steel cutter, *Capitaine Browne,* and Italian Alex Carrozzo in a 66-foot ketch named *Gancia Americana* (who only scraped into the race by leaving Cowes minutes before the deadline on 31 October then immediately anchoring outside the harbour for another few weeks to finish his preparations – later he retired with a bad ulcer brought on by stress).

So having thought he was in front of the game, Knox-Johnston found himself embroiled in the middle of a race, which he really didn't want to enter, with some apparently formidable opponents. Having such a slow boat Robin knew his only hope was to be the first to start, hopefully months or weeks before anyone else. He immediately decided to aim to leave before the end of May. He believed that Moitessier, whom he viewed as the most likely to beat him, was not going to leave until September, if he left at all.

His greatest difficulty was to fit *Suhaili* with some form of self steering. (In those days these were wind driven and needed a large wind vane which could be aligned with the direction of the wind.) A mizzen boom extending six feet over the stern of *Suhaili* did not help. Robin eventually came up with the idea of a metal framework holding two vanes port and starboard, clear of the sails and spars, linked by pulleys to an auxiliary rudder fitted aft of the main rudder. The windward vane could then be engaged and the leeward one left to weathercock. He got this idea after seeing David Lewis's Mudie designed catamaran *Rehu Moana* which had a similar set up. The system looked like a piece of agricultural equipment but it worked after a fashion. Robin christened his 'the Admiral'. Next he had to load and stow on the boat 1,500 tins, 250 pounds of onions, 350 pounds of potatoes and more. He renewed the rigging, re-caulked the bottom seam of the hull and gave the whole bottom a coat of anti-fouling paint. He fitted a new lighter mizzen mast, a new generator and a radio telephone. He was nearly ready to go but before he left the *Sunday Mirror* sent Robin to a psychiatrist to compare his state of mind before he left (and when he returned). On both occasions he was deemed to be 'distressingly normal'.

The voyage

Robin and *Suhaili* left Falmouth on 14 June 1968, later than he had hoped for. He was not the first to leave in the 'Race' but he was the first proper competitor with any hope of success. John Ridgway had left two weeks before and Chay Blyth one week after him. These two were very inexperienced (Blyth had no sailing experience whatsoever) and were in totally unsuitable boats. Ridgway was in a 30-foot Westerly weekend cruiser, plucked from the production line and lent to him for the voyage. Blyth was in an almost identical 30-foot boat, equally unsuitable. How these two (and the people who loaned them their boats) thought they could get round the world in such unfit boats is quite extraordinary. Neither lasted long. Ridgway soon retired and sailed back to Scotland, suffering mental anguish at having given up. Blyth actually got as far as South Africa before he too gave up (more on this in chapter 16).

The account of Knox-Johnston's voyage has been told many times before in several books and I will not repeat it all here. What I will do, however, is to recount several incidents from the voyage which demonstrate what a consummate seaman Knox-Johnston was and why it was really obvious from the start as to who would be the winner. We will also look at his passage round Cape Horn.

At first the Admiral did not work. Some people would have turned round at this point but Robin was determined to sort out the problem himself. And he did, gradually loosening up the system until it began to react properly. Robin soon settled in and adopted a routine which would be inconceivable to today's generation of single-handed round the world racers, who survive on twenty minute catnaps. Depending on conditions, Robin went to sleep at ten p.m. and, apart from a check at two a.m., slept through to six a.m. After a fry up for breakfast he would, if the day was warm, go for a swim. Diving off the bowsprit he would swim as fast as possible until the stern came level, then he would grab a safety line he trailed behind the boat and pull himself on board.

The most alarming thing during the first few weeks was that *Suhaili*'s bilges kept filling with water. He was close to the Cape Verde Islands when he used a period of calm to investigate. He dived over the side and saw that about a foot above the keel a large gap was showing in a seam for about eight feet. It was the same on the other side. As *Suhaili* rolled lazily in a slight swell Robin could see the gap opening and closing slightly. What worried Robin was the thought that the floors, transverse structural timbers, which join the boat's frames and planking to the keel, were working loose and that this might be the start of some serious trouble. If that was the case it would be suicidal to carry on. He had a good think and concluded that some re-caulking would cure the problem. But how was he going to do this on his own five feet below the waterline?

He got out his roll of caulking cotton and twisted up some in eighteen inch lengths. He lowered a hammer over the side on a length of line and, dressed in dark clothing so as not to attract sharks, lowered himself over the side. First he tried using a screwdriver and then a caulking iron, to hammer the cotton into the seam. It was impossible from the start. He ran out of breath before he had hammered in enough cotton to hold it and when he came up for air he lost all the work he had done. He had to come up with another way.

Next he sewed the cotton onto a strip of canvas one and a half inches wide and about seven feet long, which he gave a coating of Stockholm tar. He then forced copper tacks through the canvas at six inch intervals. He got back into the water and placed the cotton in the seam with the canvas on the outside. Next he hammered the tacks into the hull and then he tacked a copper strip over the canvas. He was half way through the job when he spied a shark. Robin hoped it would go away but eventually had to shoot it. The job had taken many hours and he still had the other side to do before he knew if it worked. Two days later he went over the side again and repeated the job on the other side. It worked and the leak stopped almost completely.

Only a consummate seaman would have been able to do this and it took a very brave man to finish such a job and carry on as if nothing had happened.

On 11 September 1968 Robin and *Suhaili* crossed the 40° South parallel and entered the Southern Ocean, the most feared piece of sea in the world. Two days later they ran into their first Southern Ocean gale. Whilst Robin was asleep below *Suhaili* was knocked down by a huge wave. Robin was thrown across the boat together with food, boxes, tins, tools, books and clothing. Clambering over the mess Robin went on deck quite expecting to see the masts gone. They were still standing but the port vane of the Admiral was buckled and jammed. Whilst clearing up below Robin noticed water pouring into the cabin each time a wave broke on board. He saw ominous cracks round the edges of the cabin top and also saw the interior bulkheads had shifted. Robin feared for the integrity of the weakened cabintop, which could be washed away by another wave breaking on board. This would leave a gaping hole six feet by twelve feet in the deck. Robin shuddered at the thought. He was 700 miles south-west of Cape Town and there was no way he could get back there in what would amount to an open boat. He felt the whole cabintop wince when another wave hit but it did not shift. Well, he thought, if it gets any worse I shall just have to put lashings over it until I have time to put in some extra fastenings. He fell asleep on a piece of canvas waiting for dawn.

He spent the whole of the next day putting in extra bolts and screws to strengthen the cabin. Two days later he replaced the damaged wind vane. It is hardly surprising that Robin felt tired and irritable for the next few days contemplating being thrown about with constant soakings for the next 150 days or so. Then his self-steering auxiliary rudder broke which took three days to repair. A lesser man than Knox-Johnston would surely have been very tempted to give up at this stage. But not R K-J.

The next problem to hit him was the discovery that the water in his forward fresh water tank was contaminated with seawater and quite unusable. He then tested his other tank and found it the same. They held eighty-five gallons between them. He also had fifteen gallons in plastic containers of which he had used five, giving him enough water for forty days at least. He was in no immediate danger but should he go on or return to Cape Town, 400 miles to his north? He had already been catching rainwater and there was plenty of rain in the Southern Ocean, so he believed he would be able to catch enough to see him the fifty days it would take to reach Australia. Also he had 300 tins of fruit juices and beer to supplement this. So he decided to keep going and see how things went. Again, many people would have retired at this point. A day later he heard via his radio that Chay Blyth had given up and had put into East London in South Africa.

If all of this was not enough, there now came a series of accidents and problems which would surely have dispirited a lesser man. Whilst heading north-east for a few days seeking an improvement in the weather, he decided to repair the spinnaker which had split down one side. He had tied the sail to opposite ends of the cabin to keep the seam tight. When he was sewing in the middle of the seam, he sewed his moustache into the sail and could not reach to free the tied ends. Neither could he reach a knife also just out of reach. There was nothing for it. Robin closed his eyes, gritted his teeth and jerked his head back tearing himself free. He said it hurt like hell and tears filled his eyes. Next, he accidentally spilled acid from his batteries into one of his eyes when the boat gave a sudden lurch whilst he was using a hydrometer. It took a week before his eye stopped throbbing but, luckily, appeared undamaged. The next day was his one-hundredth at sea.

Then, when he was asleep below, he heard a loud bang on deck and went to investigate. He saw that the main gooseneck jaw had sheared and the boom was no longer attached to the mast. He managed to fix it temporarily by lashings but he now could not reef the sail properly. He thought that this could be the end. But, undaunted, the next day he started to repair the fitting. This meant drilling out, by hand, the old jaw and bolting it to the mast. At this stage with another gale on its way and the boom not fully repaired Robin admitted to feeling 'a bit depressed'. The next day he succeeded in re-attaching the boom to the mast but then had to sew up a seam in the mainsail before he could hoist it.

On 13 October 1968 Robin ran into the worst weather he had ever experienced and thought the game was up. He wrote in his log: '*the terrifying shudders and cracks every time a wave hits the hull convinced me that the boat would not last long... water was coming into the boat as if out of a tap from leaks all round the coachhouse.*' Robin even thought he should get his liferaft out, despite being a couple of thousand miles from any land. Even streaming warps *Suhaili*, remained lying beam on to the sea. He streamed even more warps and eventually managed to bring her stern round to face the seas. Things improved.

Next, when well into the Australian Bight on 23 October, the self steering rudder broke yet again. The next day Robin dived into freezing water to fit his last remaining usable rudder. A week later this broke again, this time the metal shaft sheared in a different place and the bottom half was lost. There was no way he could repair it at sea.

Robin was not even half way round the world with no form of self steering. Could he really go on without it? In addition, the main rudder and tiller were showing signs of weakness and he had put lashings on the rudder to hold it in case the pintles went. He could no longer communicate with the shore as his transmitter had stopped working. He headed for Melbourne contemplating giving up. The more he considered it the more he felt it would be foolish to go on, what with Cape Horn still ahead of him. And yet, and yet, he thought, Ridgway and Blyth had given up and he was in the lead. Robin prevaricated, and who would not in those circumstances. He decided to carry on to New Zealand to see if he could manage without self steering. He knew he could get *Suhaili* to sail close-hauled without attention but sailing down wind was another matter. He reminded himself that Joshua Slocum could get *Spray* to sail herself on any course he wanted.

He sailed close past the entrance to Melbourne and met with a pilot boat to whom he passed a package of mail, articles and photographs. He used the opportunity of a calm sea to climb the mast and retrieve a stack of mainsail slides which had come free and stuck up the mast. He then passed through the Bass Strait, writing in his log *'Homeward Bound'*. Gradually he learned how to balance the rig to get *Suhaili* to steer a reasonably straight course with the wind behind her or on a reach. He began to think that the long sail across the Pacific may be possible after all.

As he got close to New Zealand he received a radio message from Bruce Maxwell of the *Sunday Mirror* saying he must rendezvous outside Bluff Harbour and in daylight. Bluff, of course was the harbour where Alec Rose had such a hard time entering and Knox-Johnston experienced similar problems. The weather was terrible, with a forecast of Force 9 and Force 10 winds, and the area round Bluff is riddled with unlit rocks and islands (Robin now wished he had never heard the radio message). It was dark as he approached the channel into Bluff. He was streaming a sea anchor to slow him down and was very uncertain of his position. As it got light he saw land dead to leeward and he set more sail to try to claw his way free. He doubted if the mast would stand it but it was better than doing nothing! With huge difficulty he got the sea anchor in and very slowly hauled clear of the headland. He tried for the harbour entrance but the wind pushed him remorselessly clear. Two days later he made it to a harbour called Otago further along the coast. He sailed in and promptly went aground on a falling tide – he had no proper chart of the harbour. Fending off many offers of assistance he waited for Bruce Maxwell to arrive. Robin was expecting to be given some mail with news from home but was told the rules had been altered and no material assistance of any kind was allowed – this included mail. Robin thought then (and still does) that this was silly and childish and an unnecessary restriction. He was however allowed spoken news from ashore. He was told that Bernard Moitessier was 4,000 miles behind and that if Robin carried on at the same speed he might just beat him. As the tide came in *Suhaili* lifted and he sailed out of the harbour and headed for Cape Horn. It was day 160 of his voyage.

After his travails in the Indian Ocean, Robin had a reasonably uneventful passage across the Pacific to Cape Horn, which he reached on 17 January 1969, day 217, having faced more and more gear failures. His mainsail split right across, the forestay started to strand and then the main gooseneck broke again. Even worse for him, he was running out of cigarettes (and matches). Early on 17 January he sighted Diego Ramirez Island and by seven o'clock in the evening he was some eight miles south of the Horn which he passed in a light westerly wind. He wrote *'YIPPEE !!!!'* in his log.

He rounded the Cape quite alone. No aeroplanes or Royal Navy ships for him. As his radio transmitter was not working he was not able to tell anyone at home of his achievement.

He still had 9,000 miles to go and the race was now centred on the two leading boats, *Suhaili* and Moitessier in *Joshua*, who was now only 1,500 miles behind. John Ridgway, Chay Blyth, Bill King and Louis Fougeron had all retired and Tetley, Crowhurst and Carrozzo were much too far behind to catch up. Robin's decision to leave England early was paying off and, buoyed at being first to the Horn, he now believed there was no reason why he should not make a run for it back home. His food supplies were lasting well (despite some tins going off) and whilst his water was down to four and a half gallons he was confident he would be able to collect sufficient rain water as he headed north.

Passing to the west of the Falkland Islands he made it to the Equator in twenty days. Breakages continued and for the rest of the voyage Robin was continually having to sew up sails and repair or replace ropes and halyards (and he even had to sew up his own clothes, which were beginning to disintegrate). On the day he crossed the Equator he smoked his last cigarette. He began to see other shipping and Robin tried to get their attention to pass a message back to England but at least five passed close by ignoring his attempts to attract their attention. As a trained merchant seaman Robin was disgusted by the lack of any proper lookout on these ships. It was not until he was west of the Azores with 1,200 miles to go that Robin was able to speak to and pass a message to a BP tanker. He said he estimated reaching Falmouth in two weeks time. Robin was jubilant – now they would know at home that not only had he passed Cape Horn but that he was still alive and still going. On 12 April he made contact with another ship and learnt that Moitessier had retired from the race. Nothing now was stopping Robin from coming in first.

In darkness on 18 April 1969 a ship took up station about a half a mile behind *Suhaili* and then another one did the same. Robin challenged the first ship which happened to be the *Queen of the Isles* with his mother and father on board. Whilst the wind was now blowing from the southwest, progress was slow. It was not until three days later that the convoy approached Falmouth. A naval minesweeper, HMS *Warsash* now joined in, as well as many other ships and boats, with TV and press helicopters flying overhead. Eventually at a quarter past three in the afternoon of 22 April 1969 *Suhaili* crossed the finishing line at Falmouth. The first person on board was a Customs and Excise Officer who, with a straight face, asked the time honoured question:

'Where from?'

'Falmouth' Robin replied.

Knox-Johnston was the first person ever to sail non-stop alone around the world and he did it in 313 days, having covered over 30,000 miles.

After the voyage

Robin was soon back on the water again and has combined sailing with a successful career in the marine industry up until today. He left the merchant navy and at first worked developing the Mercury Marina on the River Hamble (where he was able to help Eve Tetley - see chapter 15 below) moving on to marinas at St Katharine's Dock in London and Troon in Scotland. He was a busy man.

In 1969 he and naval officer Leslie Williams bought a 71-foot GRP hull, the first of the Ocean 71 class (and the largest GRP boat ever moulded at that time). They rigged her as a ketch and with a minimal fit out below entered her in the 1970 Two-Handed Round Britain and Ireland Race. That year's race was held in atrocious weather and it was a magnificent achievement for the two men to handle such a huge vessel in those conditions with her heavy unmanageable gear. And they won the race, the only time it has not been won by a multihull.

For the next Round Britain Race held in 1974, Knox-Johnston entered a 70-foot catamaran called *British Oxygen*, designed by Rod Mcalpine-Downie. Again he won.

Then in 1976, Knox-Johnston got together again with Leslie Williams and they built a 77-foot maxi sloop called *Heath's Condor*. They co-skippered her in the 1977 Whitbread Round the World Race but with little success. They lost an experimental carbon fibre mast on the first leg to Cape Town and never really recovered.

Robin's frenzied sailing exploits continued into 1978 when he entered Chay Blyth's old 77-foot *Great Britain II* in that year's Two-Handed Round Britain and Ireland Race. She was much too big for two people to handle properly and she was in a terrible state. They could only manage to come in twelfth, the race being won by Chay Blyth and Rob James in their frail and lightweight trimaran *Great Britain IV*. Three years later, 1981, Robin was back with another 70-foot catamaran, *Sea Falcon*. Using the same moulds as *British Oxygen*, she was half the weight and proved to be a magnificent sea-boat. Knox-Johnston raced her in that year's Two-Handed Transatlantic Race, coming in fourth. His old rival, Chay Blyth with Rob James, won that race. Robin raced *Sea Falcon* again in the next Round Britain and

Ireland Race. For the 1985 race Race Knox-Johnston had a new 60-foot catamaran, called *British Airways I*. They came in fourth.

He then took a rest from short handed racing (it is interesting to note that until 2006 Robin never undertook any single-handed racing after his Golden Globe triumph – perhaps he had had enough of his own company). In 1992 he and the well known New Zealand yachtsman, Peter Blake, acquired the 85-foot Nigel Irens designed catamaran *Formula Tag*. Re-named *Enza* the two, with an experienced crew, attempted in 1993 to beat a time of eighty days to sail round the world trying to win the Jules Verne Trophy. They withdrew that year after hitting something in the Southern Ocean which seriously damaged their boat. They set off the next year and returned successfully in seventy-four days and twenty-two hours. They were the first to win the Trophy.

Robin was knighted in 1995 for services to yachting. The next year he set up Clipper Ventures allowing amateur crews in identical yachts with a professional skipper to race around the world west about through the Panama Canal, across the Pacific and then home via the Cape of Good Hope. Eight boats took part in the first race which was a great success. These races continue to this day.

In the late 1990s Knox-Johnston's life savings were wiped out by the financial disaster at the Lloyd's insurance market where he was a 'Name'. He then had what he described as five miserable years trying to pay off his debts. He suffered further tragedy when his wife, Sue, died of cancer in 2003. Sue was the childhood friend who he had first married when they went to Bombay. They fell out over the building of *Suhaili* and were divorced, getting re-married in 1972.

To try to get over his loss he decided to enter the 2006 Velux Five Oceans Race – a race owned and organised by his own company Clipper Ventures. He acquired the Open 60 *Fila* which had won the 1998 Alone Around Race. He was sixty-eight and renamed the boat, first, *Grey Power* and then *Saga Insurance,* after Saga agreed to sponsor him. This was a remarkable race for him as he was bridging the gap between the old guard of traditional sailors and the new young generation in their 'Formula One' machines - a bit like comparing a bi-plane with Concorde. He did not really enjoy the experience and was baffled by all the modern electronics (many of which failed to work) making the chart table look like the flight deck of a jet aeroplane. Neither did he take to the vibration and noise generated by the carbon fibre hull as the boat crashed through the waves reaching speeds of twenty-plus knots. However Robin put up a magnificent effort and he came in fourth out of seven starters.

In 1997 *Suhaili* was put on show at the National Maritime Museum at Greenwich and remained there until 2002. Robin removed her as the dry atmosphere of the museum was shrinking her planking and he was not prepared to see her end her days that way. He refitted her for sailing again and in 2016 completed another major refit in which he renewed all the boats fastenings, most done by him personally. Whilst he was working on her an ignorant passing yachtsman looked at Robin and then at the boat and shaking his head said 'she's not worth it, mate'. Little did he know he was looking at probably the most famous sailing boat in the world. *Suhaili* is now sailing the waters of the Solent, probably in better condition than ever in her long and much travelled life. Robin is now eighty and continues to sail and keep us amused by his writings and articles in the yachting press. He is one of the most kind, generous and likeable of men and must truly take his place as one of the greatest (if not the greatest) in the yachting hall of fame.

Chapter 14
Bernard Moitessier – Nearly twice non-stop

A French vagabond philosopher, Bernard Moitessier was never content except when he was at, on or near the sea, where he spent virtually the whole of his extraordinary life. Always controversial, sometimes contrary and unpredictable, Moitessier wrote some very fine books (and some strange ones) who became a hero to many, especially in France. He espoused many good causes, often in vain, and tried to live a simple life taking care of the environment. Whilst he lost three boats, he was a fine seaman who undertook many exceptional voyages, usually alone. He had a muddled personal life and did not always behave well to his wife but he lived life to the full. As we shall see, not all of his writings are to be believed.

Early years

He was born next to the sea in French Indo-China in 1925. As soon as the Second World War was over, and after a year's military service, he joined the crews of junks which were then still trading under sail in the waters around Vietnam and Cambodia. Then in 1952 he bought a dilapidated junk which he called *Marie-Therese*, named after his first love. He set off alone to sail her back to Europe. The first leg of the voyage took him to Singapore. There he was persuaded to make for the Seychelles where he was told he would find work. As soon as he cleared the Strait of Malacca he was faced with beating into a strong south-west monsoon. It was very slow progress. After forty days he could still see the mountains of Sumatra behind him. Eventually he was far enough south to turn west. He had no idea of his longitude as his only clock had stopped many days before hand. So he used the old sailors trick of running down the latitude to your destination. Moitessier did this along a latitude of 8° South taking a noon latitude sun sight every day. He knew that along this parallel lay the Chagos Archipelago but he had no idea whether he was a hundred miles away, or three hundred. Or fifty. Thinking he knew his latitude Moitessier aimed *Marie Therese* to sail through a thirty mile channel with Diego Garcia to the south and some small islands to the north. But it didn't work out like that. One night in the darkness, after eighty-five days at sea, *Marie Therese* ran into a reef off Diego Garcia and was wrecked. Moitessier swam and scrambled ashore to watch his yacht being torn apart on the reef.

Diego Garcia is a military area on which landing is prohibited. Moitessier was arrested and deported to Mauritius, where he landed penniless with all his possessions lost. For three years he worked ashore and built a new boat – *Marie Therese II*. She was a double-ender not unlike his first boat and he rigged her as a gaff ketch. Moitessier sailed her alone to Durban in South Africa, where he stopped and worked for a year as a shipwright. Then he set off for the Caribbean via St Helena. He arrived at Trinidad and left from there for St. Lucia. He was exhausted after his long voyage and once again he ran his ship ashore and watched as breakers smashed *Marie Therese II* to pieces on some rocks. He was taken back to Trinidad where he shipped to France as an ordinary seaman on a tanker.

Penniless in Paris, he found a job as a salesman for a pharmaceutical company. He wrote a book about his sailing experiences called *Sailing to the Reefs* and in 1958 married Françoise, who had three children from her first marriage. Her family had known the Moitessier family for two generations and had spent childhood holidays together. Before the marriage Moitessier fretted about losing his freedom but went ahead anyway. In reality he kept his freedom (not only to sail but to have affairs with different women, something Françoise knew about and accepted). Moitessier was a free spirit and, according to some, an uncontrollable anarchist. All of this may explain what happened later.

The couple set up home with her three children, initially in Paris from where they moved south to Marseilles. All the time Moitessier planned his next boat.

Joshua

Initially Moitessier conceived of a wooden cold-moulded hull which he would design and build himself. He bought all the wood he needed but, before he could start on the boat, the well known French naval architect Jean Knocker told Moitessier that he had read his book and would be pleased to design a new boat for him. Then, unbelievably, he received a six line letter from a Monsieur J Fricaud, who Moitessier had never heard of, in which he said '......I have read your book, come and see me. I think I can help.....'

M Fricaud had a large business in Chauffailles, a town in the middle of France just north of Lyons, making industrial boilers. In his factory there was a steel boat he had built some years before. Moitessier visited the factory and was impressed by the strength and quality of the boat. He later spent that summer sailing her with M Fricaud who told Moitessier he would build him a similar boat. All he had to do was to pay for the cost of the steel. It was a miracle for the Moitessiers.

They decided to build the boat to Jean Knocker's design. She was to be 39 ½ feet long, just under 34 feet on the waterline with a 12 foot beam and a draft of 5 feet and 3 inches. She was a fairly shallow draft double-ender with an outboard rudder and a short bowsprit. Moitessier insisted on a ketch rig. She had an exceptionally long keel, which made her slow to manoeuvre but very steady on the helm when under sail. They named the boat *Joshua,* after the legendary and great seaman Joshua Slocum, whose life and voyages were described earlier in this book.

Building started in the autumn and the hull was completed by the winter. This was transported to Lyons by road, launched into an icy River Saone and towed behind a barge down the River Rhone to Marseilles, where Moitessier fitted her out. He found a 58-foot-long telegraph pole which he fashioned into a main mast. A wooden mizzen mast, another telegraph pole impregnated with creosote, followed. The galvanised rigging was held together by bulldog type clamps (there was no time for splicing) and soon he was out sailing again, three years after he had lost *Marie Therese II* .

Joshua was one of the toughest and most capable boats around. She was simple, with little to go wrong and had few 'yottie' gadgets. Moitessier designed his own form of wind vane self-steering gear, which rarely let him down. She was rough down below but everything worked. For two years he ran her as a sailing school out of Marseilles, whilst Françoise worked in a local hospital. The couple dreamed of the Pacific and of making a voyage round the world. They decided to leave at the end of the 1963 sailing season.

The logical route

In October 1963 they set sail in *Joshua,* leaving Françoise's three children in a boarding school, promising them they would be back in time for the school holidays in three years time. They headed first for Casablanca, then to the Canaries and Trinidad and through the Panama Canal to the Galapagos Islands. After two years they arrived in Tahiti. They had dawdled on the way, relishing the simple life of the Pacific, and now had only eight months until the day they had promised their children they would return. Rather than sail home by the conventional route via the Indian Ocean and the Suez Canal, Moitessier decided to sail the fastest, and most dangerous, route eastabout round Cape Horn – the 'logical route' as he called it – and to do it non-stop. No one had attempted such a long passage before.

They sailed from Moorea on 23 November 1965 heading south for the Roaring Forties, where they could expect to meet favourable westerly winds to blow them home. They reached 40° South on 10 December and immediately met their wind, but there was more of it than they had hoped for. For the next six days they faced the worst gale Moitessier had ever experienced. He streamed warps and iron weights, the favoured tactic, to help keep the boat's stern on to the oncoming seas. Moitessier and Françoise huddled below taking turns in steering from the interior wheel, keeping a look out via the small windows in a circular dome. But as the wind and sea increased *Joshua* was frequently buried by breaking waves and became almost impossible to steer. She continually broached and lay broadside onto the waves, a very dangerous position. Moitessier could no longer hold her stern up. *Joshua* was becoming overwhelmed and Moitessier thought he would have to head north toward the Panama Canal if they were to survive.

Then he thought of Vito Dumas and *Lehg II* who, as we saw in chapter 7, had been here before (and in mid winter too). Moitessier wondered how Dumas had done it, doubting if he had experienced a storm like this one. What was his secret? Dumas claimed he had crowded on sail, keeping it up, and running before the wind in all weather, crossing all three southern oceans single-handed in a wooden boat half the size of *Joshua*. In Moitessier's account of the voyage he describes how, whilst struggling to keep *Joshua* on course, he asked Françoise to read from Dumas's book. She read out: *'the staysail was strong. It was left up from beginning to end'* and: *'whenever the wind strengthened I left sail up and had the boat planing on the waves at a speed exceeding fifteen knots for short moments... it is an impressive experience but one gets used to it.... with the boat moving at the same speed as the wave, the wave is no longer dangerous.'*

Moitessier pondered on this and he then recounts how a wave approached at an angle of ten degrees which picked up *Joshua* heeling her over a little and throwing her forward at a fantastic speed, despite all the warps, without burying her bow. She planed for about thirty yards whilst the wave passed safely under her. Moitessier, who always believed he could communicate with his boat, claimed he heard her say *'Look, I'll show you'* as she took off on the wave. Taking a knife and handing Françoise the helm, he went on deck and with a few blows cut free all the warps and hawsers. Below again he resumed his position at the wheel and noticed an immediate change. As each wave came up at an angle of fifteen to twenty degrees *Joshua* heeled over, took off at high speed and the wave passed under her harmlessly. Now Moitessier could easily steer and keep the stern up to the wind. Had he continued as before he is convinced that sooner or later *Joshua* would have dug her nose into a breaking sea, pitch poled and lost her masts.

For six days Moitessier and Françoise steered *Joshua* like this. On 19 December they hoisted a small jib, re-connected the self steering vane and slept. By Christmas day they had 2,200 miles to go to Cape Horn. It was now mid summer in the southern hemisphere and they had a run of reasonable weather and the nights were short. At seven o'clock in the evening of 10 January 1966, with a fair following wind they sighted the island of Diego Ramirez, a perfect landfall. The next day in a rising gale they passed Cape Horn, some thirty miles away to their north. Moitessier wrote that he felt the presence of Alfon Hansen, who had passed Cape Horn in the other direction thirty years before and was then lost, driven ashore on the rocks of the Chilean coast 1,000 miles to the north (see chapter 6). He also thought of his fellow Frenchman, Marcel Bardiaux, who had also passed the other way in his tiny *Les 4 Vents* beating into icy spray in the endless night of the southern winter (see chapter 8). It was forty-nine days since they had left Tahiti and they had sailed 5,650 miles, an average run of 115 miles a day, all without any damage. They had to get a move on if they wanted to reach France in time for the children's Easter holidays.

A gale drove them far to the east of Staten Island and then a north-east gale forced them to the west of the Falklands. They reached better weather at 50° N in the middle of January. On 22 February they crossed the Equator. By the end of February they were beating into a north-east trade wind heading for a spot 2,000 miles away to the west of the Azores, where they should pick up the westerlies to take them straight to Gibraltar, which they passed on 25 March.

They arrived at Alicante on 29 March 1966, 126 days and 14,216 miles from Moorea. It was the longest non-stop passage that had ever been made by a yacht. It put Moitessier into the record books and had made a real seaman of him.

The long way

On her return *Joshua* went back to being a sailing school for a couple of years whilst Moitessier wrote his book of their Tahiti-Alicante trip. The book was a major success, winning a literary award. Moitessier pondered what to do next and became fascinated with the idea of a new even longer voyage, and a new book. This was to be a solo round the world voyage, from France to France, south of all the major capes and without stopping. He would be the first man to achieve this and he decided he would do the whole thing entirely on his own, at a time of his own choosing and without being beholden to anyone. What could be more fitting for a man of Moitessier's vision and ability.

His Tahiti-Alicante passage had shown him what was needed to make *Joshua* into *'a superb travelling companion'* and he worked through the winter and early spring of 1968 to achieve this. He added a second bobstay to strengthen the bowsprit, welded on a sturdy bow pulpit, fixed ladder rungs up the masts so he could more easily climb them. He replaced the rigging with stainless steel wire and added four heavy duty sheet winches and two winches on the boom to aid reefing. He had a new suit of sails made. By early April he was ready and once summer arrived he would take her to Gibraltar where he would wait *'listening to the song of the wind where the sky and stars would tell me when the moment had come to set out'*

Moitessier went to Paris and signed a contract for a book to be written about the voyage. He received a substantial advance and the publishers agreed to pay Françoise a stipend for ten months. In Paris he asked the French Ministry of Youth and Sport for their support. They agreed on the spot to have the French Navy yard at Toulon haul *Joshua* out free of charge and to give him all the charts he needed plus stores and gear. They supplied him with French Navy cold-weather clothing. (Imagine asking the British Royal Navy for such help. One would get a very frigid reply).

Then, as happens to the best laid plans, something intervened and interrupted Moitessier's preparations and plans, for ever. One day in 1968 he was sitting in his favourite harbour side bistro when a man came up to him and said, in English, 'Are you Bernard?' The man explained that he was from the *Sunday Times* and wanted to talk about an interesting project. The newspaper, he said, wanted to organize a race between Moitessier and Bill King who was also, unknown to Moitessier, preparing to sail round the world alone and non-stop. The paper hoped some other sailors might join in – the more the merrier. The rules were simple – anyone leaving from a port in Great Britain between 1 June and 31 October of that year would be automatically entered and all they had to do was to return to their starting point having sailed south of all three southern Capes without stopping. There were to be two big prizes - £5,000 for the fastest passage and a splendid trophy (a Golden Globe) for the first to return. It would make, he said, the *Sunday Times* very happy if Moitessier would come to England to start his voyage from there. The man was Murray Sayle, a well known Australian journalist, who then sat back expecting Moitessier to jump up with excitement.

Instead Moitessier sat in silence for a while and then said *'Your proposal makes me want to vomit.'* Moitessier later wrote: *' such a journey, beyond time and right to our very limits, with so little chance of success, belonged to a sacred domain where the spirit of the sea had to be respected above all else. We didn't have the right to muck about in such a beautiful story with our grimy fingers, to turn it into a circus where a bunch of clowns would set out to beat each other for money and a gold globe while the media pounded the drums.'*

Murray Sayle remained rooted to the spot, thunderstruck by Moitessier's reaction to this brilliant idea thought up by the paper's high profile editor, Harold Evans. Moitessier got up making to leave, boiling with rage. Sayle kept on trying to persuade Moitessier to start from England – 'that's all you have to do', he said. He reminded Moitessier that all the publicity was in England, that his Tahiti-Alicante trip was the catalyst, that Chichester had sailed round with one stop, as had Alec Rose, and now there were up to six boats being readied to sail non-stop. Moitessier stormed out of the bistro.

A few weeks later, out of the blue, Sayle received a letter from Moitessier which said: *' I am leaving Toulon to sail to Plymouth. I've decided to start from England, it suits me in every point of view. Each of us will run the race he wants to. I'll run my race on my terms. Suppose the gods grant that I return the first one home and the fastest. In that case I will snatch the check without saying thank you, coolly auction off the Golden Globe and leave without a word for the Sunday Times. That way I'll be making a public statement of the contempt I feel for your paper's project.'*

Sayle was now able to proudly announce to the *Sunday Times* that he had 'recruited' Moitessier to join the race. It was only later that Moitessier admitted that his decision to sail from Plymouth was actually a blessing in disguise. It suited him well and had nothing to do with the race. Whilst he knew *Joshua* was ready for the challenge ahead, a shakedown cruise from Toulon to Plymouth, across the Bay of Biscay, would be a good test of the boat and would show up any problems. In his book, Moitessier mused that *'this crazy race would take place whether I liked it or not. So if I could take the Sunday Times money without compromising myself, it would be a nice tankful of fuel to help me reach my beloved escape velocity...'* Also Moitessier was flat broke.

In Plymouth Moitessier met up with some of the other competitors and they all became friends. Among them was Bill King on *Galway Blazer II* (who also hated the idea of the race) and Nigel Tetley on his trimaran *Victress* (see the next chapter). Moitessier was by far the most experienced sailor and had the best prepared boat. He was the favourite to win and was considered the one most likely to make it all the way round and to beat Knox-Johnston in *Suhaili*.

Moitessier left Plymouth on 22 August 1968, just over two months after Knox-Johnston. *Joshua* was a bigger and faster boat and should have no problem in getting home first. Françoise was there to see him off, holding back her tears with Moitessier just wanting to be left alone with his boat and the sea. '*What's eight or nine months in a lifetime*' he said to her.

Joshua's odyssey is well told in the book Moitessier wrote following his voyage, *The Long Way*, and we won't repeat the details of the first part of the voyage here. Suffice to say he made good progress all the way down the Atlantic and only got into problems when near or approaching land. He soon settled into the rhythm of the voyage, developing an almost mystical relationship with his ship and the sea. Moitessier wrote '...*we were where body and mind join in a kind of sacred union. Joshua was the flesh, I her consciousness and each became the extension of the other..*'

Fifty-nine days after leaving Plymouth he was forty miles SW of Cape Agulhas, the extreme tip of South Africa. He decided to head for land to find a ship or boat to hand over some bags of film. He headed for Walker Bay on the coast between Cape Agulhas and the Cape of Good Hope. What happened next nearly ended *Joshua's* voyage. As he neared Walker Bay he came upon an old black rusty freighter making slow progress of about eight knots. It came up too close to *Joshua*. Moitessier used his slingshot (at which he was an expert) to fire across some film canisters. The first one landed on the foredeck but no one understood what he was doing. As the ship's bridge passed by Moitessier made it clear he had a message to pass across. The captain acknowledged and, in an effort to help, swung the ship's stern in toward *Joshua*. Moitessier tossed a package across and *Joshua* began to pull clear. But by a hair's breadth the ship's stern snagged the mainmast. The main shroud pulled loose, as did the upper spreader. This all caused *Joshua* to luff up toward the freighter, hitting her with the bowsprit, which twisted some twenty-five degrees to port. Moitessier was sure this would put an end to his 'beautiful trip' and he was convinced he would have to put in to Cape Town for repairs.

Within hours he had replaced the shroud and he could not see any damage to the mast itself, He blessed the strength of his telegraph pole. However there remained the problem of the bowsprit. He could continue under much reduced canvas with the forestay attached directly to the stemhead. The bowsprit was seven feet long made of three inch steel pipe reinforced by a second pipe inside. A few days later Moitessier set up a block and tackle led back to a sheet winch and using a spare mizzen boom to increase the angle, slowly winched the bowsprit back into position. He re-set the chain bobstay, shortening it by two links, the chain having stretched in the collision, and set sail.

A week before Christmas, Moitessier reached Tasmania and once again closed with the land to get some film and photos ashore. He reached the mouth of the Entrecasteaux Channel where he found a small cove. There he anchored a plastic container with the word 'Message' on it. Inside he had put a letter with his film asking the finder to take it all to the Commodore of the Hobart Yacht Club.

As he approached New Zealand he entered an area of dangerous reefs, off lying islands and rocks and was uncertain of his position. On 27 December in a steady west wind he saw land to his north and thought he was well clear of the southern tip of New Zealand. Then, whilst below, Moitessier heard the familiar whistlings of porpoises alongside and he went up on deck. The water around him was white with their splashing and he saw up to a hundred of them. A straight line of about twenty-five porpoises swam abreast past *Joshua* and as they reached the bow they all, as of one, veered off at right angles and headed south. They did this again and again, up to ten times or more. Moitessier sensed they were trying to tell him something and he felt their nervousness. He tore himself away from the spectacle, looked at his compass and saw he was heading due north, straight toward Stewart Island. Unnoticed by him the wind had backed to the south and he was now driving straight for land. He altered course to the east and the porpoises now calmly swam alongside keeping pace with *Joshua*. One jumped ten or twelve feet in the air in a giant somersault as if he was saying to Moitessier and the other porpoises 'the man understood we were telling him to sail to the right....keep on like that and you will be fine'. The porpoises stayed with him for over two hours as he drew safely away from land. Next destination was Cape Horn.

The weather was exceptionally kind to Moitessier as he traversed the Southern Ocean, despite the occasional gale which *Joshua* took in her stride. He averaged 120 miles per day across the Pacific. In the tail end of a full gale, Moitessier passed Cape Horn during the night of 5 February 1969 some ten miles to its south. The Horn was visible to Moitessier lit by a bright full moon. He mused mystically in his log and wrote: *'I wonder. Plymouth so close, barely 10,000 miles to the north... but leaving from Plymouth and returning to Plymouth now seems like leaving from nowhere to go nowhere.'*

Moitessier continued north toward the Falkland Islands musing all the time on the pointlessness of returning to his point of departure. It would, he thought, mean accepting all the false values of the north and would wipe out everything he held most dear. He dreamed of the Pacific once more and dreaded the thought of the crowds waiting in Europe to welcome him, of the microphones and TV cameras, of the glory, frenzy and money. He turned from home and headed north-east for South Africa once again.

Off Cape Town for the second time, on 18 March he catapulted a message, addressed to the *Sunday Times,* onto a passing tanker's deck. It read: '....*I am continuing non-stop toward the Pacific islands because I am happy at sea, and perhaps also to save my soul.*'

Moitessier wrote in his log a quotation he well remembered: '*There are two terrible things for a man: not to have fulfilled his dream, and to have fulfilled it.*' He headed off east and was now quite on his own sailing, once more, toward the Pacific as fast as he could to avoid the winter winds which would blow strongly across the Indian Ocean. He passed to the south of Tasmania on 5 May and to the south of New Zealand on 12 May. He was now definitely in the southern winter and he faced a series of gales, several from the north and north-west. He suffered a series of knock downs and broken gear. He and his boat were tired but they sailed on and on 27 May 1969 he sailed out of the Roaring Forties. He had been in them since he entered on 27 October 1968, south of Cape Town the first time, a period of 218 days, having sailed the part between Cape Town and New Zealand twice.

Moitessier kept going. He headed north-east, seemingly uncertain of a destination. He had written about making for the Galapagos Islands but on 7 June he altered course to the north-west and headed for Tahiti, the near mythical destination for south sea sailors seeking rest and the seductive comforts of the land. He moored up to the town quay at Papeete on 21 June 1969, having left Plymouth on 22 August 1968 - he had been sailing non-stop for 303 days, around ten months. He felt he had come home.

Just four weeks after Moitessier's arrival in Tahiti, the Apollo 11 mission landed the first men on the moon. The Lunar Module touched down in the Sea of Tranquillity on 20 July 1969 and Armstrong and Aldrin walked on the surface of the moon for the first time. The significance of the choice of a moon landing place coming at virtually the same time as Moitessier's own 'landing' in the peaceful (or tranquil) Pacific will not have been lost on him; he would have believed there was some mystical purpose to such a coincidence.

After the voyage

Moitessier spent the next two years in Tahiti writing his book, which he titled *The Long Way*. He agonised for many months about the royalties he would earn from it and whether he should accept them. Finally, as a gesture against what he saw as the west's materialism he detested, he instructed his publishers to pay all his royalties to the Pope and to Friends of the Earth.

Papeete was not much to his liking any more. The many palm trees lining the town quay had been bulldozed to make way for a multi-lane highway. But it was still a meeting place for the many sea vagabonds and nomads, whose yachts lined the quay and over which, much to his liking, there hung a haze of marijuana smoke.

Françoise visited Moitessier on several occasions but their relationship had broken down and she soon returned to France. Just before he finished his book he met Ileana, an unattached hippie and traveller, who arrived off a ship one day with nothing but a suitcase in her hand. She rented a run-down thatched-roof hut facing the lagoon and Moitessier settled in with her. Soon she was pregnant with twins. One survived, a boy they named Stephan.

From 1969 until 1982, Moitessier, sometimes alone and sometimes with Ileana and Stephan, roamed the Pacific on *Joshua* visiting New Zealand, the Tuamotus, Suvorov, Ahe (where they lived for three years growing coconuts) and Moorea, finally visiting San Francisco and Mexico.

In 1982, Moitessier, to make some money, set off with the mercurial Hollywood actor Klaus Kinski on board *Joshua*. Kinski dreamed of sailing around the world and had paid Moitessier to take him sailing for a week to be taught by the master himself. They headed south to Mexico and stopped in the natural harbour at Cabo San Lucas at the southern end of the Bajaifornia peninsula, where Kinski was going to leave and head back to Hollywood. The harbour was sheltered but open to the east and the south. On the morning of the third day Moitessier, strangely for him, ignored warning signs of an impending gale, including an unusual swell running into the harbour. Bad weather was extremely rare at that time of year. It was December but Moitessier was aware that severe storms had hit the harbour only twice in the last one-hundred years. *Joshua* remained at anchor.

That night a hurricane struck. Twenty-five yachts were destroyed and the beach became a graveyard of boats pounded to pieces by enormous seas. *Joshua* was one of those driven ashore. She lost her masts, her rudder stock was broken, stanchions were flattened, hatches and pulpits ripped off, portholes shattered and the whole boat filled with sand and gravel. It took Moitessier and six helpers two days to recover gear and equipment buried in the sand. The hull was battered and bent in places but remained in one piece. After a week of unrelenting effort, emptying the boat of sand, they managed to refloat her.

Moitessier was now aged fifty-eight and, not for the first time, penniless facing the prospect of re-building a beached and wrecked boat. He admitted he had neither the money (a US$ 5,000 salvage fee was demanded by the harbour authorities) nor the strength to salvage his beloved boat. He decided to give her to two young Mexicans, Joe and Reto, who had helped with her rescue. He wanted to make a gift of her but the Port Official refused to register a gift, so Moitessier, much against his will (he felt he was selling his soul) agreed to sell her for US$ 20.

Soon after the hurricane, and the grounding, Moitessier wrote in the American sailing magazine '*Cruising World*' a long and detailed account of what had happened that night, stating how he and Kinski had spent the night aboard trying to save the boat. He described how his fifty-five pound CQR anchor started dragging, how he set a second anchor, how *Joshua* started to drag again until they were on the beach, with seas breaking over the deck. He described how he and Kinski had a heated argument with Kinski refusing to leave the boat. Eventually the actor went ashore leaving Moitessier on board. He described what it was like as the masts were torn out of her and how other boats piled into her, etc.,etc. This account appeared in Moitessier's own book, *Tamata and the Alliance,* and in Jean-Michel Barrault's biography of the great sailor, *Moitessier: A Sailing Legend* published in 2004.

But, according to Herb McCormick, then editor of the American yachting magazine, *Cruising World* this was all 'total bullshit'. A very different version of what happened had been told to the famous sailing couple Lin and Larry Pardey, who visited Cabo San Lucas for the US magazine *SAIL* immediately after the incident. The Pardeys say that Moitessier instantly confessed that he and Kinski had not spent the night on board but had actually been holed up in Kinski's hotel bedroom getting stoned out of their minds on a load of highly potent Mexican marijuana, probably along with some female company. All this at the time that Moitessier's boat, which he loved *'with all my soul and with every fibre of my body',* was left alone and untended to be driven ashore and wrecked. *'I was a stupid monkey',* Moitessier said to the Pardeys, *'I lost my seaman's values when I stepped ashore.*' At first Moitessier urged the Pardeys to share this true story with readers of *SAIL* (so the world could see what an idiot he had been) but he later changed his mind and gave them the fictional story which has ever since then been the accepted version.

There can be no doubt that Kinski, a strange notoriously unstable Hollywood svengali, was a malign influence on Moitessier, leading him, probably for the first time in his life, to ignore warning signs of coming bad weather and then to abandon his boat.

After this episode one wonders how much one can really rely on the truth of what Moitessier wrote in his many books and magazine articles.

Whatever happened that fateful night, *Joshua* was refitted by its two new young Mexican owners and sailed away. Some years later she was found abandoned near Port Townsend in Washington State in the north-west of the USA. She was rescued by the French and taken back to La Rochelle in Brittany where she was again refitted. She is now maintained by the La Rochelle Maritime Museum. She is sailing today, still painted Moitessier's bright red and is to take part in the 50th anniversary re-run of the Golden Globe race starting from France in July 2018.

After *Joshua* had sailed off, leaving Moitessier stranded, friends came to his rescue, not for the first time. They rallied round and clubbed together to pay for the building of a new boat for him. A 36-foot steel yacht was built in a boatyard on San Francisco Bay. She was called *Tamata* and more friends gathered together the necessary gear and equipment. During this period Moitessier wrote 600 letters to 600 USA publications demanding nuclear de-escalation. In 1984 he sailed his new boat to Tahiti, met a French lady, Veronique, with whom he returned to France in 1985. There he spent the next seven years writing his autobiography *Tamata and the Alliance,* a strange book detailing and explaining his life, but also full of lots of home spun philosophy and musings on life, the universe and everything.

Moitessier never went back to his beloved Pacific and it is not known what happened to *Tamata.* In the early 1990s he was diagnosed with prostate cancer and he died in June 1994. He is buried in a small town in Brittany, amongst sailors and fishermen.

Chapter 15
Nigel Tetley – The first trimaran

Nigel Tetley was born in South Africa in 1924 and later joined the British Royal Navy. By March 1968 he was every inch the ideal of a career English naval officer; tall, well spoken, supremely confident, always smart and well dressed with well cut short hair. He had, seemingly with ease, reached the rank of Lieutenant-Commander. Two years earlier he had married a pretty blonde, Eve, who had two boys by an earlier marriage.

In 1967 they were living *en famille* on board a 41-foot trimaran called *Victress,* moored alongside the wall in Millbay Dock, then a somewhat malodorous and dusty commercial dock in the centre of Plymouth, surrounded by dilapidated warehouses and much accumulated industrial waste and litter. It had none of the facilities a yachtsman of today would demand but it was a cheap place to live. Naval officers were not well paid in those days.

One Sunday in March of that year Eve returned from a visit ashore with the Sunday papers. Tetley spotted a headline on the front page of the *Sunday Times.* 'Round the World Race', it said. Tetley read the announcement of the Golden Globe Non-Stop Round-the-World Race. He wrote later how excitement surged down his body. He pushed the open page toward Eve and, after she had read it, said *'May I go?'*. Eve replied that she would not try to stop him.

Tetley then did what everyone else contemplating the same voyage did – tried to find a sponsor to pay for a new boat. In this Tetley, like nearly everyone else at that time, was totally unsuccessful. So Tetley did what nearly everyone else had to do – make do with what he had and go in his own boat.

The boat

Victress had been built in the winter of 1962 at Great Yarmouth and was one of a number of Victress class trimarans built by Cox Marine to an Arthur Piver design. Donald Crowhurst's boat *Teignmouth Electron,* which later played a large and tragic part in the end of Tetley's adventure, was built to the same design but without the large coachroof and wheelhouse.

Arthur Piver was an American airline pilot and an amateur yacht designer. He was a pioneer in the design of trimarans. Virtually single-handed he started the multihull movement in the USA. His designs, which look decidedly odd to today's eyes, were narrow, heavy, with 'V' shaped hulls and were principally designed for home building out of plywood. They were very definitely cruising boats – 'caravans of the sea' as Crowhurst described them. They became very popular and many were built all over the world. All this despite the bad publicity which followed Piver's loss at sea on one of his own designs – he was undertaking a qualifying cruise for the 1968 *Observer* Single- Handed Transatlantic Race. He and his boat disappeared without trace in the Pacific.

The Victress class boats, one of the largest of Piver's designs, were comfortable floating homes taking full advantage of the trimaran's configuration. They had a large main cabin and a raised enclosed wheelhouse and their main attraction over a single hulled yacht was that they sailed upright and, provided weight was kept down, sailed faster. They were 40 feet long, 22 feet wide and drew a mere 33 inches. They carried a very inefficient ketch rig and were built out of glass-fibre sheathed plywood with a large plywood bridge deck connecting the three hulls. In reality they were totally unsuitable for ocean sailing or for racing round the world.

In the first few years of his ownership Tetley cruised *Victress* to Sweden, Denmark and Holland. In 1966 he took her in for the first Two Handed Round Britain and Ireland Race. Despite breaking her rudder twice in the North Sea, Tetley completed the race in sixth place (out of 16 starters) in a creditable time of twenty-five days. In the same year he married Eve and *Victress* became their home.

To make *Victress* suitable for singlehanded sailing, Tetley equipped her with twin poled out headsails which when linked to the rudder steered the boat downwind. For upwind work he installed a self steering system of twin wind vanes, one on the stern of each float, linked to a separate rudder on the main hull, These arrangements worked amazingly well, helped by the fact that *Victress* never sailed very fast. He strengthened the rigging of the main mast by adding additional shrouds and chain plates (unlike Sir Alec Rose who minimised the rigging on *Lively Lady* with near disastrous consequences – see chapter 12). Tetley was obviously aware of the biggest risk in taking a multihull into the Southern Ocean – the risk of a capsize. However he said in his book that he considered her slowness by multihull standards might actually be an asset as the risk of capsize increases with speed. (This is not strictly correct as the risk of being flipped over by a rogue wave is still there even when a boat is stationary). Surprisingly, Tetley took no steps to strengthen his boat in vulnerable areas or to seal the decks of the floats. They each had two large opening hatches which gave access to where Tetley, perhaps unwisely, stored lots of heavy gear and spares, including a large fuel tank and spare fuel cans in the starboard float and several gas bottles in the port one. This was hardly conducive to aiding the buoyancy of the floats, so necessary to keep the boat upright.

At the last minute a music company, Music for Pleasure, heard about Tetley's entry in the race and decided to offer him some sponsorship money (helped no doubt by the *Sunday Times* writing an article about him headed 'Around the World in 80 Symphonies' following a visit from a journalist to whom Tetley demonstrated *Victress's* stereo system). Tetley now had enough money to complete the repairs and alterations he wanted to make and to pay for the self steering gear. He was now nearly ready to go.

Tetley's voyage

One day in 1968, as his preparations were nearing completion, the lock gate in Millbay opened and a weather beaten red-painted steel ketch entered the dock. Tetley thought she had 'the unmistakable stamp of the sea' about her. This was *Joshua* and Bernard Moitessier. A little later two other competitors in the race arrived – Moitessier's friend Louick Fougeron in his *Capitaine Browne* and Bill King in a new and specially constructed junk rigged schooner *Galway Blazer II* (built mainly out of King's own pocket with some help from the *Daily Express,* she was one of the boats which did not complete the race). These four skippers soon became firm friends. Throughout Moitessier's long voyage he continually thought about the other three and anguished about their fate. On the few occasions when Moitessier spoke to passing ships, he always asked specifically for the whereabouts of Tetley and *Victress*. Moitessier and Tetley were an unlikely couple. The tall upright, tight lipped and correct Royal Navy officer against the wiry self-contained philosophizing vagabond of the sea, usually to be seen going around bare footed. However, they bonded with a shared sense of purpose.

Moitessier and Fougeron left together on 22 August 1968. The 'race' was now getting into full swing. Robin Knox-Johnston had left in Suhaili on 14 June and was supposed to be in the south Atlantic. John Ridgway and his fellow marine, Chay Blyth, had left some months before but had both retired – both were in quite unsuitable boats, as we have seen, and it was surprising they got as far as they did.

Tetley left on 16 September 1968. This left two further competitors to follow on behind – the Italian Alex Carrozzo and Donald Crowhurst - both of whom left on the last permitted day, 31 October. Neither were in any way ready to leave. Carrozo got over this by crossing a start line off Cowes in the Isle of Wight and then promptly anchoring within yards of the line, where he stayed for a week completing his preparations. He soon retired off the coast of Portugal suffering from a bleeding ulcer.

Crowhurst, despite being totally unprepared and in a dreadful mental state, left anyway, with only a few hours to spare, in his unfinished and chaotic near sister-ship to *Victress*. This led to disastrous consequences, not only for Crowhurst but also, as we shall see, for Tetley.

As for Tetley's voyage, it is hard to get a real feeling for it from reading his book or from other published accounts. In somewhat turgid prose and, no doubt in a manful attempt to please his sponsors, he writes much about the music he played (and the food he ate). Much of the book is little more than a catalogue of food dishes and the titles of the music discs he played, provided by Music for Pleasure. Tetley comes across as self-contained and unemotional but, as would be expected from a Royal Navy officer, very confident and competent when coping with the unexpected,.

By 22 October he had reached the Equator, which he crossed with barely a comment in his log and without major incident (except nearly losing his mast when a spreader broke free breaking one of his jib poling-out spars and coping with a broken seacock which filled the bilges, nearly inundating the engine and sinking the boat). All he wrote was that a sun sight put him twenty-four miles south of the line and he belatedly opened a can of beer to toast Father Neptune.

Tetley's log at this stage is full of the usual descriptions of long lazy trade wind days, flying fish for breakfast and star studded nights making him think of the insignificance of man, etc. It contains barely a mention of the myriad problems he was experiencing with *Victress*.

By the end of November he was approaching the Cape of Good Hope, or as it used to be known, the Cape of Storms. Tetley admitted to feeling depressed with an almost overwhelming temptation to retire and head for Cape Town. This was not helped when, in one of the regular radio conversations he had with the *Times*, his contact expressed disappointment by Tetley's lack of any decent news. 'Haven't you fallen over the side or anything else exciting?' he was asked. He had 12,000 miles to go to Cape Horn.

He now entered the Roaring Forties and experienced his first storms. No one really knew how a trimaran would behave in really bad weather and Tetley experimented with differing tactics for dealing with it. At first he followed Moitessier's counsel to keep the boat going fast downwind by steering *Victress* to keep her stern onto the waves. This however was proving almost impossible and Tetley was concerned at the risk of pitchpoling. Then he tried heaving-to and he found that his boat, with its huge lateral stability, sat riding the waves safely like an albatross. This was the method he adopted for the rest of the voyage.

During all this time he was averaging one-hundred miles per day and had no idea of the progress of the other competitors save he heard on the radio that Loick Fougeron had retired at St Helena and that Moitessier had passed Tasmania. Knox-Johnston's position, or even if he was still afloat, was unknown.

Toward the end of December he passed close to the small islands of St Paul and Amsterdam deep in the Indian Ocean. Tetley experienced the usual mixture of light winds and gales but generally he appeared to have a relatively easy passage to Australia. In mid January, whilst south of Cape Leeuwin, he met his worst storm to date. It blew at Force 11, a near hurricane, and heavy seas continually broke aboard *Victress* causing much damage but the ship remained buoyant, seeming to elude the massive breaking crests. On 26 January Tetley reached the half way point, 132 days out from Plymouth having travelled 14,250 miles.

He passed safely through the Bass Strait, between Tasmania and Australia,and headed to pass south of New Zealand. As he closed with land he made for Dunedin to try to make a rendezvous and pass over mail and photographs. He saw no vessels there so made for Otago Harbour, 10 miles further on. (This was the same harbour which Knox-Johnston had entered on *Suhaili* some months before and where he went aground.) Tetley met with a small launch and passed over his package. It was now 3 February and Tetley headed out to sea for the Southern Ocean and Cape Horn. Tetley next remarked in his log that Sunday, 8 February was his forty-fifth birthday and the official date for his retirement from the Royal Navy.

He experienced generally good conditions, keeping to the north of 50° South. On 26 February 1969 a Force 9 gale sprang up and Tetley hove to. After the wind had moderated to a Force 7, Tetley got under way but a rogue wave on the quarter caused *Victress* to broach and she very nearly capsized. She heeled over to an angle of over 50° in a half cartwheel but then slowly righted herself. Tetley ruminated on the consequences of a capsize which he knew would in all probability have been fatal. He had hatched a half baked plan to try to right her, which involved flooding one hull and then trying to pull the boat upright from an inflated liferaft. He would of course have needed calm weather for this to work.

On 4 March, Tetley experienced the worst storm of the voyage. He was hove to, as usual, when a wave hit the side of the vessel and stove in one of the main cabin's six feet long windows. About a ton of water was sloshing around in the bilges and everything was soaked. with more water coming in as every wave hit the boat. Tetley boarded up the window and then bailed the boat dry with a bucket, the bilge pumps having become clogged with debris. During this period Tetley heard the sound of wood cracking below and a large piece of joinery had sprung away from the cabin side. Later he found that the deck edge of one of the floats had sprung, some frames had split and the cabin top had come away from the deck in several places . In despair, Tetley decided to head north to Valparaiso, retire from the race, put the trimaran up for sale and fly home.

On the day after the storm, Tetley turned the boat's head east once again, setting all sail, having decided to carry on with the race and repair the boat as best he could as he went along. He was turning out to be a very cool headed, courageous and determined competitor.

On 18 March he sighted the Il Defonso Islands, which lie close to the west of Cape Horn, and on the morning of 19 March 1969, Tetley sighted Cape Horn itself some fifteen miles to his north. 'Vicky, we've made it' he wrote in his log. He rounded in light weather and was becalmed when due south of the Cape. He wrote 'I cannot claim that the moment held any strong emotive connection. It was just another headland to round...'

Everyone rounding the Horn from west to east immediately feels that they are nearly home and that the worst is over. So it was with Tetley, although there were several months still to go, almost exactly two months in his case. He passed the Falkland Islands on 24 March and as he sailed north there occurred a moment, which had Tetley been a few miles off his actual course, could have altered the whole complexion of the race. It would have affected its outcome as well as the fate and future course of the lives of two competitors, Tetley being one of these. It would have changed everything.

What transpired was first noticed and pointed out by Chris Eakin in his book 'A Race Too Far'. What Eakin realised (and what had never been picked up before during all the years of the many retellings of the Golden Globe story) was that Tetley and Crowhurst came very close to colliding with each other.

After passing east of the Falklands, Tetley headed north-west. With all the space in the south Atlantic to sail in, Tetley was heading straight toward a bit of sea where Crowhurst (unbeknownst to the whole world) was also heading, coming in the opposite direction, on a course toward the Falkland Islands.

Crowhurst was not supposed to be anywhere near Tetley and not even supposed to be in the Atlantic at all. According to messages Crowhurst was broadcasting to the world he was in the south Pacific 'hurtling' toward Cape Horn which he expected to reach on 15 April. In fact, as we now know, he was lurking aimlessly in the south Atlantic waiting for his false position to catch up with his real position. Then he would 're-join' the race and head for home trying to catch Tetley. Had the two met, it would have been game up for Crowhurst.

The next day, when they were very close, Crowhurst suddenly made an inexplicable change of course. He turned hard to starboard and headed direct for Argentina (Eakin points out it had always been thought that Crowhurst changed course to avoid a storm but Tetley reported no bad weather, instead writing in his log that he had his first peaceful night for many weeks). Crowhurst stayed on this westerly course for two days and then resumed his course south to the Falklands. A few years after arriving home, Tetley spotted the coincidence and believed that Crowhurst had picked up Tetley's Morse transmissions which would have been loud and clear. Crowhurst would have been startled by the closeness of another vessel (and by working out that it was *Victress*) and so made this sudden and illogical change of course, to try to get out of the way. He must have had the fright of his life.

What would have happened if they had sighted each other? Crowhurst would have been exposed for the fraud he was. Tetley would have undoubtedly succeeded in nursing his failing and fragile ship home to England and in the process would have won the £5,000 prize for the fastest voyage. It is even conceivable that Tetley might have overtaken Knox-Johnston to reach home first, to take both prizes. Crowhurst would have sailed home in disgrace. What actually transpired had tragic consequences for both Tetley and Crowhurst.

When Tetley was five days further on, Crowhurst actually fell in behind him and headed north, planning to make a dramatic reappearance. Before that happened he made a series of radio messages (this was problematic as they were picked up by a Buenos Aires radio station when he was meant to be in the south Pacific but luckily no-one noticed) announcing to the world that he, Crowhurst, would round Cape Horn on 11 April. Tetley learnt of this and could see his lead disappearing unless he got a real move on.

Suddenly in the space of a few days, Tetley's chances changed dramatically. From believing Knox-Johnston and Crowhurst were missing and that he was in a great position to gain both prizes, he now had Crowhurst on his tail coming up fast. Not only that but he had learnt at about the same time that *Suhaili* and Knox-Johnston had been sighted off the Azores.

He knew he had to speed up and had to put his foot on the accelerator if he was to keep ahead of Crowhurst and beat *Suhaili*. The trouble was that *Victress* was breaking up. She was leaking badly and an inspection Tetley made of the boat revealed a myriad of problems, including broken frames and fastenings and de-laminating plywood. Tetley believed he could get her home but he would have to nurse her the whole way and avoid bad weather. Tetley did not know it but Crowhurst was breaking up mentally and was in no fit state to make it home or sail the boat so as to overtake him. Crowhurst's trimaran was also breaking up.

A few days later Tetley was approaching the point where he would cross his outward path to become the first man to circumnavigate the world in a trimaran. Fired up by this, Tetley piled on sail in a Force 6-7 wind. It was all too much for poor *Victress*. Tetley heard a splashing noise coming from forward. He went below and could see daylight where the port float should have been. The whole of the forepart of the port wing had disintegrated and the whole of the bow of the port float was breaking up. Tetley managed to patch things up sufficiently, he thought, to be able to make it back to Plymouth. He then did something quite extraordinary but which undoubtedly allowed him to continue. Instead of trying to keep the water out of the port float, he drilled holes in the bottom so as to let out the water which he could not stop from coming in!

On 22 April he achieved his circumnavigation - 20,500 miles in 179 days at an average speed of 114.5 miles per day. Not fast for a trimaran but much faster than *Suhaili*. Somehow Tetley managed to keep *Victress* sailing north and by mid May was approaching the Azores.

On 20 May Tetley who was 245 days out from Plymouth found himself in a rising gale as he aimed to pass through the Azores archipelago. The wind rose to Force 9 and as night fell he hove to and went to sleep. He was awoken at midnight by a scraping sound coming from forward - once again the bow of the port float had come adrift, this time totally and in so doing had holed the main hull. Water was coming in rapidly. Tetley went straight to the radio telephone and broadcast a May Day call. With water rising, he got his liferaft on deck and collected what he could. As he got into the liferaft he said '*Give over Vicky, I have to leave you.*'

As day broke Tetley sent out a message on an emergency radio transmitter but received no reply. Later he realised he had not set the aerial properly and, once he had, he received an immediate response. An hour later a

USAF Hercules rescue aircraft circled overhead. The nearest ship to Tetley was diverted and by five o'clock that evening a tanker was in sight, the *MV Pampero*, on charter to BP on its way to Trinidad. The ship came alongside the liferaft, a rescue ladder was lowered and Tetley scrambled up to safety.

After the voyage

On 10 July 1969, Clare Crowhurst was told by the Devon police that Donald Crowhurst's boat *Teignmouth Electron* had been found but the boat was empty and Donald was missing. This news was all over the press the next day. It was not until the 27th July, however, that details of Crowhurst's log books were published (which revealed his fraudulent voyage) when Tetley realised he had been racing a phantom and was being chased by a competitor who was not what he seemed.

The log books revealed that, after learning of Tetley's sinking, Crowhurst became aware of the supreme irony of it all and that the sinking of *Victress* had removed from him any way out of his dilemma. As the only remaining competitor, he could not but win the £5,000 prize and all the acclaim that would go with it. His fraudulent voyage would be discovered as soon as his log books were inspected, as he knew they would be. So Crowhurst took the only way out and, descending into madness, took his own life.

Outwardly, the apparently stiff upper lipped Tetley was stoic about what happened. He had become the first man to circumnavigate the world in a trimaran and had nearly beaten Knox-Johnston when he would have become as famous as Francis Chichester. But this had all been stolen from him by a liar and a cheat. It was a very sad end to a very substantial achievement.

Though back together, Tetley and Eve had lost their home and they had no money, save for his naval pension. The *Sunday Times* awarded him a £1,000 consolation prize (equivalent to £16,000 today) and hopeful of finding a sponsor, work started on a new 60-foot trimaran in Derek Kelsall's boatyard on the River Stour at Sandwich in Kent, to be called *Miss Vicky*. After the boat was launched, she was moored in the river and the Tetley's moved on board. There Tetley wrote his account of the voyage but it was a commercial failure and he received little recognition for what he had achieved. His was a very remarkable voyage but he never got the credit for it. He had not returned home in his own boat, so to many people he had failed. But it was only through Crowhurst's deceit that Tetley had failed. Tetley must have been affected by all this, which no doubt contributed to the tragedy which followed.

One Wednesday in February 1972, Tetley failed to come home. Someone said he had just received a letter from a potential sponsor turning him down. On the next Saturday, a sixteen-year-old school boy stumbled upon the body of Tetley hanging from a tree in some woods near Dover. There was immediate press coverage of his death and the national papers all reported on it, saying it appeared to have been suicide and that Tetley was depressed at his failure to get sponsorship for his new venture.

However, it was not that straightforward. No suicide note was ever found and there was something strange about the hanging. At an inquest held three weeks later it was revealed, for the first time, that Tetley had taken off some of his clothes and placed them at the foot of the tree. He had then put on some female underclothes, a white suspender belt and stockings and placed a corset round his head like a hood. He had tied his hands behind his back. A pathologist suggested that Tetley had died during some masochistic sexual episode.

It was an ignominious end to the life of a fine seaman and a total shock for his wife, Eve, who has never really recovered from it. Robin Knox-Johnston gave Eve all the help he could, including giving her a free mooring for *Miss Vicky* in his marina on the Hamble, but there was little anyone could do. Eve had to live with everyone saying 'Oh, poor Clare', referring to Crowhurst's widow. No-one ever said 'Oh, poor Eve.' She has now made a new home for herself on the island of Alderney in the Channel Islands.

Chapter 16
Chay Blyth – The first non-stop the 'wrong way'

Sir Chay Blyth's life and sailing exploits are almost too well known to be written about again but he was the last of the first eleven and his achievement in being the first man to sail non-stop alone around the world the 'wrong way' must be recorded for the achievement it was. It brings our story to an end and into the modern world, where improvements in technology and sail handling have totally transformed the 'Cape Horn experience'. After Blyth the flood gates opened wide and it is today almost impossible to keep up with the number of solo and other voyages in and around the waters of Cape Horn.

Before the voyage

Chay was born in 1940 and brought up in Hawick in Scotland. He had a happy home life and left school at sixteen to become an apprentice to a knitwear manufacturer. He soon decided that life in a factory was not for him and at eighteen he joined the Army, choosing to join the Parachute Regiment. He took to life as a 'para' like a duck to water. He enjoyed the discipline, the camaraderie and the hard physical endeavour involved. He soon became the youngest sergeant in his regiment.

Then, to test himself, he volunteered to join an officer in his Regiment, John Ridgway, in a row across the Atlantic from the USA to Great Britain. They succeeded in this triumphantly. Next Blyth, totally unprepared (he had absolutely no sailing experience whatsoever) and, in an entirely unsuitable boat, followed his former rowing partner in entering and setting off in the *Sunday Times* Golden Globe Non-Stop Round the World 'race'. Ridgway set out on 1 June 1968, and Chay left one week later in a small borrowed GRP bilge-keeled weekend family cruising yacht called *Dytiscus III*. Blyth had a bad time of it. He got lost, began to learn navigation, found his way to Madeira and beyond, crossed the Equator and then ran into a gigantic storm in the south Atlantic. His boat could not take it and began to broach uncontrollably. Blyth did not know what to do. He lowered all sails, hid below and prayed. He tried to read what some of his sailing manuals had to say. *'It was like being in hell with instructions'* he wrote later.

Bravely, he sailed on knowing that it was extremely unlikely that he would survive the Southern Ocean and the Roaring Forties. Having discovered that his supply of petrol for his battery charger had become contaminated with sea water, Blyth headed for the island of Tristan da Cunha where he was supplied with some fresh fuel. This was a clear breach of the race rules and Blyth knew it. Despite this, he carried on, now on his own terms. He struggled on to East London in South Africa where he was towed into port. He spent four days there (drinking and carousing with an old 'para' friend) awaiting spares for his self steering gear. Determined to continue he wrote: *'I wanted to see the thing through. It was my voyage of discovery and what I wanted to discover was me.'* Two days after he had left, he was faced with sixty knot winds and colossal seas, the biggest he had ever seen. He gave up and headed for land.

In reality, it was a remarkable performance from a complete novice. In three months of sailing, Knox-Johnston, the consummate seaman, who had left England six days after Blyth in a much larger and more seaworthy boat, had gained only four days on Blyth in his weekend cruiser.

This episode in Blyth's career demonstrated just what he was capable of. Once he had learned some seamanship and navigation, there would be no stopping him. It did not take Chay long to prove this to the world.

On his way home he began to think about what to do next. He toyed with two ideas - a canoe trip up the headwaters of the Amazon or a solo circumnavigation from east to west - the wrong way round against the prevailing winds. Back in England Chay settled on the latter and studied the problems likely to be met on such a voyage. He decided he needed a steel boat but he had no money to build or equip one. With a piece of luck, Chay met a public relations man, Terry Bond, who immediately hit on the solution - try to persuade the nationalised British Steel industry to build him a boat. This he did and Chay got his boat. This may make finding sponsorship sound easy, but as all who have tried to do this know (including the author) it is very far from it. Chay and Terry Bond had hit British Steel at just the right time in the evolution of the steel industry with just the right proposal.

Where did this idea to sail the wrong way round come from? According to Chay in his book of the voyage it came from his astute young wife, Maureen. She was helping Chay sail *Dytiscus III* back from South Africa when Chay complained the boat was a handful and almost impossible to keep on course when running downwind. *'Well then, why not sail around the world the other way?'* she said. This was an exceedingly perceptive thing to say for whilst sailing up wind for thousands of miles is a daunting prospect and very uncomfortable, it is actually easier on such a course to keep a boat under control and make it steer itself (a necessity for a singlehander). Running with the the wind astern is far harder for a singlehander, although quicker and more comfortable. It is interesting to note that in the years to come when Chay started the Challenge Business organising round the world races with amateur paying crews he routed the races from east to west rather than the traditional route from west to east - where following winds can be expected most of the time. In many ways this route made the race easier and safer for amateur sailors. Charging across the Roaring Forties surfing down breaking waves as big as double decker buses with spinnakers billowing is not stuff for amateur sailors!

The steel boat

In December 1969, with British Steel's money behind him, Blyth commissioned the well known yacht designer Robert Clark (he who had designed Chichester's *Gipsy Moth III and V*) to design him a yacht for this purpose. Clark produced a very attractive looking ketch 57 feet long with a beam of just under 13 feet and a draft of 8 feet. The yacht was not dissimilar to Francis Chichester's *Gipsy Moth IV*, but with none of her idiosyncrasies. She was to be named, of course, *British Steel*. Chay then started the hunt for a builder who could build her in double quick time as Chay wanted to start in the autumn of 1970. All the yacht builders he tried were full up and Chay came to realise there were only a few yards in the country who had any real experience of building a small steel yacht. It took until the middle of March for an old established boatyard in Dartmouth, Phillips & Sons, to confirm they could indeed build the yacht. Work started on 24 April 1970.

British Steel was launched on 19 August and readers who have been involved in building a boat or fitting one out for a long voyage will know the amount of work and time that has to go into such a project. Chay needed to leave by the end of October if he was to get round both Cape Horn and the Cape of Good Hope before the advent of the southern winter; he only just made it reaching the Cape of Good Hope in May, only two months before the southern mid-winter. Even with the boat launched in good time there was still an enormous amount to do. In the middle of September, Chay sailed the boat from Dartmouth to Southampton for final fitting out.

The impossible voyage

Chay and *British Steel* left the Hamble River near Southampton on Sunday 18 October 1970. He had learnt a lot since the last time he had sailed south down the Atlantic! He now had a well prepared and very suitable boat, he knew lots more about sailing than he did the first time and, although his navigation was still a bit shaky, he was at least able to work out roughly where he was.

On 29 October, he had a rendezvous off Madeira, where Blyth passed over films and his log. He crossed the Equator on 14 November having experienced fair weather most of the way. By the end of November he was off the coast of Argentina and began to experience real weather. It is always a difficult passage from then on, with an adverse current and frequent 'Pamperos', fierce storms blowing off the Argentinian mainland, usually with no warning.

Chay was running late, having made a slower passage than planned, but on 21 December, after a difficult few days of gales and headwinds, he sighted land - Staten Island, lying to the east of Tierra del Fuego. He passed to the east of the island, rather than taking the shorter passage through the Le Maire Strait. On 23 December he was eighty-seven miles from Cape Horn and met up with HMS *Endurance*. A boat from the ship came alongside and Chay passed over mail and films. They gave him fresh bread, fruit and two bottles of whisky. On Christmas Eve, he rounded the Horn some five miles off in calm weather.

The next day a Force 9 gale hit him and for the first time Chay faced the huge seas of the Southern Ocean. He described them as having '*a quality of sheer bigness that was new and menacing.*' As a warning of what was to come a huge sea hit the yacht and his self steering gear was smashed and put out of action.

Chay was now facing the daunting prospect of four or five months of continuous sailing against strong headwinds until he could reach South Africa and turn north up the Atlantic. But this what he had come for and was the crux of his voyage. Try to imagine living like this, heeled over at forty degrees day after day, with endless spray sweeping the decks, the whole boat battened down and everything below soaking wet. Always having to get dressed in oilskins and seaboots to go on deck. Regularly having to go forward to the mast to reef and unreef the mainsail or onto a heaving foredeck, often underwater, to lower, unhank and change headsails (this was all before the days of furling headsails, which can be controlled from the cockpit). And, until he had fixed his self-steering gear, he had to steer the boat by hand. By lashing the tiller he could usually get *British Steel* to sail herself but she needed constant correction.

Blyth began to head north away from the latitude of the Horn, which is at 56° South, but he was determined to keep sailing, as best he could, along the 45° South line of latitude; to go further north might get him lighter winds but would add distance to the passage.

January continued stormy and cold as Blyth clawed his way westward and in his log began to complain of myriad deck leaks which plagued him for the rest of the voyage. 25 January 1971 was his one-hundredth day at sea and gales began to alternate with calms. Six days later the Apollo Mission 14 was launched and the Lunar Module landed on 31 January 1971 for the third lunar landing. Alan Shepherd and Edgar Mitchell stood on the surface and Shepherd performed his famous golf shot. Blyth was probably too involved in keeping *British Steel* going to be much aware of what was going on in space above his head.

On 18 February, he was south of New Zealand and he made a rendez-vous with a TV crew who had put to sea to meet up with him. He passed through the Foveaux Strait, a passage some sixteen miles wide between South Island and the offlying Stewart Island. On 5 March he made his next rendezvous off Tasmania.

He was now half way round the world and was homeward bound. But he did not know he was about to enter the worst stage of the voyage. Whilst it is perceived wisdom that Cape Horn and the waters around it serve up the worst and the most difficult conditions, it is the Indian Ocean and the rounding of the Cape of Good Hope where circumnavigators often find even worse weather.

Most circumnavigators go round from west to east where they expect to have following westerly winds for most of the passage between South Africa and South America, making their passage that much easier. But even then ferocious winds and seas can be found off the Cape of Good Hope, where the westerly winds kick up huge and ferocious seas when they meet the south-west going Agulhas current.

Before Blyth took on the Indian Ocean, only two solo circumnaviga-tors heading west had passed south of both Cape Horn and the Cape of Good Hope - Marcel Bardiaux (chapter 8) and Edward Allcard (chapter 10). They both avoided the worst of the Indian Ocean by heading north into the calmer waters north of Australia before reaching the east coast of Africa and then hugging that coast to the Cape. Blyth did no such thing but bashed on, meeting the full force of the stormy westerly winds head on as he assailed the worst ocean in the world. As before, Blyth decided to stay south of the 45° South line of latitude, unless bad weather forced him north.

He had a frustrating crossing of the Great Australian Bight, reaching Cape Leeuwin, at the far south-western end of Australia, at the end of March. He also began to have problems with his sails, which were beginning to fall apart and from now on they needed constant patching and attention.

At the beginning of April, when he was way past any land, Chay nearly fell overboard. He described this incident in a letter home to a friend but made no mention of it in his log book (in case this was collected at a rendez-vous off South Africa and got home for Maureen to read before he himself got home). He wrote: '....*Maureen was almost a widow and this isn't in my log.... I didn't have a safety-harness on (this is happening too often, forgetting to put it on). And I'd forgotten to lash down the after end of the boom. At this stage you have to think of her crashing against the oncoming waves, the boom banging and pitching up and down, the yacht heeling to 35 deg. Also you have the waves unhindered sweep across the deck. Well, a nasty one hit me. I took its weight on the boom, but the boom moved and I was thrown to the lee side where the water was roaring along, with the lee rail under. I lay amongst the water, luckily pressed against the stanchion. I had to scale the deck, like climbing a cliff, to get to windward.*'

This incident shook him and he wrote how at this stage of the voyage he felt he was subjected to a continuous wearing-down process and it was like being knocked down every time you stood up. He began to hate the damp and discomfort which came with it. He knew he just had to hang on and drive *British Steel* to the Cape whereupon he could turn north and get to the 'Trades', where all would be well.

By 20 April he was half-way between Australia and South Africa. Chay's problem now was that he was nearing South Africa with the southern winter and the onset of bad weather approaching . For the next month he experienced a series of storms worse than anything he had experienced before. During the weeks between 20 April and 21 May, when he rounded Cape Agulhas, the southernmost point of Africa, he experienced almost continuous squalls with heavy seas. He tried to keep going through the worst of them but they took their toll, with damage to his halyards, a mast spreader coming adrift (he could have lost his mast) and the mizzen ripped in five different places. He even got locked inside the cabin when loose ropes in the cockpit jammed the main companion way door! Chay was loath to heave to and never considered running before the seas (which would have been the prudent thing to do).

During this period Blyth calculated that he had travelled 11,384 miles to windward and that this must be the longest windward sail ever undertaken. With two weeks to go to the Cape, Blyth dropped all sail in a Force 12 hurricane and lay a-hull, the boat being thrown on its side to over 50°. This was the worst storm of them all and it lasted for twenty-four hours. At the end Blyth was left bruised, battered and drained, facing a number of problems. The worst was that all his headsail halyards had parted. so he could not set any foresails, without which the yacht would not sail properly.

On the morning of 2 May, the wind had calmed sufficiently for Chay to climb the mast and reeve new halyards. He managed a sun sight which showed he had been driven back 160 miles by the storm. It must be remembered that through all this, and all the way from Cape Horn, Chay had no proper form of self-steering.

On 22 May he reached the Cape of Good Hope, where he exchanged mail with a ship from the South African navy. After that, apart from the constant work needed to keep his boat and gear together, it was all reasonably plain sailing until he reached Southampton and the Hamble River, landing back home and stepping ashore to huge acclaim on 12 August 1971.

Five days before he stepped onto dry land , David Scott and James Irwin had also landed back home at the conclusion of the Apollo 15 Mission, the two being the seventh and eighth astronauts to land on the moon. Chay, the eleventh and last of the Cape Horn astronauts, had had a far harder time of it than the two lunar voyagers.

Chay's achievement in completing his voyage was truly exceptional. He had taken long distance solo sailing to a new level and into another dimension, leading directly to what we see today. From Blyth's time of 292 days, we recently saw a Frenchman, Francois Gabart, circumnavigate the world solo and non-stop in the extraordinary time of forty-two days sixteen hours and forty minutes aboard his 100-foot trimaran *Macif*. Gabart sailed at an average speed of twenty-seven knots (equivalent to thirty-one miles per hour), achieved a maximum speed of forty-seven knots (fifty-four miles per hour) and sailed 851 miles in one twenty-four hour period. Most sailors reading this book will find these figures almost inconceivable. It will not be long before these times too will be beaten.

Later life

Blyth went on to a life of considerable achievement both on and off the water and he has become one of the grand old men of British sailing.

He took to long distance ocean racing, fully crewed, two handed and singlehanded. With financial backing initially from 'Union' Jack Hayward, a Bermudan based financier and rabid Anglophile, he built and raced three yachts, *Great Britain II, III* and *IV*. (Some years before this Jack Hayward had paid for the original *Great Britain*, the world's first screw driven ocean going ship, to be brought back from the Falkland Islands to be berthed in the original dry dock in the harbour in Bristol where she had been built and where she remains today.)

The first was a 77-foot sloop, which took part in all six Whitbread Round the World Races. Blyth skippered the yacht with a crew of paratroopers in the first race. *Great Britain III* was an 80 foot long trimaran built originally for Chay to race in the *Observer* Single-Handed Transatlantic Race. She proved too much of a handful for one man and was not a great success. She suffered from collisions and a capsize and Blyth abandoned the OSTAR attempt because he could not get any insurance. *Great Britain IV*, a 56-foot trimaran was built for (and won) the 1978 Two Handed Round Britain Race, co-skippered by Chay and Rob James.

Blyth then built the 60-foot trimaran, *Brittany Ferries GB*, in which he and Rob James won the Two Handed Transatlantic Race held in 1981. He raced this boat to second place in the next year's Round Britain Race.

After that he attempted to beat the record for sailing from New York to San Francisco on board a trimaran *Beefeater II* but capsized off Cape Horn and he and his crew were rescued after being in very cold water for nineteen hours.

He was co-skipper with Richard Branson on two attempts to beat the time for a powered crossing of the Atlantic. The first attempt ended in failure when the boat *Atlantic Challenger I* sank just off Lands End. The second attempt in *Atlantic Challenger II* was successful, beating the record by two days.

In 1989 Chay founded the Challenge Business to organise a series of round the world races (east to west) with amateur novice crews aboard a fleet of specially constructed and professionally skippered yachts. These ran from 1992 until 2005, when the business ceased due to failure to raise sufficient sponsorship money. Blyth took on several marketing and business positions and became a well known motivational speaker at business events. He was knighted by the Queen in 1997 for services to yachting He is now seventy-eight, retired from competitive sailing and back living in his native Scotland.

Chapter 17
Two who nearly made it

No-one actually sailed past the Horn alone during the remainder of 1971 after Chay's arrival home, or during 1972. The fifth lunar landing (Apollo 16 Mission) took place on 16 April 1972 and the the last one, the Apollo 17 Mission, was on 7 December 1972.

But one person nearly made it round the Horn and one person pretended to make it by time of the last moon landing in December 1972. Bill King in *Galway Blazer II* never made it in time, despite setting out from England in the same month as Moitessier. The one who pretended was, of course, Donald Crowhurst on *Teignmouth Electron* who broadcast to the world that he had sailed past Cape Horn in April 1969, whilst he was actually dawdling, hiding in plain sight in the south Atlantic, having got no further. As we saw earlier, he was waiting for his fake position to catch up with his real one.

Bill King

Bill King, a retired Royal Navy submariner, set off on the Golden Globe race in his junk rigged *Galway Blazer II* around the same time as Bernard Moitessier and Nigel Tetley. He was one of the favourites to win as he had a purpose built boat, was an expert navigator and was almost as experienced an ocean sailor as Moitessier. His boat was the brain child of Angus Primrose and Blondie Hasler. She was rigged as a schooner with two unstayed masts carrying fully battened Chinese junk sails. She had a turtle deck enclosing the entire hull with just two openings from which King could reef and control the sails without having to go on deck. She was exceptionally well thought out and even carried a purpose made jury rig in case of a de-masting.

Unfortunately, this is just what happened. *Galway Blazer II* was knocked down and capsized in a severe storm off the coast of south Africa. King was able to hoist the jury mast and set sail for Cape Town, making slow progress. An intrepid yachtsman from the Royal Cape Town Yacht Club, who had a large powerfully engined yacht, agreed to rendezvous with King some

200 miles off Cape Town and tow him in. This he did and King arrived in Cape Town in late November 1968. King then had *Galway Blazer II* shipped home to England, determined to have her repaired so he could set out again in 1969.

In 1969 he did set out again in a re-masted *Galway Blazer II*, with improved sails, hoping for better light weather speed. Unfortunately the new rig was unmanageable in heavy weather and King, after putting into Gibraltar, sailed her home to Cowes, where she was re-rigged yet again.

In September the next year, 1970, King set off for the third time. Again, King had to abandon his attempt at a non-stop circumnavigation. When approaching Australia he put his back out and could barely move, added to which a long standing problem he had with his hands resurfaced. Being perpetually wet they began to shed skin from the fingertips, making it impossible for him to handle ropes or make any repairs. He put into Fremantle in western Australia. He left *Galway Blazer II* there and returned to Ireland for the southern winter.

By the middle of 1971 he was back in Australia preparing for the 17,000 -mile-voyage home to Ireland via Cape Horn. If all had gone well on that trip, and he was hopeful it would after all his previous travails, he would have made the Horn by January or February 1972 and would have become the twelfth Cape Horn astronaut.

But misfortune hit King once again. Having left Fremantle on 12 December 1971 he immediately ran into strong headwinds. By 19 December he was settling into his routine for the voyage in good weather, enjoying the sense of freedom he always felt when alone at sea on his boat. He was below when suddenly there was a rasping sound and a bang, as if a terrific fist had hit the hull, and in front of King's eyes a large section of splintered wood was stove in. King could see blue water through the bulge in the hull and water poured in. He rushed on deck to see what had hit him but saw nothing except a green swirl astern and a dark form making off fast. He thought he could see blood in the water.

He set about saving his boat. He tacked and brought the wind onto the other side.. This raised the hole above the waterline but he was sailing in the wrong direction away from land. He pumped the boat dry whilst deciding what to do but knew that if the wind died, or if there was a storm, *Galway Blazer II* would surely sink. He tried the classic remedy of lashing a sail over the side to try to cover the hull, but this did not work. Then he stuffed towelling, foam rubber and rubber strips into the gashes and holes and nailed a piece of sail cloth over the opening. This helped. Then he cut off a piece of the spare main boom to act as a shore to stop one remaining frame from springing inwards. He wedged this in place.

He now believed the leak was under control for the time being but things would not hold if he ran into bad weather. He sent out a May Day distress call but received no response. He was in a very empty piece of ocean. He spent the next few days trying to cobble together a better form of collision mat to cover the hole. He was now sailing slowly away from the coast (he was 400 miles off when the collision occurred - he was now, two days later, 600 miles off). He tried further distress calls. He also tried to contact Perth radio but without success.

Day followed day whilst King prayed for the wind to go round to the west which would have enabled him to tack and head back to land. Eventually it did and he found he could head north. On 26 December he succeeded at last in making contact with Perth Radio. He continued on his way and eventually made it home to land. It took three days to get back to the point where he was holed and another fourteen days to reach land. It was a piece of exceptional seamanship. The boat was quickly repaired and King considered setting off again, hoping to make the Horn before the bad weather took over but he was too exhausted to continue. He decided to leave it for another year, not ready to give up the whole venture. The consensus in Australia was that it was a great white shark that had attacked *Galway Blazer II*.

A year passed and on 4 December 1972 King left Fremantle for the last time, three days before the launch of the Apollo 17 Mission for what turned out to be the last Lunar landing. This time all went well and King had an uneventful, but sometimes rough, passage around the south of New Zealand and across the Pacific. He had constant following winds and sailed 7,000 miles in sixty days. He passed Cape Horn on 5 February 1973 under bare poles in storm force winds with low black clouds down to the top of his masts. He had little more than a glimpse of Cape Horn itself. He arrived back in Plymouth in May, five years after he had left.

Donald Crowhurst

Now we come to Donald Crowhurst, whose exploits are well known to the whole world having been the subject of numerous books and several films.

As we saw in chapter 15, Crowhurst tried to deceive the world that he was sailing fast across the bottom of the world south of the Cape of Good Hope then on to Cape Horn, whilst he was in fact scuttling around off the coast of Argentina, hoping not to be seen and waiting for his false position to catch up and meet his actual position. Then he planned to re-join the race and head for home to fame and glory.

None of this was to be of course. It was an impossible dream and even a chancer like Crowhurst could never have pulled it off. During his waiting period in purdah he had two narrow escapes.

The first was when he had to head for shore to get help with repairing his disintegrating boat. He found a likely looking out of the way spot to land and try to get some spare timber. Crowhurst did not know it but there was a Coastguard station at this small inlet, charged with watching shipping entering and leaving the mouth of the River Plate. But luckily for Crowhurst, and somewhat improbably, the station had no telephone and the Coastguard entered his name in their log simply as Edward Alfred - the Donald in his passport was assumed to be a honorific like the Spanish Don and his surname was omitted entirely. Thus his visit to Argentina, at a time when he was supposed to be hurtling across the Southern Ocean was never discovered until after his death.

Second, as described earlier, Crowhurst nearly bumped into Nigel Tetley and *Victress*, whilst sailing south instead of north and at a time when he should have been in another ocean entirely.

Having got over these danger points, Crowhurst began to face up to the fact that he would never be able to carry it all off had he come in first or had he won the prize for the fastest time. He would have been feted as a hero, hounded by the press and his log books would have been examined in detail. Many people in England, especially Sir Francis Chichester, were already becoming sceptical about Crowhurst's claims.

The strain of all this, and the many months alone at sea, led to a mental collapse as the fate which awaited him sank in. It seems that he decided to slow down and try to creep in second or third behind Tetley. He hoped he could slink unnoticed into some out of the way harbour and avoid all the brouhaha offered to a winner.

Then, the ultimate irony arose when Tetley, believing Crowhurst's claims that he was coming up fast behind him, pushed his disintegrating trimaran too far too fast and *Victress* sank. This left Crowhurst in a position where he could not but win the prize. Crowhurst turned his boat away from England and drifted uselessly in the wilds of the Sargasso Sea whilst he collapsed mentally. Eventually, he walked off the stern of his boat into the sea clutching his chronometer. His body was never found although his boat was, along with all his log books and the evidence which told the whole sad and sorry tale.

Crowhurst would have been the eleventh had he actually rounded Cape

Horn in April 1969 and Chay Blyth would have become the twelfth, thus equalling the number of men who have walked on the moon.

Postscript

After the end of 1972 the floodgates began to open and, inspired by these pioneers, four people rounded the Horn alone in 1973/4, five in 1974/5 and by the end of the 1980s, thirty people in all had been round alone.

After that, the waters around Cape Horn became positively crowded. It began to be used as a turning point in a number of the round-the-world yacht races as more and more yachts, both single-handed and fully crewed, either racing or cruising, with one, two or three hulls began to pass south of the Horn in both directions.

In 1983 the first single-handed round the world race with pit stops took place. Called the BOC Challenge it started and ended at Newport in the USA with stops at Cape Town, Sydney and Rio de Janeiro. Competitors had to pass south of all southern capes including Cape Horn. Sixteen boats started and ten finished. The race was won by Frenchman Phillippe Jeantot in *Credit Agricole*, in a time of 159 days, by far the fastest circumnavigation so far. This race established the French domination in this sport and fed the appetite for large French corporations to pour sponsorship money into it. Something no other country has followed to the same extent. The next BOC Challenge took place in 1986/7 with twenty one starters, the favourite being Phillippe Jeantot, back with a new boat, *Credit Agricole II*. He finished first in a time of 134 days with French sailors coming in second and third. Sixteen competitors finished.

Two more BOC Challenge races were held but the race began to lose popularity, particularly amongst the French, as the challenge of a stopping round the world race was eclipsed by the emergence of a solo non-stop race, the Vendée Globe, which has evolved into the massive event it is today. To race solo without stopping from and back to Les Sables-d'Olonne on the Brittany coast in France is without doubt the greatest challenge of all and the hardest event in the whole of the yachting calender. The Vendée Globe was founded by Phillippe Jeantot in 1989 and the first race held in 1989/90. There were thirteen starters, of whom eleven were French. Eight competitors finished (all French) and the winner was Titouan Lamazou in a time of 109 days. Since then the race has been held every four years.

It has been won every time by a Frenchman but the British woman, Ellen MacArthur, came in second in the 2000/1 race and a British man, Alex Thompson, also came second in the 2016/7 race. This, the latest race, was won in a record time of seventy-four days, with Thompson coming in only sixteen hours later.

In addition to these single-handed races there have been a number of fully crewed affairs, starting with the Whitbread Round the World Races, the first having been run in 1973. As mentioned above, Chay Blyth entered this race in the purpose built yacht, *Great Britain II*. This race has been run every four years and in 2005 changed its name (and sponsor) to the Volvo Ocean Race. It is now held in a one-design class of 65-footers.

Chay Blyth then started the series of Global Challenge Races in which amateur novice paying crews assisted by a professional skipper sailed identical 67-foot and then 72-foot cutters around the world 'the wrong way' i.e. from east to west following the route pioneered by him in *British Steel*.

Apart from these fleets of race boats speeding past Cape Horn there is today a continuous procession of cruising yachts sailing in and around these waters. The harbours of Ushuaia in Argentina and Puerto Williams in Chile have become yachting centres, welcoming passing yachts. Newly built yacht marinas form the base for a fleet of charter yachts, which today ply the waters of Cape Horn, some descending further south across the Drake Strait to visit Antarctica.

Having been deserted for generations, Patagonia has become the 'must go to' destination for sailors, tourists and skiers alike. One fears for its future. Large cruise liners regularly appear here and in the waters of Antarctica. There are severe concerns as to the environmental consequences of so many ships and travellers frequenting these unspoilt waters. Recently Chile has tried to stop or limit this exploitation by banning large cruise ships from its waters and limiting the numbers of others. The Chilean authorities strictly control the movement of yachts in and around the islands and the passages of Tierra del Fuego. They prohibit yachts from using various inter island passes and anchorages, many of which were used by the sailors described earlier in this book. However, the Chilean authorities face a losing battle in the face of large and powerful operators and the huge amounts of money which these activities bring to a very poor part of the world.

In addition to all this there is a small but growing band of adventurers who go to Cape Horn and with the aid of support vessels and by picking their weather, have succeeded in sailing past (or rounding) Cape Horn in a variety of craft, including 16-foot Hobie Catamarans, dinghies, windsurfers, kiteboards and other novelty craft. Others have paddled round in canoes or kayaks.

Worse is to come. With the advent of global warming and with the 'hot spot' tropical and sub-tropical cruising areas becoming ever more over-developed and over-crowded, more and more sailors are going to travel to the so-far relatively deserted high latitude waters, both north and south, to find the seclusion, peace and solitude so many people in an overcrowded world desire. They are not going to find this in the region of Cape Horn for very much longer.

It is salutary to remember that when Edward Allcard, alone in his yacht *Sea Wanderer*, spent a whole season in and around Patagonia in 1965/6 there were no other yachts sailing in the area, except for Bill Tilman, who followed a few weeks behind him in his Bristol Channel Pilot Cutter *Mischief*. Today there would be hundreds.

Since the last moon landing in 1972, 46 years ago, many hundreds if not thousands of people, both men and women, have sailed past and south of Cape Horn, many in their own yachts, many more on board charter yachts and many on cruise liners of all shapes and size from many different countries. Tourism to this uttermost part of the earth, and to Antarctica, has become well established and increases every year. The same thing may be about to happen to the moon.

Whilst no-one has been on or even near the moon since 1972 this is going to change. Space tourism within the earth's orbit has already started and it will not be long before the first tourists leave orbit and head for the moon. Between 2001 and 2009 seven tourists (although they do not like being called this) visited the International Space Station, orbiting 400 kilometres above the earth, at a cost of between US$ 20 million and US$ 40 million for each visit. These space tourists were transported by the Russian Soyuz rockets.

NASA was proposing to offer something similar until the first non-NASA citizen-astronaut, Christina McAuliffe, was killed in the Challenger Space Shuttle when it blew up and disintegrated on lift off in January 1986. NASA cancelled this programme but it did not take long for the private sector to step in.

Two of the planet's biggest egos, in the form of Elon Musk and Richard Branson, soon decided to use their own money (or, as is usual in the case of Branson, other people's money) to be the first to offer tourists trips into space. Branson's effort has been the most troubled (one of his 'spaceplanes' recently broke up on a test flight) and is the least enterprising. He promises only to offer short hops some sixty to ninety miles high to experience six minutes of weightlessness and to get a glimpse of the curved earth before coming back to earth. For this they would pay around US$ 250,000. His project is year's behind schedule and may never take off. Despite all these setbacks Branson is still maintaining that flights will take place before the end of 2018. We shall see.

Elon Musk's plans however are daring and seemingly well advanced. He reports having received deposits from two individuals who will go on a moon loop flight on his Dragon re-usable spacecraft some time during 2018. These two will see the far side of the moon before returning to earth. Musk will in the future offer moon landings to tourists. His Dragon spaceship is already in use ferrying satellites into orbit. He has developed and has successfully launched a reusable rocket, the Falcon 9, sufficiently powerful to launch heavy payloads into space (the first one 'launched' one of his Tesla electric cars into earth orbit). Musk is even talking about offering one way trips to Mars.

More will inevitably follow and it may not be too many years before tourists are visiting the site of the first human landing in the Sea of Tranquillity and photographing Buzz Aldrin's boot print still visible there. In anticipation of all this, the State of California has listed the first moon landing site on the state's Heritage Register and NASA has issued a request for visitors to keep at least seventy five metres away from it.

So it will not be too long before it all changes, as it has on earth, and those twelve original visitors will soon be forgotten amongst the hordes of camera hugging tourists walking and leaping (and no doubt playing golf) unsteadily in the moon's low gravity.   This is similar to what is happening back here on earth. The first eleven men who sailed the Horn are in the process of being forgotten amongst the motley collection of sailors, walkers, climbers, skiers, paddlers and gawpers who are despoiling the beauty of the virgin waters of Cape Horn and its surrounding islands.

Whilst no-one trod on the moon before the twelve astronauts, it is worth reflecting on the fact that those who today paddle their canoes and kayaks round the headland we call Cape Horn are merely emulating what the very first mariners to pass that way would have done. They would have been Yaghan Indian natives, probably naked and in primitive canoes, in search of food. They are the real true pioneers who should be remembered as the first people to go round the Horn. We Europeans, Americans, and others from far away who go there are only following in the footsteps of these native Yaghan Indians. We should salute their memory, take care never to forget them and, most importantly of all, not destroy such a very special part of the world - the uttermost part of the earth.

THE END

ACKNOWLEDGEMENTS

My thanks go to Robin Knox-Johnston who first pointed out the extraordinary fact of their being only eleven solo Cape Horners (of whom he was one) as against twelve men who had stood on the moon. My thanks also to Paul Heiney for writing such a stimulating Preface. I received much help, as always, from Clare Allcard and her late husband, Edward, before his death in July 2017 at the age of 102. They have given me permission to use extracts and material from his books. This book is dedicated to his memory.

I would like to thank the Conrad Press, especially James Essinger for his boundless enthusiasm for the project (and for coming up with a title for the book), and Charlotte Mouncey for her excellent design work. My thanks also to Roger Robinson for his illustrations and chart, for imparting to me so much of his knowledge of all things 'Vertue' and 'Cape Horn' and for reading and improving the text. Also my thanks to Nic Nicholas (for the index), Chris Eakin, Mick McKeon, Jeremy Atkins, Rob Peake, Sam Llewellyn, Katy Stickland, David Stickland, Julian Mustoe, Renee Forsyth, David Dillistone, Bob Brinton, Steve Parish, Rodney and Maura Pell. Also thanks to Henrietta Barnes and Claire Lloyd Simpson for helping me understand the intricacies of the internet and social media.

In the USA, I thank Marie and Bill Nance, who gave me much information about Bill's life after I had tracked him down to Oregon in the USA; and my thanks for that, and more, go to Pam Wall of Fort Lauderdale. I would also thank Jeanie Stahl and John Jacobsen from Marblehead, Virginia Jones from Martha's Vineyard and Herb McCormick of *Cruising World* who, with Lin Pardey, gave me new information about Bernard Moitessier and the wrecking of *Joshua*.

I gratefully acknowledge and thank the authors and publishers of the books listed in the Bibliography, many of which I have used as source material and from which excerpts have been reproduced.

The chapter on Edward Allcard first appeared, in a slightly revised version, in the spring 2017 edition of the Marine Quarterly, published by The Marine Quarterly Ltd.

If any acknowledgements due to other authors and publishers have been inadvertently omitted I hope they will accept my apologies.

Finally my thanks, as always, to my wife Josephine who has taken well to my new found fondness for writing books, which she helps bring to fruition in so many ways. Her proof-reading skills have been put to good use.

Nicholas Gray
  Sandwich
  March 2018

BIBLIOGRAPHY

Allcard, Clare. *A Gipsy Life*. Ashford, Buchan & Enright 1994
Allcard, Edward. *Single Handed Passage*. Putnam & Co 1950
_____ *Temptress Returns*. Putnam & Co 1952
_____ *Voyage Alone*. Robert Hale 1967
_____ *Solo Round Cape Horn and beyond*. Imperator Publishing 2017
Bardiaux, Marcel. *The Four Winds of Adventure*. Adlard Coles Ltd 1961
Bernicot, Louis (translated by Edward Allcard). *The Voyage of Anahita - Single Handed Round the World*. Rupert Hart-Davis 1953
Blyth, Chay & Ridgway, John, *A Fighting Chance - How We Rowed the Atlantic in 92 Days* Hamlyn. 1967
_____ *The Impossible Voyage*. Hodder & Stoughton 1971
Borden, Charles. *Sea Quest, Small Craft Adventures*. Robert Hale 1968
Chichester, Francis. *The Lonely Sea and the Sky*. Hodder & Stoughton 1964
_____ *Along the Clipper Way*. Pan 1966
_____*Gipsy Moth Circles the World*. Hodder & Stoughton 1967
Clements, Rex. *A Gipsy of the Horn*. Rupert Hart-Davis 1951
Darwin, Charles. *The Voyage of the Beagle*. First published 1839
Dana, Richard H. *Two Years Before the Mast*. T Nelson & Sons 1840
Dumas, Vito. *Alone Through the Roaring Forties*. Adlard Coles Ltd 1960
Eakin, Chris. *A Race Too Far*. Ebury Press 2009
Gerbault, Alain. *The Fight of the Firecrest*. Penguin 1939
_____*In Quest of the Sun*. Hodder & Stoughton 1929
_____*The Gospel of the Sun*. Hodder & Stoughton 1933
Heaton, Peter *The Singlehanders*. Michael Joseph Ltd 1976
Heiney, Paul. *One Wild Song*. Bloomsbury 2015
Holm, Donald. *The Circumnavigators*. Angus & Robertson 1975
Kearns, Des. *World Wanderer-100,000 Miles Under Sail*. Angus Robertson 1972
King, Bill. *Capsize*. Nautical Publishing Co. Ltd *1969*
_____*Adventure in Depth*. Nautical Publishing Co. Ltd 1976
_____ *The Wheeling Stars*. Faber & Faber Ltd. 1989
Knox-Johnston, Robin. *A World of My Own*. Cassel & Co 1969
_____*Force of Nature*. Michael Joseph 2007

Mailer, Norman. *Of a Fire on the Moon* Little, Brown & Co 1970

McCormick, Herb. *As Long as it's Fun: The Epic Voyages and Extraordinary Times of Lin & Larry Pardey.* Paradise Cay Publications 2014

Moitessier, Bernard. *Cape Horn: The Logical Route.* Adlard Coles Ltd, 1969

_____*The Long Way.* Sheridan House 1995

_____*Tamata and the Alliance.* Waterline Books 1995

Nicholls, Peter. *A Voyage for Madmen.* Profile Books 2001

O'Brien, Conor. *Across Three Oceans. A Colonial Voyage in the Yacht Saorsie.* Edward Arnold & Co, 1926

_____*From Three Yachts.* Edward Arnold & Co 1928

_____*The Small Ocean-Going Yacht.* Oxford University Press 1931

Pidgeon, Harry. *Around the World Single-Handed.* D Appleton-Century Co 1932

Rose, Alec. *My Lively Lady.* Nautical Publishing Co 1968

Slocum, Joshua. *Sailing Alone Around the World* Sampson Low, Marston & Co 1900

Smeeton, Miles. *Because the Horn is There.* Nautical Publishing Co 1970

Smith, Andrew. *Moondust.* Bloomsbury 2005

Southby-Tailyour, Ewen. *Blondie: A Biography of Lieutenant-Colonel H G Hasler.* Pen & Sword Books 1998

Spencer, Ann. *Alone at Sea, the Adventures of Joshua Slocum.* Firefly Books, 1999

Tetley, Nigel. *Trimaran Solo.* Nautical Publishing Co 1970

Tomalin, Nicholas & Hall, Robin. *The Strange Voyage of Donald Crowhurst.* Hodder & Stoughton 1970

Turnill, Reginald. *The Moonlandings: An Eyewitness Account.* Cambridge University Press 2002

Riesenberg, Felix. *Cape Horn.* Robert Hale Ltd 1941

Roth, Hal. *Two Against Cape Horn.* W W Norton & Co 1978

Woolass, Peter. *Vertue.* Peter Woolass, 1973

LIST OF PLATES

1. Map of Cape Horn, drawing © Roger Robinson, used with his permission

2. Joshua Slocum (1899) by Hollinger & Co. [Public domain], via Wikimedia Commons

3. Joshua Slocum's boat *Spray* (1898). Source: [Public domain], via Wikimedia Commons

4. Yacht *Coronet* - First yacht to round Cape Horn in 1888. John S. Johnston [Public domain], via Wikimedia Commons

5. Alain Gerbault in the Pacific with Queen Marau of Tahiti (between 1925 and 1929). Source: [Public domain], via Wikimedia Commons

6. Alan Gerbault arriving at Le Havre at the end of his circumnavigation in 1929. Source: Agence de presse Meurisse [Public domain], via Wikimedia Commons

7. Photograph of Edward Miles on board *Sturdy II*. Photo dated 1931. Print of photograph in possession of the author and from his collection. (Rear of print states "1931 credit line must read: "ACME" SF1787- (San Francisco Branch).

8. Louis Bernicot on board his yacht *Anahita* (1952) by F2gm (Own work), via Wikimedia Commons

9. Louis Bernicot's yacht *Anahita* by Jean Bernicot (Personnal photo) [Public domain], via Wikimedia Commons

10. Vito Dumas on board *Lehg II* by El Gráfico [Public domain], via Wikimedia Commons

11. Vito Dumas and Alfon Hansen with his cat and dog. By El Gráfico [Public domain], via Wikimedia Commons

12. Vito Dumas's first yacht *Lehg I* by DumasDiego (Own work), via Wikimedia Commons

INDEX

Images are denoted by 'P' followed by the plate number, both in *italics*. Books are listed under the author's name.